UNDERSTANDING HOUSING POLICY

Other titles in the series

Understanding the finance of welfare
What welfare costs and how to pay for it
Howard Glennerster, Department of Social Administration, London School of Economics and Political Science

"... a brilliant and lively textbook that students will enjoy."
Ian Shaw, School of Sociology and Social Policy, University of Nottingham
PB £17.99 (US$26.95) ISBN-10 1 86134 405 8 ISBN-13 978 1 86134 405 2
HB £50.00 (US$59.95) ISBN-10 1 86134 406 6 ISBN-13 978 1 86134 406 9
240 x 172mm 256 pages May 2003

Understanding social security
Issues for policy and practice
Jane Millar, Department of Social and Policy Sciences, University of Bath

"This first-class text provides students with the most up-to-date review and analysis of social security issues. It will fast become the definitive guide to the subject." **Jonathan Bradshaw, Department of Social Policy and Social Work, University of York**
PB £17.99 (US$26.95) ISBN-10 1 86134 419 8 ISBN-13 978 1 86134 419 9
HB £50.00 (US$59.95) ISBN-10 1 86134 420 1 ISBN-13 978 1 86134 421 2
240 x 172mm 360 pages May 2003

Understanding social citizenship
Themes and perspectives for policy and practice
Peter Dwyer, Department of Sociology and Social Policy, University of Leeds

"An excellent introduction to current debates about citizenship and the only general social policy text on the subject. Highly recommended. Students will certainly benefit from reading this book."
Nick Ellison, Department of Sociology and Social Policy, University of Durham
PB £17.99 (US$28.95) ISBN-10 1 86134 415 5 ISBN-13 978 1 86134 415 1
HB £50.00 (US$75.00) ISBN-10 1 86134 416 3 ISBN-13 978 1 86134 416 8
240 x 172mm 240 pages May 2004

Understanding the policy process
Analysing welfare policy and practice
John Hudson and **Stuart Lowe**, Department of Social Policy and Social Work, University of York

"Hudson and Lowe's book provides an excellent review of the issues about the policy process in a changing society and a changing world." **Michael Hill, Visiting Professor in the Health and Social Policy Research Centre, University of Brighton**
PB £17.99 (US$28.95) ISBN-10 1 86134 540 2 ISBN-13 978 1 86134 540 0
HB £50.00 (US$75.00) ISBN-10 1 86134 539 9 ISBN-13 978 1 86134 539 4
240 x 172mm 304 pages June 2004

Forthcoming
Understanding the mixed economy of welfare
Edited by Martin Powell
PB £22.99 (US$39.95)
ISBN-10 1 86134 759 6
ISBN-13 978 1 86134 759 6
HB £50.00 (US$80.00)
ISBN-10 1 86134 760 X
ISBN-13 978 1 86134 760 2
240 x 172mm 256 pages tbc February 2007

If you are interested in submitting a proposal for the series, please contact
The Policy Press
e-mail tpp-info@bristol.ac.uk
tel +44 (0)117 331 4054
fax +44 (0)117 331 4093

INSPECTION COPIES AND ORDERS AVAILABLE FROM:
Marston Book Services
PO Box 269 • Abingdon • Oxon
OX14 4YN UK
INSPECTION COPIES
Tel: +44 (0) 1235 465500
Fax: +44 (0) 1235 465556
Email: inspections@marston.co.uk
ORDERS
Tel: +44 (0) 1235 465500
Fax: +44 (0) 1235 465556
Email: direct.orders@marston.co.uk

www.policypress.org.uk

UNDERSTANDING
HOUSING POLICY

Brian Lund

First published in Great Britain in March 2006 by

The Policy Press
University of Bristol
Fourth Floor, Beacon House
Queen's Road
Bristol BS8 1QU
UK

Tel +44 (0)117 331 4054
Fax +44 (0)117 331 4093
e-mail tpp-info@bristol.ac.uk
www.policypress.org.uk

© The Policy Press and the Social Policy Association 2006
Reprinted 2008

British Library Cataloguing in Publication Data
A catalogue record for this book is available from the British Library

Library of Congress Cataloging-in-Publication Data
A catalog record for this book has been requested

ISBN 978 1 86134 618 6 paperback
ISBN 978 1 86134 624 7 hardcover

Brian Lund is Principal Lecturer in Social Policy at the Manchester Metropolitan University, UK.

Cover design by Qube Design Associates, Bristol.
Front cover: photograph 'Stress of city life' by Steve Allen kindly supplied by Alamy Images.
Printed and bound in Great Britain by MPG Books, Bodmin.

Contents

Detailed contents

List of boxes, figures and tables

Boxes

Figures

Tables

Preface

Housing policy is about why the state has intervened in the housing market, the forms this intervention has taken and the impact it has made. Chapter One sets out various theoretical approaches to understanding housing policy, indicating how each approach carries assumptions about the nature of housing problems and how they ought to be tackled. Readers who find this chapter too abstract might start with Chapter Two and then return to the first chapter. Chapter Two outlines the history of state involvement in housing. In *The Road to Wigan Pier* (1937) George Orwell records that 'Talking once with a miner I asked him when the housing shortage first became acute in his district: he answered "When we were told about it"'. The miner's response to Orwell's question illustrates the approach to housing policy adopted in Chapter Two and throughout the book. Housing problems are not obvious and 'out there' – an awareness that a housing problem exists and a proposed solution based on a notion of causation have to be created through a political process. Chapter Three sets out the broad outlines of New Labour's housing policy in the institutional context that generates and implements policy change. A comparative dimension is added in Chapter Four with the accounts of housing policy in selected countries aimed at promoting an appreciation of the importance of the specific national contexts in which housing policy has developed. Chapter Five explores the idea of 'affordable' housing and the various ways that the state has attempted to reduce the housing costs to below its market price. Homelessness, a problem that has received considerable academic, media and political attention, is discussed in Chapter Six in the context of the different meanings attributed to the term and the ways these meanings have been reflected in policy.

At the current housing construction rate in the UK only 1% is added to the housing pool each year, demonstrating the importance of keeping the existing stock in good condition, upgrading when feasible and replacing when necessary. This is the subject of Chapter Seven on 'decent homes'. Overcrowding and the multiple occupation of a single dwelling, problems linked together in the past, are analysed in Chapter Eight, with overcrowding identified as a neglected social condition. Chapter Nine explores 'low demand', the latest term applied to an issue that has also been labelled 'problem estates', 'unpopular housing' and 'deprived neighbourhoods'.

In the past, housing problems have tended to be identified as pathological conditions that can be remedied without too much disruption to the existing social and economic order. Chapter Ten, using the notions of class, gender, ethnicity and disability, supplies a different standpoint, examining what is problematic from a social justice perspective. The conclusion (Chapter Eleven) sets out New Labour's future housing policies in the context of the 'Third Way' politics it has adopted.

Acknowledgements

Thanks are due to a number of people who have contributed to the publication of this book. I am indebted to Saul Becker, the editor of the Understanding Welfare series, and to the staff of The Policy Press for their help. I would also like to thank all the people in the housing policy community, especially the two referees, who made valuable comments on draft versions of the book. My more personal gratitude is to Sukey, Daniel, Rachel, Milligan and Stanley for their continual support and encouragement.

Understanding housing policy

Summary

- Housing policy is concerned with the processes involved in state intervention in the housing market.
- There are a number of approaches to the study of housing policy, each containing:
  - a normative order against which housing problems are identified;
  - causal explanations;
  - accounts of how and why the state has intervened in the housing market.

- This chapter examines five approaches to understanding housing policy:
  - laissez-faire economics;
  - social reformism;
  - Marxist political economy;
  - behavioural;
  - social constructionism.

What is housing policy?

Housing has been described as 'the wobbly pillar under the welfare state' (Torgersen, 1987, p 116) because, unlike health and education, the state has not seen its role as the main service provider. Indeed, housing is intrinsically different from education and health care in that it represents a 'home' rather than a locale for a temporary activity such as 'going to school' or 'entering hospital'. Nevertheless, although housing has not attained the status of a universal social service to be distributed primarily according to need, the state has intervened in the housing market in a number of ways. Thus housing policy is best understood as the government attempting to modify the housing market to achieve social objectives such as delivering 'a better balance between housing supply and demand' and ensuring that 'people have decent places to live' (ODPM, 2004a, p 12).

This book adopts a broad view of housing policy as involving:

- state regulation, that is, the rules set down to govern the conduct of people involved in the housing market;
- financial policies designed, for example, to increase or reduce the borrowing cost of house purchase, such as the setting of interest rates;
- taxation measures aimed at encouraging or discouraging housing investment and consumption, for example, Stamp Duty Tax – payable on purchasing a house – from which people living in disadvantaged areas may be exempt if the purchase price is below a specified threshold;
- the basis on which people have rights and obligations in a dwelling – sometimes called tenure (see Box 1.1);
- direct subsidies to producers and consumers of housing;
- infrastructure support for housing construction to make developments sustainable, for example, it has been estimated that each new home in the new growth areas around London will cost the government between £45,000 and £65,000 on roads, schools and other infrastructure support (Power, 2004);
- services to support tenants and homeowners, for example, supported housing and home improvement agencies;
- physical planning constraints and incentives;
- supply, allocation and management policies in the social housing sector;
- security for the 'quiet enjoyment' of a home and the lifestyle choices that such security promotes;
- the promotion of social capital, that is, the value of the social networks people can draw on accruing from living in a neighbourhood;
- housing-related policies aimed at reducing social exclusion.

Understanding housing policy

Currently the dominant theoretical approaches used in housing studies tend to assume that the problems housing policy addresses are objective and self-evident and that different governments respond to these problems according to their ideological tendencies (Jacobs et al, 2003). However, housing problems are not objective and 'out there' waiting to be exposed by social investigation. They are constructed through the social processes of claims-making via problem definition and attaching notions of causation to a problem. Thus, when used as a verb, 'housing' refers to a process or activity – to quote one dictionary definition, 'to take or put into a house' (Wordnet, 2004). This process involves

Box 1.1: Tenure

In the past the term 'tenure' was related to privileges and duties involved in land possession but today it is usually used to refer to the rights and obligations involved in occupying a dwelling. It is now conventional to identify four main types of tenure:

- **Owner-occupation:** where the occupier owns the land freehold or, as a leaseholder, rents it for a specified period after which the land and the dwelling revert back to the freeholder. Under the 2002 Commonhold and Leasehold Reform Act people who occupy units in a multi-occupied building can share their freeholds through a system of 'commonhold'.
- **Renting from a local authority:** where, as a 'secure' tenant, the occupier has a Right to Buy and good protection from eviction if the tenancy agreement is kept.
- **Renting from a private landlord:** usually as an 'assured shorthold' tenant with the presumption that the landlord has the right to possession at the end of the agreement.
- **Renting from a housing association:** usually as an 'assured' tenant and, if the housing association is registered with The Housing Corporation, then the tenant has the added protection of The Housing Corporation's regulatory regime.

a number of stages whereby housing conditions *become* housing problems and policy develops from the causative notions *attributed* to these problems. This is not to deny the reality of the housing conditions experienced by people but to draw attention to the ways these conditions have been construed as problematic.

The adoption of a normative order against which problems are identified is an integral part of the housing policy process. The social policy literature contains a number of normative order classifications that frame the recognition of housing problems and point to policy responses.

Laissez-faire economics

Being a revival of the classical economic theories of the 18th century this approach is sometimes called neoclassical economics. Following the basic premises of Adam Smith (1970 [1776]), laissez-faire economists claim that:

- free exchange allows the division and specialisation of labour so that individuals can concentrate on producing the goods they are most suited to create;

- the state should confine itself to doing what only the state can do – the maintenance of law and order, the policing of contracts and the production of large infrastructure projects which can never be in the interest of any individual to produce;
- if the state obeys these rules then, because individuals are rational maximisers of their self-interest, the market's 'invisible hand' will promote the welfare of all.

Laissez-faire economics dominated housing policy for most of the 19th century. State involvement in the housing market embraced the removal of 'nuisances' to public health and the elimination of obstacles to social order but not the stimulation of housing supply by direct state provision or the offer of subsidies. However, during the 20th century economic liberalism was on the defensive as the state assumed a larger role in shaping and partially replacing the market through subsidised local authority housing, improvement grants, rent control and the creation of a favourable tax regime for homeownership. Friedrich Hayek (1960, 1973) was the most important figure in restoring free market ideas in the 1970s. He embraced Adam Smith's notion of the market, added lessons drawn from the experience of state intervention and set out ideas for the renewed application of market principles to economic life. Various 'think tanks' converted Hayek's beliefs into concrete policy proposals and, by the mid-1970s, a developed critique of the alleged unjustified activities of the state was available. This approach is sometimes called the 'New Right'.

Market efficiency

The New Right believe that housing is a commodity with no intrinsic merit: the value of a dwelling is its exchange price as determined by the interaction between supply and demand. Consumers have different views about how much to spend on housing and different preferences about the style, location and amenities of the dwellings they want to occupy. The price of house reflects its value according to consumer preferences and the other ways the site, labour and materials could be deployed. Only two exceptions are permitted to the general rule that the state should 'leave to be'. First, the state can eliminate externalities. An externality is a side impact of an activity that affects other parties without being reflected in the price of the good or service involved. According to laissez-faire economic theory, slum dwellings generate externalities because they influence the health of people living outside slum areas and thus they can be demolished at public expense. Writing in 1841, Nassau Senior, a prominent advocate of free markets, put the matter clearly when he said:

> With all our reverence for the principle of non-interference, we cannot doubt that in this matter [slums] it has been pushed too far.

> We believe that both the ground landlord and the speculating builder ought to be compelled by law ... to take measures which will prevent the towns which they create from being the centre of disease. (quoted in Holmans, 1987, p 25)

Second, some market economic theorists also permit an income subsidy to the poor to enable them to afford a minimum housing standard supplied by the market.

Market distortions

The laissez–faire economic approach claims that state intervention in the housing market has caused more problems than it has solved. Rent control and subsidised council housing are regarded as the primary culprits. Rent control, introduced in 1915, had the following undesirable consequences:

- It prevented private savers investing in houses to let.
- It limited labour mobility because workers benefiting from rent control were reluctant to move and thereby lose their protected status.
- It produced under–investment by landlords in their properties.

Subsidised council housing is also regarded by the New Right as part of the housing problem rather than part of its solution (see Box 1.2). Some neoclassical economists also condemn the physical planning system for restricting the land supply thereby pushing up house prices and increasing overcrowding and homelessness (Evans, 1988).

Government failure

The New Right believe that state intervention in the housing market not only generates problems but that state housing provision is likely to be inefficient. Only competition can supply the incentives necessary for efficiency and, if the state becomes a monopoly supplier of accommodation as it did for family rented housing in the 1970s, then it is bound to be wasteful.

Social Reformism

Two main elements in the development of Social Reformism can be identified. Social Liberalism and Fabian Socialism emerged at the end of the 19th century and both claimed that market capitalist economies produce unjust outcomes. Social Liberals asserted that, because land values were created not by individuals but by the community, then such enhanced land values should be used for community purposes. Fabians agreed but identified other unfair advantages accruing to capitalists such as the gains obtained by paying skilled workers less

Box 1.2: Hayek on subsidised council housing

Hayek presents the most polished exposition of the case against state provision of subsidised dwellings. He argues that:

> The old buildings which at most stages of the growth of a city will exist at the centre … will often provide for those of low productivity an opportunity to benefit from what the city offers at the price of very congested living. (Hayek, 1960, pp 346-7)

Thus slum-dwellers gain opportunities to live in the city but at the cost of poor living conditions. So, says Hayek:

> If we want to abolish the slums we must choose between two alternatives. We must either prevent these people from taking advantage of what to them is part of their opportunity, by removing the cheap but squalid dwellings from where their earning opportunities lie, and effectively squeeze them out of the cities by insisting on certain minimum standards for all town dwellings; or we must provide them with better facilities at a price which does not cover costs and thus subsidise both their staying in the city and the movement of more people into the city of the same kind. (Hayek, 1960, p 348)

Hence, according to Hayek, subsidised council housing promotes the movement of poor people into areas where they cannot afford to live without subsidy. Once subsidised council housing has been provided then more people move to an area to take advantage of the new, low-cost, housing opportunities thereby promoting more urban growth and pressures for yet more subsidised council housing.

than the value of their labour. During the 20th century, Fabian Socialism and Social Liberalism coalesced into a broad social democratic, reformist approach that emphasised the gradual change to be achieved by tackling specific housing problems through state action.

Today Social Reformists maintain that housing has special characteristics, which, taken together, mean that markets will operate inefficiently (see Box 1.3). In addition they argue that the market is incapable of resolving certain housing issues. Glennerster (2003, p 163), for example, extends the idea of externalities – recognised by the laissez-faire approach but only in a limited way – to cover:

- The concentration of poor accommodation in a neighbourhood giving it a shabby appearance and discouraging investment in the area. State action to improve the entire district 'can spark a virtuous circle of revival'.

Box 1.3: Why is housing 'special'?

- Housing is expensive relative to incomes and the requirement for independent accommodation comes at an inconvenient time in the life span, that is, before people have been able to accumulate wealth. Thus purchasing a home usually involves borrowing from institutional lenders who may have the power to influence the ways the market operates. For example in the 1970s some building societies 'red-lined' certain areas where they were unwilling to lend because they believed such areas were bad risks.
- Houses are durable and therefore have a value for future generations. Anticipating the future may involve building to high standards that existing consumers cannot afford. The durability of housing also means that it is both a consumption good, because of the flow of services involved in living in a house, and an investment good with potential gains to be made from increases in price.
- Housing supply does not respond quickly to changes in demand. The housing market is 'made' by the existing supply of dwellings; the best year of housing production in the UK was 1968 when, although 400,000 dwellings were built, only 2% was added to the housing stock.
- The housing stock is immobile and so there is limited opportunity to switch existing supply to areas of new demand. This is reflected in wide variations in house prices in different parts of the country. Moreover, since houses are fixed to a specific location, house values are linked to a particular neighbourhood.
- Housing is built on land, which is an absolute scare resource, made scarcer by planning controls. Thus land supply is not automatically responsive to demand.
- Housing is a basic necessity – people cannot opt out of consumption. Moreover, unlike other goods, it is difficult to vary consumption on a day-by-day basis.

- Unregulated building can produce urban sprawl, making journeys to work long, depopulating city centres and wasting urban infrastructure assets.
- Market forces can exclude people with low incomes from middle-class areas and 'produce ghettos where crime and disorder flourish'.

Some Social Reformists go further, claiming that housing – good enough to be called a home – is so fundamental to the formation of personal integrity and a sense of individual identity that it should be regarded as a 'merit' good. The state should encourage housing consumption because income levels generated by market transactions will be insufficient for many to afford the decent housing necessary for character development. Moreover, many consumers will be unwilling to purchase appropriate quantities of housing.

Marxist political economy

Marxist political economy maintains that relationships between individuals and social institutions are determined by the mode of production used in a particular society. Capitalism is a form of production based on two classes: a capitalist class that owns the means of production and a proletariat or working class that, because it does not own capital, is forced to work for the capitalist class in order to subsist. Whereas Fabian Socialists and Social Liberals believe that capitalist exploitation is partial, to Marxists it is total. This exploitative economic relationship is the real foundation of all other legal, political and ideological 'superstructures', including the state.

When applied to housing this approach generates a number of propositions:

• The real exploitation of the worker takes place at the point of production when building workers are paid less for their labour than the exchange (market) value of the houses they create. In addition, because housing is expensive relative to worker earnings, special institutions are necessary to realise the value of the house. These institutions – building societies, banks, private landlords, and so on – spread the cost of housing over the lifetime of the worker. By demanding a share of the surplus value created when houses are constructed such exchange institutions add to working-class exploitation.
• There are factions of housing capital with different short-term interests but the same long-term interest in ensuring the continuation of the capitalist system. Industrial capital wants to ensure that its workers can be housed at minimal cost; land capital wants to maintain high land values whereas development capital wants to secure access to cheap land. Unrestricted competition between these factions may undermine the overall system so it is the state's business to ensure that their activities are complementary rather than contradictory. Thus the state uses its power to assist the development process in an attempt to ensure maximum profitability for all.
• Capitalism needs a contented, efficient labour force and a 'reserve army of labour' that can be injected into the economy when required and ejected when superfluous. It is the role of state housing policy to provide such a flexible, efficient workforce, to 'reproduce labour power' in ways that reflect capitalist values. Homeownership – designed to convince working people that they have an investment stake in capitalism, to promote an ethic of possessive individualism and to provide the psychic benefits of security, independence and respectability – will be encouraged.
• Housing has an exchange value to capitalists – its efficiency in generating profits – but a use value in meeting human needs to the working class. Therefore, in a market capitalist economy, housing will be affected by its investment value as well as by its utility in meeting needs.
• 'Capitalist rule cannot allow itself the pleasure of creating epidemic diseases among the working class with importunity; the consequences fall back on

it and the angel of death rages in its ranks as ruthlessly as in the ranks of the workers' (Engels, 1872). Thus attempts will be made to eradicate areas of social malaise to protect the bourgeoisie but, given that the housing conditions of the poorest members of the working class are determined by the capitalist system, such action merely displaces the problem elsewhere.

Behavioural approaches

The approaches to understanding housing policy examined so far have been 'structural' in that the causes of housing problems have been located in the operations of the economic and social systems. In contrast, there is a tradition of thinking about housing issues that places blame for housing problems on the behaviour of certain people living in the housing. This approach can be traced back to Malthus who, in his *Essay on the Principle of Population* (1803), argued that, because population increases in geometrical ratio whereas agricultural production grows only arithmetically, the consequences of unrestrained population growth will be famine and disease. Malthus advocated 'moral restraint' – delayed marriage – as the check on population growth and, to the extent that the labouring classes did not practice such restraint, then they were to blame for famine and disease. He believed that any form of help to enable the working class to secure better housing would, by encouraging early marriage and more children, make matters worse.

During the second part of the 19th century, behavioural approaches to explaining housing problems were very influential. Octavia Hill, often regarded as the founder of housing management, succinctly expressed the approach when she said:

> The people's homes are bad, partly because their habits and lives are what they are. Transplant them tomorrow to a healthy and commodious home, and they would pollute and destroy them. (Hill, 1883, cited in Goodwin and Grant, 1997, p 30)

For Hill, action to improve physical housing conditions had to be accompanied by 'character' reform.

In the first part of the 20th century, behavioural approaches became subservient to structural approaches but, in the 1980s, they returned to prominence in the form of underclass theories. Charles Murray (1984) asserted that an underclass had developed in the US characterised by young females reliant on state welfare to maintain their children, and young males, separated from the necessity to support their offspring, adopting an irresponsible and criminal lifestyle. He applied the underclass idea to Britain, claiming to have identified similar trends – escalating illegitimacy, rising crime and growing aversion to work (Murray, 1992). Other authors have recognised a tendency for the underclass to become concentrated in certain areas thereby compounding the impact of their behaviour (Anderson, 1992; Hill, 2003).

Although often associated with New Right the behavioural approach has also featured in Marxism and has been a strong undercurrent in Social Reformism. Marx referred to the 'lumpen-proletariat' as a 'passive putrefaction of the lowest strata of the old society' (Marx, 1848, cited in Bovenkerk, 1994, p 13) whose 'local inter-connection' meant that it could not form the basis for class action (Marx and Engels, 1969 p 278). The New Liberals and Fabian Socialists identified a 'residuum' requiring a paternalist, disciplinary state to improve their conduct (Lund, 2002, pp 77-82). Tony Blair has resurrected this behavioural approach in social reformist thinking:

> I have chosen this housing estate to deliver my first speech as Prime Minister.... There is a case not just in moral terms but in enlightened self-interest to act, to tackle what we all know exists – an underclass of people cut off from society's mainstream, without any sense of shared purpose. The basis of this modern civic society is an ethic of mutual responsibility or duty. It is something for something. A society where we play by the rules. You only take out if you put in. (Blair, 1997)

Social constructionism

Social constructionism is a dimension of the post-modernism thinking that came to prominence in the 1980s. Social constructionism challenges 'modern' thinking by questioning global, all-encompassing, rational views that claim to capture objective knowledge of reality. In its most zealous form – sometimes called the strong version – social constructionism rejects the notion of 'essentialism' – the idea that the external world exists independently of our representations of it. Its objective is to supply an account of the processes by which phenomena are socially constructed and thereby expose the ways that certain understandings have become privileged and regarded as 'the truth'. In its less zealous forms social constructionism allows for the possibility of an objective world but claims '*our access* to the material world is mediated through language and discourse' (Jacobs et al, 2004, p 3; emphasis in original). Social constructionism's key concepts are 'meaning' and 'power'. According to the approach, language, codified into 'discourses', is the key to meaning. These 'discourses' – systems of knowledge – classify and order events and persons. They give some groups power over others because dominant discourses frame the image and often the self-perception of the subjects of the discourses (see Box 1.4).

Social constructionism both liberates agency – the capacity of people to formulate the discourses that frame their identity – and points to the factors

that may inhibit such agency. It opens the door to examining different perceptions of the meaning of housing to different family and household members, the ways these meanings change according to time and place and the roles of housing consumers as 'creative agents, acting upon, negotiating and developing their own strategies of welfare' (Williams and Popay, 1999, p 44). It also provides a vehicle for the examination of what Foucault has called 'governmentality' – the ways in which power is exercised by the creation of 'technologies of the self' whereby people absorb socially constructed norms of responsible conduct (Foucault, 1991).

The strong social constructionists' claim that we cannot know reality apart from our interpretation of it has led to accusations of moral relativism and lack of political purchase. Nonetheless, there is a form of politics implicit in the social constructionist approach. In deconstructing dominant 'grand narratives', social constructionists have helped to release the subjects of these constructions and enabled them to promote different interpretations of their circumstances with claims to legitimacy as valid as those promoted in 'grand narratives'. This has produced an interest in identity politics, that is, the personal liberation of groups that have been marginalised from mainstream politics. In the past, dominant constructions of reality have categorised certain people as 'lesser beings' but, by denying the capacity of social science to generate transcendent truths, social constructionism claims to have liberated 'difference'.

Box 1.4: The social construction of homelessness

In *Citizen Hobo: How a Century of Homelessness Shaped America* (2003) Todd Depastino explores how homelessness was identified as a social problem in the US. Different labels were applied to homeless people at different times – 'tramp', 'hobohemian', 'transient', 'skid row bum' – to reflect the dominant concerns of US society. All the terms applied were discourses on a lifestyle rather than descriptions of the condition of lacking shelter. These dominant discourses were not always shared by their subjects. For many hobos an 'unsettled way of living' was an acceptable, even attractive, way of life – 'a civilisation without a home' to quote the title of one of the chapters in Depastino's book. It took a significant expansion of the US welfare state after the Second World War in the form of subsidised mortgages, unemployment compensation and grants for higher and vocational education to ensure that many of the returning GIs did not go back to their former hobo way of life. Dominant discourses on homelessness as an unnatural, pathological way of life triumphed when the 'hobohemians' accepted this representation of their condition.

Explanations of continuity and change in housing policy

Each of the normative approaches to housing outlined above contains explanations of continuity and change in housing policy.

Public choice theory

Laissez-faire economics has adopted public choice theory as its principal explanation of why the state has intervened in the housing market. Public choice theorists divide the political system into three elements: the voting system, the activities of interest groups and the behaviour of state officials organised into bureaucracies. All the participants in the political process are thought of in terms of the basic premise of neoclassical economics – they act rationally to promote their self-interest. Politicians want power, prestige and material advantage and, to secure them, they must win more votes than their rivals. To obtain these votes they will try to attract the 'median voter' – the additional voter necessary to secure a majority – and will pursue policies that redistribute income from the rich to middle-income groups and the poor. In their pursuit of power, politicians are susceptible to the influence of interest groups. Interest groups exist to take a free ride on their fellow citizens. They seek to persuade politicians to give special privileges to the domains of life in which they have a vested interest. Politicians may rely on interest groups to secure a winning coalition in elections and, when in power, they may respond to the demands of interest groups to ensure cooperation in regulating a complex sphere of activity. Interest groups will engage in a variety of tactics to enhance their control over politicians and bureaucrats, for example 'log rolling', where a variety of interest groups may act together against unorganised groups. Thus, for example, the construction industry, estate agents, landowners and the financial institutions may combine to demand government intervention to kick-start the housing market in a period of stagnant house prices. They will make their demands in the public interest but there will be losers – new entrants to the housing market who would benefit from falling prices – if the government agrees to the demands.

Bureaucratic self-interest is the third influence on the growth of state housing systems identified by public choice theorists. State officials are perceived as motivated by 'salary, prerequisites of the office, public reputation, power, patronage and the ease of managing the bureau' (Niskanen, 1973, pp 22-3). They can behave as 'knaves', promoting their self-interest, not 'knights' upholding the public good (Le Grand, 2003) and their interests are served by maximising the agency's budget. Niskanen asserts that, because bureaucrats have a virtual monopoly on information about the costs of the organisation, there will always be a degree of inefficiency in the delivery of services to the consumer.

Functionalism

Functionalism as an explanatory theory was at the heart of Fabian Socialism and Social Liberalism. Functionalism used the analogy of human society as a biological organism – a system of interdependent parts that function for the benefit of the whole. The social scientist's role was to specify how the parts of the social system were interrelated with a view to identifying the dysfunctional elements. Given that the identification of the 'dysfunctional' elements was perceived to be an objective, rational process then it followed that the very act of identification must lead, in time, to action from the political system. Thus, for example, functionalists believe that slums are dysfunctional for society because they generate communicable disease, crime and immorality, and a rational state will take action to eliminate the slum.

Marxist theories of the state

Academic interpretations of the work of Marx and Engels have identified two major models of the role of the state in capitalism: the instrumental model and the arbiter model.

In the 1970s 'instrumental Marxism' claimed that the state is a straightforward instrument used by the ruling class to dominate society and to ensure that the capitalist system continues. The capitalist class uses the state for a variety of purposes:

- to take the steam out of radical movements by means of temporary concessions at times of social unrest thereby preventing the development of class consciousness and the working class becoming a 'class for itself';
- to maintain profits in times of surplus production;
- to sustain capitalist ideology through the nature of the institutions supported by the state;
- to keep workers fit to work in a capitalist economy;
- to maintain the reserve labour army that capitalism needs in order to be able to respond to its boom/bust cycle of production.

The arbiter model is grounded on the earlier works of Marx in which – while disputing the notion, propagated by social reformists, that the capitalist state could act in accordance with the common good – he recognised that the state may obtain a degree of neutrality from capitalism. The state can act in the proletariat's interest at certain moments in history. This arbiter model allows the organised working class some enduring influence in the historical construction of state housing policy and offers a degree of optimism about the outcome of future struggles within and against the state. By placing its emphasis on class power as the mechanism for viable change within the existing state apparatus, the arbiter model promises the possible erosion of capitalism by ceaseless pressure from the working class arising from its everyday experience as producers and recipients of welfare. It also allows Marxists to provide a more convincing account of the evolution of housing policy with genuine improvements being made in working–class housing provision at times when the labour movement was strong as, for example, between 1945 and 1951. However, although the attribution of relative autonomy to the state makes the Marxist account more plausible, it reduces its distinctness when compared to the Social Reformist perspective.

Systematic scepticism

Social constructionism is more of an epistemological position – a view on the nature of knowledge – than an explanatory theory. Social constructionists claim that all discourses are situated historically and are best understood when located in the circumstances of their development. Value and significance are culturally and historically specific. Power influences the extent to which a particular discourse becomes 'realised', that is, widely regarded as an objective account of the real world. Thus, when applied to housing problems social constructionism adopts a systematically sceptical approach. It asks a series of questions about all *claims* that a given housing situation constitutes a housing problem:

- Who says so?
- What interests do they represent?
- Why do they say that a condition is a social problem? Does it threaten social order with the people concerned regarded as *being* a social problem or does it perpetuate social injustice with the people affected regarded as *having* a social problem?
- How do they justify their views?
- What are the implications of their assumptions? (Saraga, 1998, p 192)

Answers to these questions are found through a detailed examination of the *specific* contexts of a condition *becoming* a social problem and the responses made to the problem in accordance with the dominant discourses of the times.

Behavioural explanations

Behavioural approaches do not seek to explain changes in housing policy but they do attempt to explain changes in the behaviour of the people who cause the housing problems to which the state may respond. The development of an underclass has been explained in two principal ways. In *Neighbours from Hell: The Politics of Behaviour*, Field (2003) claims that the family is no longer functional in transmitting social values.

> Manners, sentiments and moral opinions are learned best in families. It is the breakdown in a growing number of families in the teaching of social virtues that is becoming a central issue to voters. To talk of transmitting social virtues is already a foreign language to a minority, but growing number of households. (Field, 2003, p 5)

Others stress the growing detachment of rights from obligations. According to this line of argument the 'underclass' started to grow when, in the 1960s, rights to welfare began to supersede the obligations involved in the receipt of welfare. Marquand, for example, claims that under the influence of the welfare rights approach 'the notions that rights should be balanced by duties, that activity was better than dependence and that the point of collective provision was to foster self-reliance and civic activism came to be seen as patronising or elitist or (horror of horrors) "judgemental"' (Marquand, 1996, p 19). It is alleged that this emphasis on rights created a culture that generates 'antisocial behaviour' because civil society is seen as condoning such conduct by its failure to apply appropriate sanctions. The idea that rights must be attached to obligations and that these obligations need to be enforced by sanctions became known as 'communitarianism'.

Overview

- Housing policy is about the state making corrections to the housing market.
- There are a number of approaches to understanding housing policy. Each approach is linked to a political agenda and contains an explanation of why the state became involved in housing and, explicitly or implicitly, a normative theory used to establish the nature of the housing problems to be tackled by the state.

Questions for discussion

(1) According to the laissez-faire economic perspective what is the legitimate role of the state in the housing market?

(2) Why do Social Reformists insist that the supply and distribution of housing cannot be left to the free play of market forces?

(3) Examine the websites of the 'think tanks' listed below. On which approach to the study of housing policy are they based?

(4) What are the major differences between the 'instrumental' and 'arbiter' approaches to understanding the development of housing policy?

(5) Should state help with housing costs be linked to the behaviour of the recipients?

Further reading

Theorising Welfare: Enlightenment and Modern Society by **O'Brien and Penna (1998)** is a good introduction to normative and explanatory theories of welfare. Such theories are linked to the development of the British welfare state in **Lund's (2002)** *Understanding State Welfare*. The idea of social construction is explained in **Saraga's (1998)** *Embodying the Social: Constructions of Difference*. **Depastino's (2003)** *Citizen Hobo: How a Century of Homelessness Shaped America* is an excellent example of the application of the social constructionist approach to understanding housing problems, although Depastino may not recognise it as such.

Website resources

Various 'think tanks' reflect the diversity of approaches to understanding housing policy and the development of policy prescriptions. See, as examples, the websites of:

- The Adam Smith Institute [www.adamsmith.org/]
- Centre for Policy Studies [www.cps.org.uk/]
- Catalyst [www.catalystforum.org.uk/]
- Fabian Society [www.fabian-society.org.uk/int.asp]
- Civitas [www.civitas.org.uk/]
- Institute of Economic Affairs [www.iea.org.uk/]
- Institute for Public Policy Research [www.ippr.org.uk/]
- New Policy Institute [www.npi.org.uk/]

two

The politics of housing policy

Summary

- Poor housing conditions became recognised as a social problem because they were seen as a threat to the social, moral and physical well-being of the nation.
- At the end of the 19th century a housing shortage was identified and many ideas were in circulation about how this shortage could be rectified.
- Homeownership and council housing developed rapidly in the inter-war period.
- The Labour government (1945-51) attempted to tackle the housing deficit by promoting subsidised local authority housing in planned new towns and local authority estates.
- The Conservative Party initially maintained a robust council house building programme but gradually switched emphasis from building for 'general needs' to building to facilitate slum clearance. Owner-occupation was promoted and an attempt was made to revive private landlordism by relaxing rent controls.
- The Labour Party, in office between 1964 and 1970 and between 1974 and 1979, tried to secure a balance between council housing and homeownership.
- Both the major political parties encouraged the improvement of older homes and, from the early 1960s, the development of housing associations.
- In the 1980s and 1990s the Conservatives applied market forces to the supply and distribution of houses via the Right to Buy, rent decontrol, the transfer of local authority housing to alternative landlords and by pushing rents in the social sector closer to market rents.

Housing becomes a social problem

The industrialisation and urbanisation of the late 18th and early 19th centuries created the conditions necessary for housing to become a social problem. Housing standards were extremely low in rural areas (Gauldie, 1974; Holmans, 1987) but it was the identification of the 'externalities' involved in the concentration of poor housing that transformed housing into a social problem. Urban growth developed through short-distance moves of less than 30 miles by young people in search of better-paid work and freedom from village norms, supplemented by the migration from Ireland and the highlands of Scotland. These migrants were of child-bearing age and those born in urban areas soon provided the main source of population growth. The provision of dwellings, drainage and sewerage could not keep pace with this billowing population with the result that people were crammed together in poor-quality, unsanitary accommodation. However, poor housing conditions are not necessarily problematic to those with political power. Housing had to be constructed as a social problem and this was accomplished through the attentions of a new group of experts in the 'public good' who thought it necessary to centralise administration to secure a more wholesome nation.

Housing, health and the public good

Edwin Chadwick (1800-90) was the most formidable exponent of sanitary reform to promote the 'public good'. His *Report on the Sanitary Condition of the Labouring Population of Great Britain* (1842) assembled a variety of statistics and opinions to demonstrate that existing sanitary arrangements generated a variety of 'externalities' (see Box 2.1).

Chadwick was so anxious to ensure his findings produced action that he consulted Charles Dickens on how to present his report for maximum impact. He also ignored alternative analyses circulating at the time that stressed 'work, wages and food' as causal agents of poor health in favour of the politically less controversial notion of a polluted atmosphere (Hamlin, 1998). Nonetheless, Chadwick's report did not produce immediate results and it required pressure group activity from the Health of Towns Association to promote the measures included in the 1848 Public Health Act. This Act set up a Central Board of Health with powers to establish local boards to regulate offensive trades, provide parks and public baths, remove nuisances and manage sewers in areas where the death rate exceeded 23 per 1,000.

Public health and local democracy

The attempts of Chadwick, the Secretary to the Board, to use the Board's powers to cajole the localities into action were firmly resisted on the grounds that he was interfering with the right to local governance. In 1858 such

Box 2.1: Extracts from the *Report on the Sanitary Condition of the Labouring Population of Great Britain* (Chadwick, 1842)

- That of the 43,000 cases of widowhood, and 112,000 cases of destitute orphanage relieved from the poor rates in England and Wales alone, it appears that the greatest proportion of deaths of the heads of families occurred from [insanitary conditions] and other removable causes.
- That the ravages of epidemics and other diseases do not diminish but tend to increase the pressure of population.
- That the younger population, bred up under noxious physical agencies, is inferior in physical organization and general health.
- That the population so exposed is less susceptible of moral influences, and the effects of education are more transient than with a healthy population.
- That these adverse circumstances tend to produce an adult population short-lived, improvident, reckless, and intemperate, and with habitual avidity for sensual gratifications.
- That these habits lead to the abandonment of all the conveniences and decencies of life, and especially lead to the overcrowding of their homes, which is destructive to the morality as well as the health of large classes of both sexes.

resistance led to the Board's abolition in a climate of opinion well captured by *The Lancet*:

> ... a few doctrinaires nursed in the narrow conceits of bureaucracy, scornful alike of popular knowledge and of popular government, seized upon the sanitary theory as a means of exercising central power of domiciliary inspection and irresponsible interference with the conduct and property of Englishmen.... The truth is we do not like paternal governments. (*The Lancet*, 12 February 1858)

Despite Chadwick's demise, gradual progress was made towards improving public health through better understanding of the causes of ill-health, the middle-class panic during the periodic outbreaks of cholera – spread by contaminated water into areas of middle-class residences – and the work of 'ad hoc' health authorities set up in some localities under private legislation. The 1875 Public Health Act, which consolidated and enhanced earlier legislation – notably the 1866 Sanitary Act that enforced the connection of all houses to sewers – was a major progressive step having implications for future housing conditions as well as for public health. It set out the duties of sanitary authorities – to be established in every locality – as supervising street widths and securing the provision of an adequate sewage disposal system, a water supply and a method of drainage. Under the Act, the Local Government Board, established in 1871, issued a new code of model by-laws, which, although not compulsory, was adopted by many local authorities. Tens of thousands of the terraced dwellings were built under these by-laws, each with an indoor water supply and a walled yard containing a privy and perhaps a coalhouse, laid out in such a way as to facilitate sewage removal and provide ventilation. Sir John Simon, who framed the Act, described it as 'the end of a great argument'. So it was. Commenting on the application of the by-laws to Preston, Morgan (1993, p 59) asked: 'Was Preston's housing revolutionised?' and concluded that 'the short answer is that most new housing was, and that it was good enough to have survived to the present day, still mostly in good condition'. However, not all authorities adopted the by-laws and, even when adopted, they were not always enforced. In Leeds, for example, the building of back-to-back houses continued until 1937, justified by the arguments that they were warmer and that their lower building cost brought rents within the limits of poor people.

The slum

The 1875 Public Health Act ensured that new dwellings were built to sanitary standards and the gradual municipalisation of water and sewerage – paid collectively through the rates – made basic hygienic standards more affordable. Yet there remained the problem of the unwholesome dwellings built before the adoption of sanitary regulations. These dwellings became known as slums, a term referring both to individual houses deemed 'unfit for human habitation' and entire districts – *the* slum – regarded as areas of social pathology, the breeding grounds of disease, crime and immorality. The slum 'nuisance' was to be eradicated either by forcing the landlord to repair or demolish an individual unfit dwelling or by the demolition of entire slum areas. Local government's role was not to build, except in exceptional circumstances and with special permission, but to demolish the slums and assemble a site for rebuilding by private enterprise or by philanthropic organisations whose shareholders restricted the return on their investment.

In 1885 the Royal Commission on the Housing of the Working Classes investigated the impact of this 'nuisance removal' and the activities of the railway companies and street-widening schemes. It concluded that the situation had deteriorated since the 1850s and made a number of recommendations to improve housing conditions. Local authorities should be allowed to build outside clearance areas; the lowest possible rate of interest, without making a loss, should be charged by the Treasury for housing schemes; the 1883 Cheap Trains Act, requiring railway companies to operate cheap workman's trains, should be enforced; and the existing legislation requiring railway companies to build houses to replace those demolished to make way for new stations should be implemented more diligently. In 1890, the Housing of the Working

Classes Act permitted local authorities to erect houses outside clearance areas provided that they did not make a loss on any scheme. As Morton (1991, p 2) has pointed out: 'There was no question at this point of any agency operating on other than commercial terms. Authorities were expected to act like commercial companies and seek a return not exceeding 5 per cent'. Although some authorities ignored the 'no loss' requirement, only 20,000 local authority houses had been built by 1914.

The housing issue circa 1906

During the 19th century the housing issue was constructed as a matter of public health, public order and public morality. The role of the state was to mitigate urban externalities without too much disturbance to the operations of the housing market. Some commentators were prepared to accept municipal house building to replace slums demolished in the public interest but subsidised housing was regarded as illegitimate. As one Member of Parliament said, 'If such a principle were admitted he did not know where it could stop. The next demand made on them [Parliament] might be to provide clothing if not carriages and horses' (quoted in Wohl, 1983, p 314). However, towards the end of the 19th century – prompted by a slump in house building, sensational press accounts of 'the condition of England' and the growth of the labour movement – debate started to focus on the ability of the capitalist market economy to meet the housing requirements of the working class. Many ideas on how to end the 'housing famine' – as it was called at the time – were in circulation.

Employer-provided housing

Housing provided by employers contributed about 10% of the Victorian dwelling stock. Some estates were built as 'model villages' linked to factories and provided high-quality accommodation but the paternalism and social control involved in their management made them unacceptable to the independently minded working class. As Ravetz (2001, p 37) comments:

> For the most part the model villages were admired as the single harmonious communities their founders wanted them to be.... The price was, of course, the acceptance of paternalism and the elimination of deviance and militancy. We are told that when Lever toured his village it was, among other things, to confirm that any worker off sick had placed his boots in the window, as proof that he really was indoors and not truanting in the big city ... as a trade unionist wrote to Lever in 1919, 'No man of an independent turn of mind can breathe long in the atmosphere of Port Sunlight'.

Land and the Liberals

Housing policy was not a matter that divided the Liberal and Conservative Parties in the second part of the 19th century but, by the turn of the century, fissures had started to appear. These divisions can be traced to 1886 when a large number of Liberal landowners defected from the Party over home rule for Ireland. This split enabled the Liberal Party to concentrate on land reform both as an issue in itself and as a means to end the housing shortage and thereby counter the growing influence of the organised labour movement. The 'land issue' had been brought to prominence by Henry George who, in *Progress and Poverty* (1979 [1879]), argued that land values were created by the community. He advocated a single land tax that would reclaim for the community any rise in land values not due to the landlord's efforts.

Many members of the Liberal Party, adopting George's approach, argued that the housing famine was caused by landowners who were hoarding land in anticipation of future higher values. Moreover, in urban areas, where landowners leased their land to developers, they were avoiding local taxation in the form of the rates and were paying no tax on their 'unearned' capital appreciation. Winston Churchill put the issue bluntly in 1909:

> Roads are made, streets are made, railway services are improved, electric lights turns night into day … water is brought from reservoirs a hundred miles off in the mountains – and all the while the landlord sits still…. To not one of those improvements does the land monopolist … contribute and yet by every one of them the value of his land is enhanced. He renders no service to the community, he contributes nothing to the general welfare; he contributes nothing even to the process from which his own enrichment is derived. (Churchill, 1909)

Taxation of land at its potential use value, so the National Liberal Federation claimed, would persuade landowners to release land and make them pay their fair share of local taxation. Lloyd George introduced land taxation in his 1909 'People's Budget' but problems with land valuation and adverse court judgments meant that, by 1914, only £612,787 had been collected (Packer, 2001).

Garden cities

Land values formed an important element in Ebenezer Howard's advocacy of garden cities. In *Garden Cities of Tomorrow* (1902) he argued that the 'magnets' of living in the city or the country could be combined in a planned garden city surrounded by a rural 'green belt' and organised through a not-for-profit trust. An important element of Howard's scheme was the retention of enhanced land values by the community. As the city grew, land values within its boundaries would increase and this 'betterment gain' could be used by the not-for-profit trust to provide community facilities and stimulate cooperative housing ventures.

Planning the suburbs

Despite some experimental schemes in new town planning, the garden city idea failed to gain momentum and its advocates turned their attention to influencing the suburban development occurring at the time. Between 1893 and 1908 cheap public transport had allowed half a million acres of land to be used for building and it was argued that suburbia had to be planned if the mistakes of the past were to be avoided. The 1909 Housing and Planning Act was a diluted version of an attempt to allow local government to plan the shape of the emerging suburbs by permitting them to acquire land by compulsory purpose. Rather than grant such a power the Act gave local authorities the permissive power to control the development of new estates after a lengthy exercise in public consultation. Few local authorities used the Act's powers.

Municipal housing

The first Manifesto of the Labour Representation Committee, formed in 1900 to establish a voice in Parliament for the working class, declared its objective as 'the emancipation of labour from the domination of capitalism and landlordism' (quoted in Mellor, 1989, p 585). It demanded the general public provision of better houses, a demand that marked a step change in the perception of the housing issue away from sanitary matters and towards the general shortage of affordable, quality homes and the need to plan housing developments in line with transportation systems (Thompson, 1903). Nevertheless, there were divergent views within the labour movement about how to improve the housing situation, with a significant group, including the Marxist Social Democratic Federation and the Independent Labour Party, claiming that higher wages, not the public provision of dwellings, was the solution. The most radical factions advocated land nationalisation whereas others joined the more progressive Liberals in adopting Henry George's ideas. Some activists favoured 'co-partnership' schemes that had built about 7,000 houses before 1914. In such schemes tenants were shareholders in a holding company entitled to low-interest loans under the 1909 Housing and Planning Act. The Fabians and the Workmen's National Housing Council supported municipal housing with the arguments that building by direct labour organisations would eliminate the developer's profits and that local authority housing would retain enhanced land values in the community. They pressed for Treasury grants to local government to reduce the cost of municipal housing.

Refurbishing places and people

Octavia Hill (1838-1912) was against tenant subsidies because she thought that state support would produce a 'pauper mentality'. She believed that slum dwellings were the product of two influences, both linked to 'character'. Uneducated slum landlords tried to make a quick profit from dilapidated dwellings – she was fond of quoting a slum landlord and undertaker who claimed to be in the private landlord business for 'the bodies it produced'! Such private landlords had to be replaced by 'fit and proper' housing managers. She also believed that tenants contributed to their housing conditions by ill-disciplined behaviour. Her housing management philosophy was the 'tough love' of combining the efficient administration of reconditioned older property with character reformation. Such reformation was to be achieved through the personal influence of a housing worker sustained by a home visit for weekly rent collection and a system of sanctions and incentives to promote good conduct. Drunk and disorderly behaviour and rent arrears were punished by summary eviction whereas good conduct was rewarded by speedy repairs and extra rooms.

> As soon as I entered possession, each family had an opportunity of doing better: those who would not pay, or who led clearly immoral lives, were ejected. The rooms they vacated were cleansed, the tenants who showed signs of improvement moved into them. (Hill, 1883, p 25)

The Conservative Party and housing policy

Confronted by radical demands for land reform the Conservative Party assumed a defensive position and surrounded itself by pressure groups such as the Liberty and Property Defence League and the Land Union set up to fortify the position of landowners. The Conservatives denied the need for radical change citing Census evidence that between 1891 and 1911 the overcrowding problem had abated but they were prepared to concede that the 'slum problem must be grappled within the slum' by building multi-storey flats (Mayne, 1993, p 85).

Housing policy 1914-39

Landlord–tenant relationships

In 1914 about 90% of households rented from a private landlord. Most private landlords owned only a few houses and financed their purchases from personal savings plus borrowing from insurance companies, building clubs and building societies (Lund, 2002). In the early part of the 20th century the residential property market experienced a slump but, contrary to market theory, vacant properties existed close to overcrowded and unfit dwellings. This was because the private landlord sector was divided into sub-markets and many landlords were reluctant to move 'downmarket' to house a 'lower class' of tenant who may not be able to pay the rent on a regular basis. This reluctance also reflected divisions within the working class. At the time it was conventional to refer to the 'working classes' – artisans (skilled) and labourers (unskilled) – and the 'respectable' artisan element was unwilling to live in the same neighbourhood as 'rough' manual labourers. Landlord–tenant relationships at the lower levels of the market were strained, it being a constant battle to extract rent from poor families prone to 'moonlight flits' and aggressive behaviour.

Rent control

House building stopped on the outbreak of the First World War and the movement of workers into the munitions factories led to rent increases. Faced with working-class unrest, notably in Glasgow, the government introduced rent control and restricted interest rates on the associated mortgages. Rent control was buttressed by giving tenants security of tenure to prevent landlords from evicting sitting tenants to extract a higher rent. Rent control was due to be revoked six months after the end of hostilities but fear of social unrest prevented such a move. The Conservatives – in power for most of the inter-war period – attempted to back out of rent control gradually. Their general approach was to classify dwellings according to their markets and decontrol those sectors where it was thought that supply and demand were in balance. New building for rent was decontrolled soon after the end of the war and, by 1939, dwellings with a high rateable value had been decontrolled and houses with middle-range rateable values became decontrolled on vacant possession. Only low-value houses – about 44% of the total rented stock – remained controlled and the Conservatives had declared their intention to abolish all rent control as soon as possible. There was a modest revival of private landlordism in the mid-1930s. The political dominance of the Conservative Party making a return to rent control unlikely, there were favourable economic conditions for residential construction (Kemp, 2004) and the 1933 Housing (Financial Provisions) Act allowed local authorities to guarantee building society loans made for building rented accommodation.

Council houses for the working class

The Fabian Society, whose members occupied influential positions on the various wartime reconstruction committees (Orbach, 1977), played a significant role in framing the 1919 Housing and Town Planning Act. This Act made it mandatory for each authority to compile a plan to meet the housing needs in its area and granted open-ended central subsidies to local authorities to meet the cost of house building above a set contribution from the rates. The Fabians received valuable support from the garden city advocates who, while maintaining that building a hundred garden cities was the best way to create a 'land fit for heroes to live in', endorsed the view that community provision, not profit-motivated private enterprise, was the right path. Opposition to subsidised local authority provision came from the Treasury but was overcome by the need to provide work for the demobilised troops and by the fear of social unrest. Lloyd George put the issue bluntly to the Cabinet meeting that endorsed the measures contained in the 1919 Act. 'Even at the cost of £100,000,000', he said, 'what was that compared with the stability of the State' (quoted in Johnson, 1968, p 346). Although subsidised local authority housing was regarded as a temporary expedient, scheduled to end in 1927, the new homes were to be built to high standards. The Tudor Walters Committee Report (Tudor Walters, 1918) – mainly written by the Fabian Socialist, Raymond Unwin – stated that the temptation to build on small urban sites should be resisted. Rather, the new homes should be built on suburban sites at low densities and have bathrooms, gardens and, in some cases, parlours. As Burnett (1986, p 255) has stated, 'every Englishman was, or felt he was, a disinherited country gentleman' and social stability would be created by mimicking the 'manor' in suburban estates. The 1919 Act gave local authorities the power to control densities and estate layouts in homeownership schemes as well as in council estates.

Central subsidies to local government to build houses acted as a butterfly valve in the inter-war period serving to direct local authorities towards central government priorities. In 1921, when the 1919 Housing and Town Planning Act ran into difficulties because the housing market was overheated by too many local authorities competing for limited construction industry capacity, the Conservatives ended central subsidies. Two years later the 1921 Housing Act introduced fixed subsidies to assist local authorities to build houses but councils were able to build only when they had demonstrated that the private sector could not meet the need for new dwellings. The contrast between the Conservatives' 'residual' view of council housing and Labour's more comprehensive 'suburban solution' was revealed in the 1924 Housing (Financial Provisions) Act passed by a minority Labour government. Negotiated with housing producers – the building workers' trade unions and their employers – it was aimed at guaranteeing a long-term demand for housing built by traditional methods. The Act granted higher subsidies than the 1921 Housing Act and removed the restrictions on local authority house building. The 1930 Housing Act, also passed by a Labour government, introduced special subsidies, in addition to those for 'general needs', to encourage local authorities to tackle the problem of unfit dwellings.

Council housing to replace the slums

In the inter-war period homeownership started to develop at a rapid rate (see Box 2.2; Figure 2.1) and its growth influenced the attitude of the Conservative Party to council housing

The Conservatives maintained the local authority subsidy of the 1924 Housing (Financial Provisions) Act – albeit at reducing levels – but, in the early 1930s, leading Conservatives expressed concern about the growing involvement of local government in housing supply (Yelling, 1992). The 1933 Housing (Financial Provisions) Act ended general subsidies for local authority housing, retaining only the subsidy arising from the building to clear the slums to which the 1935 Housing Act added a subsidy for the relief of

Box 2.2: The growth of homeownership

Homeownership increased from an estimated 10% in 1914 to 34% in 1939 (Holmans, 2000). This growth can be explained by the following:

- State assistance was provided in the form of:
  - subsidies for inexpensive houses owner-occupied under the 1919 Housing (Additional Powers) Act and the 1923 Housing Act;
  - tax relief on mortgage interest, although the impact of such relief was modest because Schedule A tax on imputed rental income had to be paid;
  - mortgage guarantees and cheap loans from local authorities, for example the 1936 Small Dwellings Acquisition Act.
- The extension of suburban railways made it possible for more people to live at a distance from their workplace. This trend, together with the dearth of planning controls, enabled builders to erect dwellings on cheap 'greenfield' sites making houses affordable to more people. In the 1930s real interest rates declined and the availability of cheap labour made homeownership more affordable for those in secure employment.
- Finance for house purchase became more accessible because savings invested with building societies increased rapidly. The numerous building society offices offered a convenient and generally safe haven for the savings of the middle class and the skilled working class. Housing became regarded as a secure form of investment and payment periods were extended from 10-12 years to 25 years. Deposits were reduced from about a third before the war to 'almost nothing' by the 1930s (Offer, 2003, p 15). The continuance of rent control had made a traditional repository of such savings – direct investment in houses to let – less attractive.
- Some landlords, concerned about rent control and security of tenure for tenants, sold their properties to sitting tenants.

Figure 2.1: **Housing tenure: England and Wales, 1919-2004**

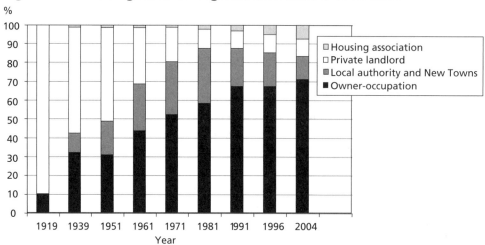

Sources: Adapted from Holmans (2000); ODPM (2005a)

overcrowding. It is clear that in the 1930s the Conservatives' housing strategy was to confine the state to removing 'pathological' conditions in the cities leaving private enterprise to build the vast majority of new dwellings for homeowners on suburban sites. Council housing, as a proportion of total building, declined from 44.4% of housing output between 1919 and 1924 to 21.5% in the late 1930s (Glynn and Oxborrow, 1976).

Labour and housing policy 1945-51: a planned solution

On the outbreak of the Second World War, the government did not wait for social unrest before putting rent controls in place. Except for very high-value properties, rents were frozen for the duration of hostilities.

Despite the progress made between the wars there was still a serious housing shortage. The war intensified the problem with 458,000 houses destroyed and 250,000 badly damaged and at the end of hostilities household formation accelerated and the birth rate increased. Housing became *the* political issue and a squatting movement developed with homeless people, sometimes led by the Communist Party, taking over disused army camps and empty luxury flats. Despite these problems, there was no housing equivalent of Beveridge's report on social security (Beveridge, 1942). This absence of a comprehensive housing policy review may have been a reflection of the urgent and obvious nature of the problem – a massive shortage of houses – and the self-evident nature of the solution – state-directed production that had been so successful in meeting the needs of the war economy. The *Daily Mirror* declared in 1945 that 'Housing will have to be tackled like a problem of war. We make, as if by miracle, tanks,

Box 2.3: Housing between the wars: an assessment

The absence of Census data for 1941 and the dearth of national housing statistics on housing quality make it difficult to assess the impact of housing policy between the wars. Without doubt substantial progress was made in improving housing conditions. Housing investment, averaging about 19% of total domestic investment between 1870 and 1914, increased to 33% between 1930 and 1938 (Glynn and Oxborrow, 1976). Four million houses were completed: 1.3 million in the public sector, 470,000 in the private sector with state aid, and 2.5 million by unsubsidised private enterprise. 250,000 unfit properties were demolished (Bowley, 1945). Rowntree (1941) found that overcrowding in York had been reduced by two thirds since 1900. Unfit property had decreased from 26% of the housing stock in 1900 to 12% in 1936.

aircraft, battleships, pipelines, harbours! Are we then incapable of building houses?'.

Although the Coalition government had been lukewarm on the long-term dominance of local authorities in supplying new homes, Aneurin Bevan, who became the minister responsible for the housing programme in 1945, favoured local authorities because they were plannable instruments and could meet, in a direct manner, the need of poor people for rented accommodation. No attempt was made to change the natures of either homeownership or private landlordism that were basically frozen in their 1930s forms. Neither did the Labour Party nationalise the building industry, so most of the new council homes were built by private builders. The government offered local authorities a new flat-rate subsidy for 'general needs' houses, which tripled the subsidies on offer in the late 1930s and made them available for 60 rather than 40 years. Bevan made it mandatory for local authorities to make a rate contribution to house building and allowed local authorities to borrow from the Public Works Loans Board at a rate of interest below the market rate. The supply of local authority houses would form part of a planned physical environment: see Box 2.4.

Mixed communities

Bevan wanted to ensure that all new housing schemes promoted mixed communities and demanded that three out of four new houses should be owned by local authorities or New Town Corporations and built to high standards. He asserted that 'We don't want a country of East Ends and West Ends, with all the petty snobberies this involves' (quoted in Foot, 1975, p 78). Bevan's vision of local authority housing as replicating the social mix of the Welsh village with its 'living tapestry of a mixed community' (quoted in Foot, 1975, p 78) was reflected in the 1949 Housing Act. This removed the

> **Box 2.4:** Post-war planning
>
> The 1947 Town and Country Planning Act:
>
> - imposed taxes of between 40% and 100% on the 'betterment' value of land used for development;
> - set up a Central Land Board with powers to purchase land compulsorily;
> - made provision for grants to be paid to local government for land assembly;
> - placed a duty on local authorities to prepare development plans;
> - allowed local authorities to acquire land by compulsion;
> - required most development to have planning permission.
>
> The 1946 New Towns Act made provision for the establishment of New Towns as a method of relieving congestion in the major cities, reviving the fortunes of the 'depressed areas' of the inter-war period and creating balanced communities.

requirement – present in all previous housing legislation – that local authority housing was to be supplied only to the working class. In the face of opposition from other Cabinet members he insisted on higher standards than had been provided in the inter-war period. Space in each house was increased by 134 square feet compared to pre-war houses, an outbuilding was added and there were water closets, both upstairs and downstairs, in each family dwelling. Such improvements increased the cost of council housing by 35% compared to pre-war levels (Morgan, 2005). In 1948 Bevan ended the prefabricated bungalows programme, started in 1944, arguing that such homes were 'rabbit hutches' of insufficient quality and limited space. Although it controlled building for homeownership with a system of licences, Labour was not opposed to homeownership in principle. For Bevan, politics was about priorities and priority was to be given to people who could not afford to buy. Four fifths of the houses built between 1945 and 1951 were local authority houses and Labour's 1951 Manifesto stated that, in future, 'Most of these houses will as now be built for rent and not for sale, and for the benefit of those whose housing need is greatest' (Labour Party, 1951, p 4).

The Conservatives and housing policy 1951-64

The 'people's house'

Housing construction was sluggish between 1945 and 1951 and actually declined between 1950 and 1951. In the late 1940s the Conservatives began to blame state involvement for this slow progress, arguing that restrictions on the private sector and the taxation of land values were impeding the housing drive. At the 1950 Conservative Party Conference the delegates passed a resolution – against the wishes of the leadership – calling for a target of 300,000 houses per year. This target was used in the 1951 Conservative Party Manifesto and started a political numbers auction that lasted until the early 1970s. Although the Manifesto declared that 'In a property-owning democracy, the more people who own their homes the better' (Conservative Party, 1951, p 3) the Party recognised that there was little hope of meeting its housing target through private enterprise alone. The private sector had built only 26,000 dwellings in the previous year and, in 1951, there was still a crude housing shortage with 800,000 more households than dwellings. Thus, for a time, the Conservatives continued to rely on local government. By reducing standards – the so-called 'people's house' was 15% smaller than those built in the 1940s – encouraging terrace building and increasing subsidies, 300,000 new dwellings were built in 1953. Nevertheless, a Party committee established in 1951 to discuss ways to restore the free market in housing set out the Conservative's long-term housing policy as:

- the encouragement of house ownership;
- the limitation of subsidies to slum clearance;
- the majority of people – tenants and owner-occupiers – should pay the full cost of the accommodation they occupy (Weiler, 2003, pp 362-3).

The Conservative Party was set to return to the 'bifurcation' of housing policy (Kleinman, 1996) – a market-based approach, assisted by fiscal incentives for the mainstream and state housing for the urban poor.

Stimulating the private sector

In a series of measures introduced in the mid-1950s – reminiscent of the strategy pursued in the late 1930s and with portents of the measures introduced in the 1980s – the Conservatives took some tentative steps towards applying free market principles to housing. The policies were heralded in the White Paper, *Housing: The Next Step*, which acclaimed homeownership as 'the most satisfying to the individual and most beneficial to the nation' (Ministry of Housing and Local Government, 1953, p 3). Local authorities were forced to borrow from the capital markets at higher rates of interest than had been available from the Public Works Loan Board, subsidies to local authorities to build for 'general needs' were withdrawn and the available central resources were concentrated on slum clearance. Housing policy again became a matter of containing urban England and, in 1955, this was reinforced by the codification of Green Belt policy and its extension to areas other than London. The statutory contribution from the rates to council housing was ended and an attempt was made to persuade local authorities to charge more 'realistic' rents with local rent rebate schemes to cushion the impact on low-income households. Private sector solutions to the problem of unsatisfactory dwellings were encouraged by the introduction of mandatory improvement grants for the installation of basic amenities.

In line with the 1930s policy of relaxing rent control as dwelling supply increased, the 1954 Rent and Repairs Act allowed limited rent increases in return for repairs. This Act was opposed by the Labour Party on the argument that landlords could not be trusted to spend any rent increase on repairs. Labour proposed to make rented housing a social service via the municipalisation of the private landlord. In 1957 the Conservatives made a major attempt to stop the decline of private landlordism by relaxing rent controls. Under the 1957 Rent Act the rents of dwellings above a specified value were decontrolled and creeping decontrol was introduced by ending rent control when a house became vacant. This experiment in free market economics was a political disaster. Decontrol failed to increase the pool of private rented houses and did not even stop the decline. In 1957 there were 4.5 million privately rented homes but by 1965 the total had fallen to 3.5 million. Rent decontrol generated a political storm as the vicious tactics of a small number of slum landlords to secure vacant possession added a new term to the English language – 'Rachmanism'– named after Perec Rachman, the most notorious practitioner of the abuses. The already tarnished reputation of private landlordism was stained again. In an attempt to ease the housing problem and cool the political controversy, 'general needs' subsidies were restored to local authorities in 1961 and, in 1963, owner-occupation was stimulated by the abolition of Schedule A Tax: see Box 2.5.

Labour and housing policy 1964-70

Despite the emotional atmosphere in which the housing issue was debated during the 1964 election campaign, the policies of the two major parties were similar. The Conservative Party, although lukewarm on local authority housing, had to give it a role. Private landlordism had been totally discredited by the publicity given to the activities of Rachman and an attempt, started in 1962, to create a 'third sector' of non-profit landlords through 'cost-rent societies' – a form of housing association – needed time to make an impact. A ten-year plan (Ministry of Housing and Local Government, 1963) promised 400,000 houses each year with a substantial portion being local authority homes. Labour outbid the Conservatives by setting an annual target of 500,000 houses by 1970. The Party had a stronger commitment to public housing than its rival but thought it necessary to declare its support for owner-occupation by a promise to reduce the interest rate on mortgages to 4%.

The Labour government of 1964-70 attempted to adopt an even-handed approach to local authority tenants and homeowners. Its five-year housing programme promised to split new building 50/50 between the two sectors. Labour's growing taste for homeownership was reflected in the declaration that public sector growth was a response to 'exceptional needs' whereas 'the

Box 2.5: Taxation and homeownership

Schedule A was a tax levied on the rental income all owner-occupiers were assumed to have paid to themselves. It ensured that a homeowner was treated in the same way as a private landlord who had to pay tax on rental income. As part of the package involved in Schedule A payment both owner-occupiers and private landlords were allowed to deduct their mortgage interest payments from their Income Tax liability. Schedule A Tax had a diminishing impact in the years after the Second World War because the house values on which it was based were fixed at 1936 levels. Thus, as the real impact of Schedule A Tax abated, tax relief on mortgage interest became more valuable to homeowners. When Schedule A Tax was abolished for resident owners in 1963, mortgage interest tax relief continued and thereby the subsidy to homeowners was enhanced. The tax concession was important to people paying the standard rate of taxation and valuable to those people paying the higher rates of tax, especially when interest and taxation rates were high.

expansion of buildings for owner occupancy ... is normal' (Ministry of Housing and Local Government, 1965, p 3). Owner-occupation was stimulated by the introduction of an option mortgage scheme allowing a person with a low income who did not benefit from tax relief on mortgage interest to receive a low-interest loan. Gradually Labour began to restore the balance between public and private sector building that had tipped in favour of owner-occupation in the late 1950s and early 1960s and encouraged local authorities to adopt better space and amenity standards. The annual production gap between the two sectors narrowed from 96,000 in 1964 to 23,000 in 1969 but, as Dunleavy (1981, p 24) has commented, 'if Labour's strategy was successful in terms of the numbers of public housing completions, it contained the seeds of its own demise in the type of housing being completed'.

Cities in the sky

The story of high-rise housing is complicated with a number of factors contributing to its construction (see Box 2.6). The Conservatives provided a central subsidy for high-rise housing in 1956 and, after gaining momentum in the 1960s, high-rise construction did not start to decline until after the 1968 collapse of a high-rise block of flats – Ronan Point – when seven people were killed. Other forms of innovative housing design and estate arrangement were introduced in the 1960s. Deck access, in which entry to flats was attained from walkways to enhance social interaction, became established and many low-rise estates were designed on Radburn principles, which separated vehicle and pedestrian access.

Private landlords and the improvement of older dwellings

The Labour government set up new mechanisms to regulate rents, giving tenants and landlords the opportunity to ask for a rent assessment committee to determine a 'fair' rent – one that ignored scarcity value – for a property. Theoretically this was impossible but the device enabled market rents to be moderated. Cross-party consensus was generated around a switch in emphasis from clearance to improvement based on a degree of targeting of funds on designated neighbourhoods. Labour promoted this change in emphasis as a positive measure, stressing the ways that clearance disrupted established communities, but the policy was also a response to the financial crisis of 1967 and the demands of the International Monetary Fund for cutbacks in public expenditure. Rehabilitation was cheaper than demolition and new building.

Box 2.6: High-rise housing

Flats were never popular with the people they were designed to house. Their form was alien to the ground-level terraced property familiar to the English working class and flats 'were the products of monolithic and large-scale design which gave little scope for the users to modify through their ordinary domestic behaviour' (Ravetz and Turkington, 1995, p 57). Until the mid-1950s, technological limitations restricted the height of blocks of flats to about seven storeys but advances in construction techniques allowed high-rise building. By 1966-67, 25% of the dwellings constructed were high-rise and, in the major cities, the proportion was far higher – up to 70% in Greater London. Over 60% of all tower blocks were built by industrialised systems (Dunleavy, 1981).

High-rise building was the product of a number of influences. The architectural profession was dominated by 'modernism'. The Bauhaus School argued that structural form should reflect the functional mechanisms within the building and hence dwellings should have clear, angular lines and incorporate materials such as glass, steel and concrete. Le Corbusier (1927) claimed that houses should be 'machines for living in'. Well-spaced tower blocks, providing homes with equal access to daylight, should be linked by 'streets in the air' allowing the area around and beneath the blocks to be used as parkland. The major building firms, who possessed the techniques for system building, regarded high-rise building as a source of profit and used their influence on the National Building Agency and with senior politicians to promote tower blocks. Central government wanted housing units to be built quickly and regarded system building as a way to achieve this objective. Many city authorities demanded more homes within their boundaries in order to retain rateable value and preserve civic status whereas rural authorities – assisted by the Green Belt policy – resisted most attempts to move the 'overspill' of people from clearance schemes to their areas.

The Conservatives and housing policy 1970-74

'Fair' rents and rent rebates

The 1972 Housing Finance Act made provision for local authority rents to move towards the 'fair' rents charged in the private landlord sector, with poorer tenants protected from the consequent rent increases by a national rent rebate scheme. If, having charged 'fair' rents, a particular local authority housing revenue account made a surplus – the 'fair rents' producing more than the costs of providing council houses – this surplus had to be paid to the government.

It is possible to construe the 1972 Housing Finance Act in two ways. It can be interpreted as a move towards restoring a free market in rented accommodation, especially if one accepts that there was a potential link to be made between 'fair' rents and future 'market' rents. Alternatively the Act can be seen as a rational/technical measure designed to make more effective use of available resources. It was presented in this way in the White Paper *Fair Deal For Housing* (DoE, 1971, p 4), which condemned the system of distributing housing subsidies based on the historical entitlements of earlier legislation as providing 'subsidy for housing authorities which do not need it' and 'giving too little to authorities with the worst problems of slum clearance and overcrowding'. The Act also introduced a national allowance scheme for tenants in the private landlord and housing association sectors.

Labour and housing policy 1974-79: the party's over

Labour recast the policy contained in the 1972 Housing Finance Act. The national system of rent rebates and allowances was retained but local authorities were instructed to charge only 'reasonable' rents. A new form of central government subsidy was introduced by the 1975 Housing Rents and Subsidies Act that consolidated all existing assistance and granted a subsidy of 66% of the loan charges for new capital investment. The ideas contained in the Conservative White Paper *Better Homes: The Next Priorities* (DoE, 1973) were adopted and incorporated into the 1974 Housing Act. Housing associations were given a major role by the legislation. Associations registered with The Housing Corporation became entitled to Housing Association Grant designed to pay, as a capital sum, the difference between the cost of a project and the amount that could be raised by charging 'fair' rents. Between 1974 and 1976 local authorities and housing associations were provided with resources to purchase and refurbish properties owned by private landlords in 'stress' areas – partly meeting the long-standing demand from Labour Party activists to 'socialise' the private landlord sector. In addition, housing associations were encouraged to build new homes. These measures – combined with the financial impact of the more generous improvement grant regime and the subsidies needed to boost council house construction because of high interest rates – meant that housing expenditure increased rapidly.

The sterling crisis of late 1976 and the agreements made with the International Monetary Fund produced big cuts in capital expenditure. Anthony Crosland, Secretary of State for the Environment, declared that 'the party's over' and a housing review concluded:

> We should no longer think about [housing] only in terms of national totals; we must try to secure a better balance between investment in new houses and the improvement and repair of older houses ... we must increase the scope for mobility in housing ... and we must make it easier for people to obtain the tenure they want. (DoE, 1977, p 7)

Economic circumstances and the growing popularity of owner-occupation – described in the housing review as a 'basic and natural desire of all people' (DoE, 1977, p 50) – had combined to modify Labour's traditional faith in public housing. Thus, although the review acknowledged that, in the long term, local authority housing meant inexpensive housing because investments were held at fixed historic costs and older houses could be used to 'cross-subsidise' newer houses, the council building programme was cut back. The freedom of local authorities to decide how many new houses to build, subject only to meeting 'cost yardsticks' was ended. Improvement grants were scaled back and the policy of bringing private landlords into the social sector was curtailed. Local authority housing construction fell from 110,000 in 1975 to 47,000 in 1979 and housing association production fell from 27,000 in 1976 to 14,000 in 1979 (Newton, 1994, p 24).

Despite changes in emphasis, the improvement of older homes was consensus politics and produced significant improvements in housing conditions. Table 2.1 and Figure 2.2 set out the statistics on housing changes in the period under examination, and Box 2.7 assesses the impact of the policies pursued.

The New Right and housing policy

In 1975 the Conservative Party acquired a leader with firm anti-collectivist beliefs as was demonstrated in Ranelagh's record of Margaret Thatcher's only visit to the Conservative Research Department.

Box 2.7: Housing policy 1945-79: an assessment

The post Second World War years are often seen as a period of consensus in social policy but this is only partially true of housing policy. The Labour Party was ideologically opposed to private landlordism and the 1957 Rent Act was bitterly contested. There were periods of consensus on the respective roles of homeownership and local authority housing but also times of conflict especially concerning the respective roles of means-tested consumer and general producer subsidies in helping to reduce housing costs to below market levels.

The loss of six years of house building, the damage to the existing stock in the war years and the backlog of need unmet in the inter-war years meant that post-war housing politics was dominated by a numbers game with success accessed according to the number of new units erected in any year. Unfortunately quality was often sacrificed for quantity – not of internal amenities, but in the design, density and environment of the new dwellings. Tower- and 'slab'-block housing was to taint the image of local authority housing for years to come.

Table 2.1: *Housing 1945-81: England and Wales*[a]

	1951	1981
Rooms per person	1.36	1.86
Local authority rents at 1997 values	£10.30	£18.80[b]
Household/dwelling balance (000s)[c]	−1660	440[b]
Dwellings without bath or shower (millions)	4.8[d]	0.5[b]
Without hot water supply (millions)	7.4	0.7[b]

Notes:
[a] The available statistics do not match the political phase under analysis. Thus figures are given for 1951 and 1981.
[b] England only.
[c] Estimated surplus or deficit (–) between the number of separate households and the number of separate dwellings.
[d] 1947 figure.
Source: Adapted from Holmans (2000)

Figure 2.2: **Housing construction: UK, 1919-2004 (000s)**

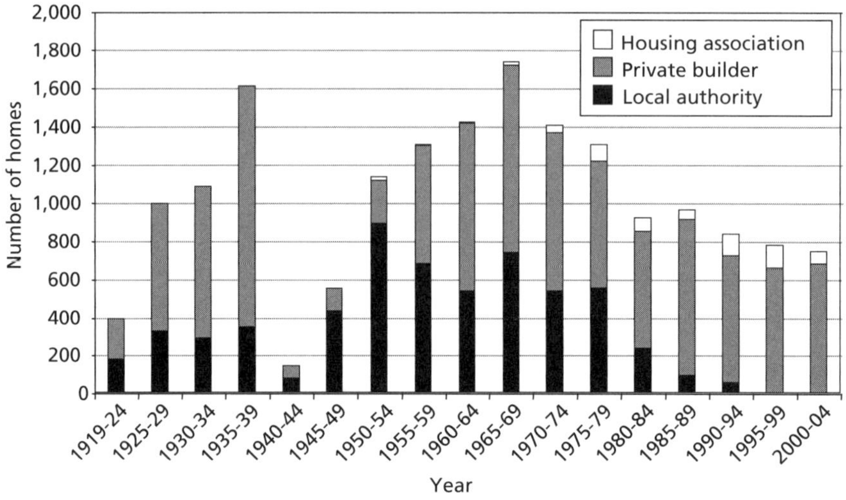

Sources: Adapted from Holmans (2000); ODPM (2005a)

Another colleague had also prepared a paper arguing that the 'middle way' was the pragmatic path for the Conservative Party to take, avoiding the extremes of Left and Right. Before he had finished speaking to his paper, the new Party leader reached into her briefcase and took out a book. It was Friedrich von Hayek's *The Constitution of Liberty*. Interrupting our pragmatist, she held the book up for all of us to see. 'This,' she said sternly, 'is what we believe' and banged Hayek down on the table. (Ranelagh, 1991, p ix)

By 1975 there were years of experience of state intervention in housing against which laissez-faire ideas could be tested. It was the predictions made by such theorists as Hayek that made their arguments so powerful. In 1960 Hayek had warned that subsidised state housing would result in uncontrollable expenditure and the increase in state subsidies to council housing in the late 1970s could be interpreted as confirmation of Hayek's prediction. The experience of state housing also created concern about lack of consumer influence in the local authority sector. It was alleged that architects working for local authorities had ignored the views of potential tenants in designing their 'urban utopias'. The negative features of state housing were contrasted with the positive aspects of owner-occupation that, so it was argued, encouraged personal responsibility and gave people a capital stake in society.

The Right to Buy

In the 1970s council house sales began to feature more strongly on the Conservative Party's agenda. Selling council houses was not a new idea – it had started in the late 19th century – but its impact had been limited despite the government granting local authorities a general consent to sell in 1952. In the early 1970s some Conservative-controlled councils started to promote council house sales and, in the election campaign of 1974, the Conservatives promised to allow council tenants to buy their homes at 33% less than the market value. In 1975, a member of the Shadow Cabinet suggested that council tenants who had occupied their houses for 20 years should be given their homes. According to Gilmour (1992, p 142), 'Mrs Thatcher feared that those on the Wates estates, the least well-off owner occupiers, whom she regarded as 'our people' would have resented council house occupiers being given something for nothing...' and hence the outright gift proposal was changed to the 1974 discount system but on more generous terms. Conservative ideas on the sale of council houses caused great concern in among Harold Wilson's advisors and a scheme for the sale of council homes was prepared in secret by Labour (Haines, 1977). However, when Labour's housing review was published in 1977, there was no mention of any new scheme for council house sales. Instead, proposals were put forward to enhance the status of tenants by offering more involvement in council house management and more legal rights. These proposals were incorporated into a Bill introduced into Parliament in 1979. The Bill fell with the defeat of the government but its provisions were included in the 1980 Housing Act (see Box 2.8).

The Conservative Party was on firm political ground in selling council houses. Opinion surveys conducted in the late 1970s revealed that less than 20% of council tenants under the age of 55 stated that their ideal choice of tenure in two years' time was the council sector and 59% of council tenants gave negative reasons for living in their present accommodation. Even the letter sent in 1979 by Mrs Thatcher's Private Secretary to a tenant who had complained about the condition of her home probably demoralised as many council tenants as it angered. It said:

> I hope you will not think me too blunt if I say that it may well be that your council accommodation is unsatisfactory but considering the fact you have been unable to buy your own accommodation you are lucky to have been given something which the rest of us are paying for out of our taxes. (quoted in *The Times*, 9 April, 1979)

> **Box 2.8:** The 1980 Housing Act
>
> The privatisation of council housing was neatly linked with Labour's notion of tenants' rights in the 1980 Housing Act and the 1980 Tenants' Rights (Scotland) Act. Local authority tenants became 'secure tenants' with a clearer set of rights regarding possession and people who had been 'secure tenants' for three years (later reduced to two) were given an individual right to purchase their homes at a substantial discount on the market value. This was 33% for a three-year tenancy rising by 1% per year to a 50% maximum in the early stages of the policy and was later extended to 60% on houses and 70% on flats subject to a 'cost floor' based on the capital expenditure on the house made by the local authority in the previous eight years. Non-charitable housing association tenants were given similar rights. The 1980 Housing Act added the push of higher rents to the pull of discounts by introducing a new subsidy system that withdrew subsidy from local authorities on the assumption that they would increase their rents according to ministerial guidelines. Later, eligibility for Housing Benefit was restricted so that, by 1988, only households on less than 50% of average male gross earnings were able to claim, compared to those on 110% of average male gross earnings in 1983.

Liberalising the private sector

In the early 1980s some circumspect moves aimed at reviving private landlordism were introduced. The remaining controlled tenancies were brought into the regulated sector and landlords could let property as 'shorthold' tenancies subject to 'fair' rents but with the landlord able to repossess after a fixed term. New 'assured' tenancies allowed approved landlords to let newly constructed property at market rents. A number of innovative but limited schemes to promote low-cost homeownership were also set up and, in 1986, the Building Societies Act completed a process of allowing building societies and banks to compete in a deregulated mortgage market. This mortgage market deregulation made it possible to expand homeownership with deregulation shifting 'the market to one where consumers could obtain the funding they wanted at the market price rather than being subject to market restrictions' (ODPM, 2005b, para 3.34).

Changing the nature of housing associations

From the early 1960s both the major political parties showed an increasing interest in housing associations as a housing 'third arm' but for different reasons – Labour regarding them as a means of 'socialising' the private landlord sector and the Conservatives viewing them as an alternative to local authority housing. Until the late 1980s housing associations obtained their capital finance from the government and therefore their borrowing counted in determining the size of the Public Sector Borrowing Requirement (PSBR). The 1988 Housing Act transformed the nature of housing associations and paved the way for their expansion as part of the 'independent' sector whose borrowing did not count in calculating the PSBR. The Act placed all new housing association tenants under the formal legal regime governing tenant–landlord relationships in the private landlord sector – pleas from the National Federation of Housing Associations for a distinct housing association tenure were ignored. The Right to Buy was abolished for new housing association tenants, making private sector investment in housing association stock more attractive. Housing associations had to rely on private finance for an increasing proportion of their investment and had to compete to secure grants according to which associations could meet the government's objectives at the lowest cost. Rents were expected to move towards market rents with Housing Benefit mitigating the impact of higher rents on low-income households.

Ending council housing and reviving the private landlord

The 1987 Conservative Party Manifesto was aimed at a further reduction of the role of local authorities as housing suppliers and at using market forces, underpinned by a more selective system of housing assistance, to promote private rented accommodation. Homeownership retained its dominant position in the Party's ideology but the new policy initiatives were directed mainly at the rented sector. A White Paper was published setting out the government's view of the impact of past policies and giving four aims for the future:

> First to reverse the decline of private rented housing and improve its quality; second to give council tenants the right to transfer to other landlords if they choose to do so; third to target money more accurately on the most acute problems; and fourth to continue to promote the growth of owner occupation. (DoE, 1987, p 3)

The Conservatives had mixed success in achieving these aims.

Private landlords

Private landlordism was promoted by:

- removing rent controls on new private sector lettings with Housing Benefit 'taking the strain' from low-income households;
- ending security of tenure;
- allowing investors in private landlordism to claim up to 40% of their investment against their tax liability for five years through the Business Expansion Scheme;

• enabling housing associations to manage property on behalf of private landlords.

These measures helped to halt the decline of the private landlord sector and its share of the housing stock increased by 1% between 1987 and 1997 but at a high cost in terms of additional expenditure on Housing Benefit and the income forgone under the Business Expansion Scheme. Housing Investment Trusts, designed to encourage investment by financial institutions in private landlordism, had little impact (Crook, 2002).

Local authority housing

Under the 1988 Housing Act a statutory procedure was established to enable local authority tenants to change landlords via individual action or a 'tenant's choice' ballot. In addition, Housing Action Trusts were to be set up to take over local authority estates, improve them and then sell the stock into a variety of tenures. However, as Margaret Thatcher (1993) recognised in her memoirs, the implementation of this policy was troublesome. Despite extensive publicity, tenants showed little interest in leaving their local authority. Housing Action Trusts encountered local opposition and gained modest momentum only when tenants were given assurances that they could return to their local authority when the improvements had been made. Initially moves towards ending the local government provider role came more from local authorities using large-scale *voluntary* transfer than from tenants concerned about the quality of local authority management. The sale of council homes to special housing associations set up to receive the dwellings allowed local authorities to keep homes for rent in their areas by avoiding the Right to Buy, enabled extra spending on repairs and maintenance through private finance and produced substantial capital receipts. Between 1989 and 1995, 41 councils, mainly in the South, transferred over 185,000 homes to the housing association sector. Limitations on capital finance to local authorities significantly reduced council house building and, by the late 1990s, housing policy had 'come to be seen increasingly as an arm of regeneration policy for low-income inner cities and marginal estates, rather than an end in itself' (Hills, 1998, p 124) – a familiar theme in the history of Conservative housing policy.

Selectivity

Targeting money more accurately on the most acute problems was achieved by means testing improvement grants and limiting their application to the 'fitness' standard (see Chapter Seven). Rent increases plus greater targeting of Housing Benefit continued the trend towards reliance on means-tested consumer subsidies rather than producer subsidies. Between 1978/79 and 1996/97 government housing expenditure declined from 5.8% to 1.5% of total expenditure whereas spending on Housing Benefit increased from 1.2% to 3.8% (Hills, 2004, p 130).

Homeownership

Promoting owner-occupation was knocked off course by the crisis in homeownership of the late 1980s and early 1990s. The removal of restrictions on borrowing in the mid-1980s and the announcement by the Chancellor that tax relief on mortgage interest would be limited to one person per house rather than two for an unmarried couple helped to kick-start a sharp increase in the price of houses (see Figure 2.3). Feeling confident and affluent on the basis of the current value of their dwellings, many homeowners began to spend on consumer durables. In addition, a large amount of equity, estimated at over £50 billion between 1985 and 1989 was taken out of the accumulated value of housing by re-mortgaging. The subsequent rise in consumer spending followed by use of interest rates to dampen the housing boom – the mortgage interest rate reached 15.4% in February 1990 – led to a slump in house prices. Mortgage arrears increased, repossessions escalated and negative equity – homes where the value is less than the amount borrowed – emerged as a significant problem. In order to prevent a further downward spiral in house prices the government introduced a housing market package that provided finance to housing associations to purchase unsold homes built for owner-occupation. The decline in house prices dampened tenant enthusiasm for the Right to

Figure 2.3: Real average house price: UK mix adjusted

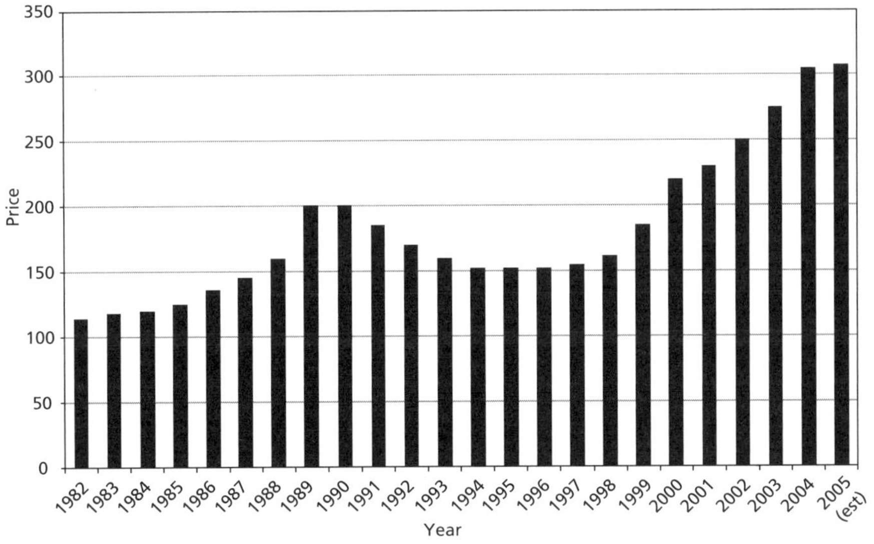

Note: 1977 = 100

Sources: Adapted from Scottish Executive (2005); ODPM (2005a)

Buy and a 'rent into mortgage' scheme had few takers. In order to reduce the PSBR produced by the recession, John Major's government started to phase out tax relief on mortgage interest so that, after reaching a peak of £800 per recipient in 1990/91, it declined to £230 in 1996/97. Table 2.2 sets out statistics on housing inputs and outputs between 1981 and 1997.

Table 2.2: *Housing inputs and outputs, 1981-97: England*[a]

	1981	**1997**
Net capital investment in housing at constant prices (£ million)	5,201	2,095
Local authority rents at 1997 values	£18.80	£41.20
Exchequer and rate fund subsidy to local authority tenants (£ million)	1,732	−614
Dwellings without bath or shower (millions)	0.5	0.1
Without hot water supply (millions)	0.7	0.2
Local authority rents (% of average earnings)	6.9	13
Households without one or more basic amenities (millions)	0.9	0.2
Fewer bedrooms than standard (000s)	760	508
% of local authority tenants receiving rent rebates	40	66
Number of households accepted as homeless under the 1977 Housing (Homeless Persons) Act (000s)	60.4	103.3
Publicly funded renovations (private and housing associations) (000s)	100.3[b]	56
Households in temporary accommodation	5,372[b]	44,360
Unfit dwellings (%)	6.3	7.5[c]
In serious disrepair (%)	5.8	6.1[c]
Housing Benefit expenditure (£ million)[d]	3,766	12,313
% of national housing subsidies spend on Housing Benefit	11.7	57.4
Average value of tax relief on mortgage interest (£)	335	230

Notes:

[a] The available statistics do not match the time period under analysis. Thus figures are given for 1981 and 1997 unless stated otherwise.

[b] 1979 figure.

[c] 1996 figure: the definitions of unfitness and disrepair changed between 1981 and 1997.

[d] Great Britain figure.

Sources: Adapted from Barr et al (1998); Wilcox (1998); Hills (1990); Holmans (2000)

Overview

- In the 19th century the housing issue was constructed as a sanitary problem related to 'externalities' of order, health and morality.
- Initially the provision of state-subsidised houses supplied by local authorities was perceived as a 'temporary expedient' made necessary by the abnormal circumstances of war.
- The Labour Party adopted council housing as its principal means of delivering affordable housing in planned environments but, when in government in the 1960s and late 1970s, moved towards promoting homeownership.
- The Conservative Party, although prepared to support council housing to overcome extreme housing shortages and to contain urban England, preferred homeownership.
- From the 1960s both the major political parties showed an interest in housing associations – Labour to replace the private landlord and the Conservatives to replace council housing.
- Between 1979 and 1997 the Conservative Party applied market principles to the supply and distribution of housing but with a bias towards owner-occupation.

Questions for discussion

(1) What were the arguments for and against sanitary reform in the 19th century?
(2) How was the land question related to the housing issue at the end of the 19th century?
(3) Why was private landlordism in decline for most of the 20th century?
(4) Labour was the party of council housing, the Conservatives were the party of homeownership. Discuss this statement.
(5) Why and how was council housing 'eclipsed' between 1977 and 1997?
(6) Give reasons for the growth of homeownership in the 20th century.

Further reading

Hamlin's (1998) *Public Health and Social Justice in the Age of Chadwick: Britain, 1800-54* is a perceptive account of the politics of sanitary reform. **Ravetz's (2001)** *Council Housing and Culture: The History of a Social Experiment* offers an interesting account of the rise and fall of council housing. *The Five Giants: A Biography of the Welfare State* by **Timmins (2001)** charts the politics of housing policy from 1945. *Private Renting in Transition* by **Kemp (2004)** tells the story of the decline of private landlordism and its modest revival in the 1990s. There is no up-to-date book on the development of homeownership but *Dunroamin: Suburban Semi and its Enemies* by **Oliver et al (1981)** is an appealing account of suburbia and its enemies.

Website resources

The Victorian Times website at www.victoriantimes.org contains many original documents on housing in the 19th century.

Steve Wilcox's *UK Housing Review*, containing statistics on the development of housing policy since the 1980s, can be downloaded from www.cih.org/publications/downloads/ukhr.htm

An excellent legislation time line can be found in *A Chronology of State Medicine, Public Health, Welfare and Related Services in Britain: 1066-1999* at www.chronology.org.uk/

three

New Labour and the governance of housing

Summary

- The Treasury distributes public expenditure approvals in three-year rolling cycles, each cycle being preceded by a spending review that sets performance targets for the spending ministries.
- For many years direct responsibility for housing policy has been located within a state department with a changing but broad remit covering such functions as physical planning, local government and regional economic planning.
- The Department for Work and Pensions has a key role in housing policy because it is responsible for Housing Benefit.
- Following constraints between 1997 and 2002, public expenditure on housing increased and, since the early 2000s, its distribution has shifted towards stimulating new housing supply.
- Local authorities have a 'strategic enabling' role in meeting local housing needs but their provider role is being supplanted by housing associations.
- In recent years, the regional dimension of housing market management has been strengthened.
- New Labour maintains control over housing agencies through a robust regulatory regime based on targets and performance indicators.
- Since 1998 various degrees of devolved powers have been granted to the Scottish Parliament, the National Assembly for Wales and, when sitting, the Northern Ireland Assembly.

The governance of housing

This chapter sets out the political and administrative contexts in which New Labour frames its housing policies. The term 'governance' has been chosen to convey the ambience of New Labour's style in devising and implementing policy. New Labour has adopted a pragmatic approach to policy development, placing emphasis on 'evidence-based' policy or 'what works, counts' rather than on the imposition of the 'old' ideologies of the market *or* the state. Tony Blair's 'Third Way' rhetoric promotes a diversity of suppliers connected via partnerships.

> The days of the all-purpose local authority that planned and delivered everything are gone. They are finished. It is in partnership with others – public agencies, private companies, community groups and voluntary organizations – that local government's future lies. Local authorities will still deliver some services but their distinctive leadership role will be to weave and knit together the contribution of the various local stakeholders. (Blair, 1998, p 13)

New Labour claims to seek a 'collaborative discourse' (Glendinning et al, 2002) between public and private enablers and providers to promote networks of 'joined-up' thinkers within a policy community. The term 'governance' rather than 'government' also reflects New Labour's attitude to the forces of globalisation. The 2001 White Paper *Opportunity for All in a World of Change* stated:

> There are limits to what national governments can realistically achieve on their own. In a global economy we benefit from investment by multinational companies which can go anywhere in the world. We cannot force companies to invest or to continue to invest in particular places. (Department of Trade and Industry, 2001, para 1.37)

Thus New Labour attempts to adjust housing provision to go with the grain of this world of change rather than to govern to try to buck the global trends.

The Treasury

The Treasury controls the lion's share of the resources necessary to pursue a housing policy aimed at stimulating housing supply, maintaining the existing housing stock and ensuring affordability. It allocates public expenditure in three-year rolling cycles with a spending review every two years preceding the distribution. Under New Labour the Treasury has applied two rules to government spending: the 'golden rule' that over the economic cycle – flexibly defined – borrowing should not be used to finance current expenditure and the 'sustainable investment rule' that borrowing for investment should be below 40% of GDP.

New Labour's 1997 Manifesto contained few robust pledges on housing expenditure. Unspent local authority capital receipts from Right to Buy sales would be released on a phased basis to rehabilitate older houses and build new homes via a partnership between the public, private and housing association sectors, and the problem of homeless young people would be 'attacked' (Labour Party, 1997).

Despite the release of unspent capital receipts in debt-free authorities, state expenditure on housing declined during New Labour's first term of office. Its 1997 election pledge to retain the Conservative Party's spending programme for two years – a programme anticipating a fall in housing capital expenditure – was responsible. Housing did not fare well in New Labour's first comprehensive spending review (HM Treasury, 1998), which revealed that only in 2001/02 would resources start to flow at a faster rate than in the last full year of the Conservative government. The second spending review promised that investment in housing and regeneration would increase from £4.46 billion in 2000/01 to £7 billion in 2003/04. As part of the review each Department of State entered into a Public Service Agreement with the Treasury specifying strategic targets. The principal housing target was to:

> Ensure that all social housing is of a decent standard by 2010 with the number of families living in non-decent social housing falling by one third by 2004 and with most of the improvement taking place in the most deprived local authority areas as part of a comprehensive regeneration strategy. (HM Treasury, 2000, para 9.3)

New Labour's first housing policy statement (DETR, 2000a) said little about improving supply. Rather it placed emphasis on improving the quality of the existing housing stock and promoting choice via stock transfer from local government, a new system of choice-based lettings and sustaining the private landlord sector. By 2002, however, it had become clear that, after five years of New Labour governance, the housing situation in England had deteriorated compared to the last year of John Major's government (see Box 3.1). Unrest within the parliamentary Labour Party over housing policy and the intervention of the Chancellor of the Exchequer produced what the Deputy Prime Minister called a 'step change' in policy towards encouraging housing supply – a traditional objective of 'old' Labour. The 2002 spending review extended the decent homes target to an increase in 'the proportion of private housing in decent condition occupied by vulnerable groups'. It also added the achievement of 'a better balance between housing availability and the demand for housing in all English regions …' to the Government's housing objectives (ODPM, 2004a, p 17).

The initial response of the Office of the Deputy Prime Minister (ODPM) to achieving a better balance between supply and demand was contained in *Sustainable Communities: Building for the Future* (ODPM, 2003a), which identified a housing shortage in the South East where housing construction was well below government targets. This shortfall was to be met by investment in four 'growth areas': the Thames Gateway, Ashford, Milton Keynes–South Midlands and the London–Stansted–Cambridge corridor, supported by £610 million, over three years, from the Treasury for site assembly and infrastructure work. Extra resources for affordable housing were promised with two thirds of the total national resources for new social housing earmarked for the South East. Funding, in the form of a Market Renewal Fund, was provided to allow nine 'pathfinder' authorities in the North and the Midlands to tackle low demand. The fourth spending review stated that the ODPM would have over £1.3 billion a year more to spend on its programme in 2007/08 than in 2004/05. The resources would be used to:

- increase the supply of new social house building by 50% to 'turn around the growth in homelessness';
- increase the supply and improve the affordability of housing by continued infrastructure investment in the growth areas;
- supply extra investment to regenerate localities suffering from low demand (HM Treasury, 2004, p 107).

Box 3.1: The state of housing: 2002

- New social housing completions had fallen from 32,463 in 1996/97 to 22,347 in 2001/02 mainly because the overall resources available to subsidise social housing had not kept pace with increased land and construction costs.
- In London, social housing lettings had declined by 6%.
- Overcrowding had remained static nationwide but, in London, the number of seriously overcrowded households had increased by 60% between 1991 and 2001.
- The number of households in temporary accommodation had almost doubled in five years.
- The completion of new dwellings – 175, 499 in 2001/02 – was the lowest since 1945 and had remained steady for five years.
- The annual rate of house price inflation was 18.5%.
- Household formation – the combined impact of increased life expectancy, net international in-migration and the trend towards living in separate households – was predicted to rise by 3.25 million between 2001 and 2021 (see Table 3.1).

Sources: ODPM, 2003a; Reynolds et al, 2004; Wilcox, 2004

Table 3.1: *Estimates of household formation, 2003-21*

England: population at start (2003)	Natural change (births – deaths) 2003-06 each year	Natural change (births – deaths) 2006-11 each year	Natural change (births – deaths) 2011-16 each year	Natural change (births – deaths) 2016-21 each year	Net migration per year 2003-06	Net migration per year 2006-11	Net migration per year 2011-16	Net migration per year 2016-21	England: population in 2021
49,856,000	101,000	98,000	111,000	113,000	108,000	124,000	124,000	124,000	53,954,000

England: households at start (2001)[a]									England: households in 2021
20,750,000									24,000,000

Note:

[a] Estimates of future household formation are based on population projections. Population projections are translated into projections of household formation based on known trends. For many years the rate of household formation has been faster than population increase because of an ageing population, trends in divorce and separation and the desire of young people to live independently.

Sources: Adapted from: ONS (2004a); ODPM (2005a)

House building picked up after 2001/02 with 190,186 completions and 212,056 starts in 2003/04. The government exceeded its 60% target for new dwellings – including conversions – to be provided on previously developed, 'brownfield' sites but density increased to 39 dwellings per hectare in 2004 compared with 25 dwellings per hectare between 1996 and 2001. In 2003/04, 40% of dwellings were flats, double the share in 2000/01, while new detached houses fell to 30% compared to 50% in 1995/96. In the South East the proportion of flats increased from 16% in the registered social landlord sector in 1995/96 to 66% in 2004/05 and in the private enterprise sector from 14% to 45%, raising the issue of the suitability of such accommodation for families.

The Bank of England

Setting the minimum interest rate is an important dimension of economic management and, in the past, the government has increased the interest rate to control inflation or, in times of recession, reduced it to stimulate spending. In 1998 New Labour passed interest rate control to the Bank of England in order to generate confidence from the financial institutions in the government's ability to manage the economy. The housing market has an important impact on inflation and other economic indicators because, at times of rising house prices, people use the equity in their homes to finance additional spending. Between 1998 and 2003 gradual reductions in the interest rate had fuelled house prices and helped push up inflation so, in 2004, the Bank of England increased the interest rate. This fed through to the housing market in 2005 when the rate of house price increase declined rapidly.

Department for Work and Pensions

Known as the Department of Social Security until 2001, the Department for Work and Pensions is responsible for a range of benefits and services aimed at reducing poverty and encouraging people to work. Housing Benefit, administered by local authorities under rules set by the Department for Work and Pensions, is an important instrument of housing policy. Between 1979 and 1996 housing subsidies were switched from producer subsidies towards means-tested consumer subsidies in the form of Housing Benefit.

The Office of the Deputy Prime Minister

Between 1919 and 1951 responsibility for housing policy was located in the Ministry of Health but was then transferred to the Ministry of Housing and Local Government and, in 1970, to the Department of the Environment. In 2002, after a series of different homes, housing policy became part of the

ODPM. The functions of the ODPM are coherent but its title is a consequence of the political position and interests of the Deputy Prime Minister, John Prescott. It is responsible for:

- housing policy;
- neighbourhood renewal and social inclusion;
- delivering improved public services and better local government performance;
- regional economic performance and regional assemblies.

Having received its spending allocation and its broad distributional principles from the Treasury, the ODPM allocates its resources to the agencies responsible for delivering housing services.

English Partnerships

English Partnerships, formed in 1999 by an amalgamation of the Commission for the New Towns and the Urban Regeneration Agency, is the national regeneration agency. Its role is to identify and assemble land, especially brownfield and other publicly owned land, to be used for sustainable development. It manages a number of strategic sites and, in the government's 2005 five-year housing strategy, *Sustainable Communities: Homes for All* (ODPM, 2005c), it was given the lead role in the First Time Buyers Initiative set up to help people become homeowners. Public sector land – mainly redundant National Health Service sites – was earmarked for use in creating equity sharing schemes targeted on key public service workers and others unable to buy on the open market.

The Housing Corporation

The Housing Corporation is a non-departmental public body with its board and chief executive appointed by the Deputy Prime Minister. It was set up in 1964 to distribute resources to housing associations and to monitor their activities. It defines its aims as:

- to regulate and promote a viable, properly governed and properly managed housing association (registered social landlord) sector;
- to invest for the creation and maintenance of safe and sustainable communities;
- to champion a resident focus in the housing association sector;
- to be a modern, customer-centred, forward-looking organisation, encouraging change in the sector (Housing Corporation, 2004a).

Having determined the slice of its budget to be allocated to housing associations, the ODPM establishes the broad principles for its distribution but relies on the Housing Corporation to allocate it to individual associations as Social Housing Grant. In the past this was done via a Housing Needs Index (HNI) – based on local requirements for new dwellings – and on the quality and cost-effectiveness of bids for new development from registered social landlords. However, the HNI distribution has been increasingly modified according to regionally determined priorities and, since 2003, The Housing Corporation has identified 70 registered social landlords or consortia of registered social landlords as 'preferred partners'. In 2004 private developers in England and Wales became eligible to receive Social Housing Grant directly from the Housing Corporation.

The regional dimension

In its earlier departmental forms, the ODPM maintained a regional structure of civil servants who played a significant role in distributing housing resources to local government. Within variable limits they could adjust the General Needs Index (GNI) distribution (a calculation of each local authority's housing needs based on such factors as overcrowding and housing conditions) according to their perceptions of the quality of each local authority housing strategy. In 1994 these civil servants were merged with regional officials from other departments to form Single Regional Government Offices. The Housing Corporation also had regional offices to allocate funds to local areas and Regional Planning Bodies had been set up to help determine the scale of housing provision over a 15-year period and allocate land release targets for housing to local authorities. Ad hoc arrangements such as joint commissioning were made to coordinate the decisions of these agencies but, as New Labour became more interested in regional devolution and set up unelected regional assemblies, these decision-making procedures were seen as in need of reform. In 2003 Regional Housing Boards were established to devise regional housing strategies and advise the Deputy Prime Minister on resource allocation to specific areas within each region in the form of 'supported capital expenditure'. The Boards were made up of senior officials from Government Regional Offices, the Housing Corporation, Regional Assemblies, Regional Development Agencies and English Partnerships but it was open to regions to have wider membership where they considered this to be appropriate. Although there has always been regional discretion in modifying the outcomes of the GNI and the HNI, the introduction of Regional Housing Boards enhanced the role of regional discretion. A consultative document released in 2004 by four central departments indicated that, in future, Regional Housing Boards and Regional Planning Boards would be merged and the budgets for housing, and economic development would be combined at the regional level and with Regional Assemblies responsible for advising ministers on the long-term allocation of these pooled resources (HM Treasury et al, 2004).

Local government

In England the 36 metropolitan district councils in urban areas outside London and the 33 London boroughs are responsible for all local authority functions, although the fire service, police and public transport responsibilities are exercised through Joint Boards. Until 1995 local government powers outside the urban areas were divided between county councils and district councils (see Box 3.2) but a process of local consultation between 1995 and 1998 led to the unitary model being introduced in some areas but rejected in others. There are now 34 county councils in England with 238 district councils and 46 unitary authorities. Parish and town councils cover areas up to 30,000 people, but usually far less, and have very limited responsibilities for local services and environmental improvements.

Capital expenditure

Although the difference is somewhat blurred it has become conventional to distinguish between capital expenditure – investment for the future to be financed by borrowing – and revenue expenditure to be consumed and paid for in a particular year. In the past, local authority capital expenditure was centrally controlled by 'credit approvals' for each service but under the 2003 Local Government Act local authorities can borrow up to what are called 'prudential borrowing' limits. These are set in accordance with guidelines issued by the Chartered Institute of Public Finance and Accountancy and place great stress on the ability of the local authority to repay the capital and the interest.

Box 3.2: The distribution of functions in county council/district council areas

County councils	District councils	Shared
Education	Local planning	Recreation
Social services	Housing	Cultural matters
Transport	Local highways	
Strategic planning	Building regulation	
Fire services	Environmental health	
Consumer protection	Refuse collection	
Refuse disposal	Leisure services and	
Smallholdings	parks	
Libraries		

Despite this prudential borrowing power, central control over local authority capital expenditure is maintained through what is known as 'supported capital expenditure', that is, capital expenditure that the government is prepared to support with financial aid, often by redistributing the receipts from the Right to Buy. Special allocations are made for specific government initiatives such as New Deal for Communities, the Neighbourhood Renewal Fund and the Market Renewal Fund.

The Housing Revenue Account

In 2004 local authorities owned 2,983,000 houses. Their finance is governed by a specific Housing Revenue Account that must be kept by each local authority and balanced every year. Since the early 1990s the main objective of the complex and opaque central rules governing such accounts has been to maintain central control over local authority rents to prevent those local authorities with low outgoings – the outcome of a good stock built in the past at low cost – from using this advantage to promote the interests of their tenants. In 1989 the Housing Revenue Account was 'ring-fenced' (rents could not be supported by other local government income streams) and, more importantly, the cost of Housing Benefit for council tenants was added to the expenditure side of the Housing Revenue Account. This meant that most Housing Revenue Accounts fell into deficit and local authorities had to rely on central 'subsidies' to keep rents at reasonable levels. Central government set guideline average rents for each local authority and used them to calculate subsidy entitlement in accordance with a notional housing revenue account. If, after allowing for these guideline rents, the cost of Housing Benefit to council tenants and various allowances for items such as management, maintenance and loan charges, the nominal account was in deficit then a 'subsidy' was paid by central government. If a surplus was identified this had to be paid into the local authority's 'General Fund' and was available for spending on all local services or for reducing local taxation.

These mechanisms ensured that the real rents set by local authorities were broadly in line with the guideline rents determined by central government although some local authorities did set rents outside the guidelines. Moreover, because the guideline rents were increased substantially in the 1990s, many council tenants were effectively paying for the Housing Benefit of their poorer neighbours – a sacrifice not required of other tenants or homeowners. Until the introduction in 2001/02 of the Major Repairs Allowance – an element in the Housing Revenue Account aimed at boosting a local authority's resources for maintaining its stock in its current condition – the local authority housing stock produced a substantial surplus, worth £1,834 million in 2000/01 (Wilcox, 2004).

In 2002 central government started to take control not only of the general level of local authority rents but also the specific rent of each dwelling. A target rent for each house was set according to a formula taking into account average earnings in the area plus the size and location of the dwelling and capital values but subject to a maximum rent for each type of dwelling. Existing rents of both local authority and housing association dwellings would gradually converge to the target over 10 years. The impact of these target rents is variable according to place but many local authority tenants will have to pay substantially higher rents. Rent restructuring was justified with the argument that there were anomalies in the existing rents of social housing and that consistency in social rents – relative to the qualities valued by tenants – was fairer (DETR, 2000b, ch 10). Nevertheless, rent convergence between the local authority and housing association sectors had the added bonus for the ODPM of reducing the tenant resistance to stock transfer. Direct central control of individual rents also meant that counting Housing Benefit for council tenants on the debit side of the Housing Revenue Account was no longer necessary for central control of local rents. Thus, under the 2003 Local Government Act, Housing Benefit expenditure was excluded from the Housing Revenue Account but any surplus on the account had to be paid to the ODPM for distribution to authorities with a deficit. In the eastern region of England, for example, tenants were paying £14 per week in rent to support housing costs elsewhere whereas, in London, housing costs were supported by £15 per week from tenants in other areas (Audit Commission, 2005a, p. 53).

Housing strategies

Housing strategies were introduced in the late 1970s as 'a means of controlling public expenditure while allowing resources to be allocated selectively with regard to variations in local requirements' (DoE, 1977, p 12). Local authorities had to assess their housing investment requirements, devise a strategy to meet them and submit resource bids to central government. Local housing strategies assumed a new importance in the late 1980s when the Conservative government designated local authorities as housing 'enablers' rather than housing providers and the quality of each housing strategy in enabling housing associations, private landlords and developers to supply housing became an important factor in central resource distribution. This enabling role for local housing authorities has been adopted by New Labour but with a more strategic emphasis. According to the ODPM a Housing Strategy Statement should be:

> ... an over-arching document that reviews housing-related issues in a local authority's area, sets out its housing objectives, establishes priorities for action both by the local authority and by other service providers and stakeholders, and sets out a clear Action Plan in agreement with the council's local partners. It should also be consistent with national policy and designed to deliver regional and sub-regional strategies (including those for economic

development and land use) as well as meeting the authority's wider objectives. (ODPM, 2004b, p 2)

In addition to a housing strategy the 2002 Homelessness Act required every housing authority in England to adopt and publish a homelessness strategy aimed at preventing homelessness and ensuring that accommodation and support are available for people who are homeless or at risk of becoming homeless (ODPM, 2004c).

Performance indicators and targets

Margaret Thatcher embraced the market as the means to ensure efficiency and consumer satisfaction in the delivery of public services but, in acknowledgement that the special characteristics of certain services make it difficult to apply full market principles, this was modified to the pursuit of 'quasi-markets' (see Box 3.3).

Building on the 1989 Local Government and Housing Act requiring councils to publish performance indicators to demonstrate their efficiency, John Major's administration introduced a number of 'Citizen's Charters' justified as ways of empowering individual citizens through knowledge, choice and market-testing. Performance indicators would be made available for each service to enable consumers to make informed choices and existing suppliers and 'independent' contractors would be invited to bid for contracts to manage public services. Under the 1992 Local Government Act local authorities had to start a process leading to the compulsory competitive tendering of their housing management functions – the repairs service had been subject to compulsory competitive tendering since 1980. By 1997, 69 local authorities had tendered their housing

---

Box 3.3: What is a quasi-market?

A quasi-market has been defined as:

A market in the sense of independent agents competing with one another for the custom of purchasers, but a quasi-market in that, unlike in a normal market, purchasing power came not directly from the consumer but from the state. (Le Grand, 2001)

In housing, the quasi-market took the form of:

* suppliers of rented housing – local authorities, housing associations and private landlords – competing for customers on the basis of charging market rents;
* people who could not afford to pay market rents would be subsidised by Housing Benefit available on equal terms to the tenants of all types of landlord.

management functions with most resulting in 'in-house' wins (Boyne et al, 2003). When elected, New Labour delayed the competitive tendering process and, in the 1999 Local Government Act, substituted competitive tendering with the requirement that every 'best value authority must make arrangements to secure continuous improvement in the way in which its functions are exercised, having regard to a combination of economy, efficiency and effectiveness' (1999 Local Government Act, section 3.1). The Act gave the government powers to specify:

(a) factors (performance indicators) by reference to which a best value authority's performance in exercising functions can be measured;
(b) standards (performance standards) to be met by best value authorities in relation to performance indicators specified under paragraph (a) (Local Government Act, 1999, section 4.1).

Local authorities now publish housing service best value reviews according to nationally determined performance indicators and the Housing Inspectorate, located in the Audit Commission, inspects all housing authorities in England. Services are rated on a star system from 0 to 3 with all services scoring 0 re-inspected within 18 months. Performance indicators and associated targets are part of what has been called 'the new public sector managerialism' (see Box 3.4).

Housing associations

A housing association is a not-for-profit organisation set up to supply accommodation. Housing associations are run by boards of management made up of unpaid volunteers who, unlike local councillors, are not elected, which means that a diversity of organisations and people can become involved in supplying social housing – some housing associations, for example, are run by ethnic minorities. Housing provision does not automatically qualify for

Box 3.4: The new public sector managerialism

The introduction of quasi-markets was accompanied by what has been called 'new public sector managerialism'. The 'old' bureaucratic and professional forms of organisation required a rival culture to challenge their authority. The new managerialism was defined by what it was not – it was consumer rather than state orientated, based on ends not means, stressed vertical 'contract' rather than hierarchical 'command' relationships and was geared to performance outcomes rather than rule-based accountability. New Labour has adopted and enhanced the new public sector managerialism as a means to promote and control a diversity of suppliers within a framework of state-financed services.

charitable status so some associations register as charities on the grounds that their activities are concerned with the relief of poverty, promoting education or the advancement of religion, or are of benefit to the community. Charitable status offers tax advantages and many associations have adopted group structures organised into separate legal entities under a parent body. This gives them the flexibility to pursue both charitable and non-charitable activities. If registered with the Housing Corporation under the 1996 Housing Act, housing associations become 'registered social landlords' (see Box 3.5). They are entitled to apply for financial assistance from the state but are subject to regulation by the Housing Corporation.

In the late 1980s housing associations started to be created for the specific purpose of managing stock transferred from local authorities. Transfer associations differ from many of the established housing associations in that they tend to operate in a specific geographical area and there are usually tenant and councillor representatives on their management boards. If set up as a local housing company, there is equal representation on the board for tenants, council nominees and 'independents'. Tenants transferred to the new association retain the Right to Buy.

Nomination agreements between local authorities and housing associations are important mechanisms through which local authorities can meet their obligations to homeless families and ensure that those in the greatest housing need can secure accommodation. By providing land, using local authority Social Housing Grant (now abolished) and Section 106 agreements (see Chapter Five) local authorities have been able to secure 75% to 100% nomination rights on first lets but subsequent re-lets and accommodation built without direct local authority assistance usually involve lower percentages of local authority nominations.

Central control and local autonomy

Central government now has a great deal of control over the activities of local authorities and housing associations. Local government has been declared a 'policy-free zone' with its role being 'to deliver centrally determined policies in a strategic way' (Maile and Hoggett, 2001, p 512) and the Audit Commission (2005a, p 2) has claimed that 'Council housing might more accurately be labelled 'national' housing'. Rents are set by a national formula; resource allocation is determined by central views of the quality of various local housing strategies; the regional resource distribution process lacks an elected element and the everyday activities of local government are subject to performance targets and inspection. The autonomy of housing associations, traditionally viewed as housing's independent 'third arm', is also in question. State financial assistance for new building, support service provision and the refurbishment of older properties is accompanied by detailed regulation, inspection by the Audit Commission, performance indicators and the regional discretion involved

Box 3.5: Registered social landlords: key facts

Table 3.2: Size of landlord by number of units

Number of units	Number of registered social landlords	% of total stock
Over 10,000	29	26.8
2,501-10,000	202	55.4
1,001-2,500	104	9.8
251-1,000	157	4.7
Less than 250	1,433	3.2

Table 3.3: Largest five housing associations

	Stock owned	% of total housing association stock
North British	39,140	2.2
Home Group	29,320	1.7
Anchor	27,766	1.6
Sanctuary	26,492	1.5
London and Quadrant	24,741	1.4

Table 3.4: Average weekly rent, 2004 (£s)

	Registered social landlord	Local authority
Bedsit	54.11	42.46
One bedroom	56.88	45.29
Two bedrooms	60.81	50.71
Three bedrooms	64.84	55.14
Four+ bedrooms	77.20	66.92

Table 3.5: Property size compared to local authorities (%)

	Registered social landlord	Local authority
Bedsit	3.8	2.4
One bedroom	29.3	26.4
Two bedrooms	33.3	32.7
Three bedrooms	30.4	35.7
Four+ bedrooms	3.1	2.7

Table 3.6: *Lettings, 2002-03 (general needs)*

Household type	% of lettings	Ethnic origin	% of lettings
Lone adult	50	White	86
Lone parent	23	Asian British	4
Two adults	11	Black British	7
Two adults with children	12	Mixed	2
Others	6	Refused to give ethnic origin	2

Economic status	% of lettings	Income (£s)	% of lettings
Working full time	23.1	Less than 100	5.7
Working part time	6.3	101-150	11.4
Unemployed	14.7	151-175	7.9
Retired	20.4	176-225	21.9
At home	20.9	226-275	18.5
Other	10.6	276+	34.6

Source of income	% of lettings	Housing Benefit	% of lettings
Wholly state benefits	52	In receipt	58
Partially state benefits	15	Not in receipt	23
No benefits	21	Unknown	19
Other/unknown	12		

Source: Adapted from Housing Corporation (2005a, 2005b)

in the grant distribution bidding process. Moreover, housing association rents are set by central government according to a formula similar to the one applied to local authorities. As Malpass (2000, p 259) has argued, housing associations 'are little more than agents of the state and the voluntary element has been reduced to marginal and largely symbolic importance, providing a fig-leaf for those who really hold the power'. The government has created a housing sector that is directly controllable by the central state. This control is exercised by the same new public sector management techniques used to direct the local authority sector.

Tenant participation

The Conservatives believed that the market was the best method to promote tenant empowerment in social housing. They wanted to break down local government's family rented accommodation monopoly through 'tenant's choice' and produce a system whereby, by developing a range of independent landlords, tenants could exercise 'exit' politics. If a tenant did not like the service supplied by their landlord then exit to another landlord was possible, supported, if necessary, by Housing Benefit.

Local authority tenants

Although 'tenant's choice' was a failure, finally abandoned in 1996, the Conservatives' desire to fragment local authority housing produced some fruitful innovations in tenant participation in the form of Tenant Management Organisations (TMOs). In 1994 the development of TMOs was encouraged by a 'right to manage' under the 1993 Leasehold Reform, Housing and Urban Development Act. This gave all local authority tenant groups representing 25 or more households the right to assume a variety of management and maintenance responsibilities subject to training and a ballot in favour of the change.

There are two broad types of TMOs – tenant management cooperatives and estate management boards – although, in practice, the distinction is rather blurred. Neither of the TMO forms owns the housing stock but tenant management cooperatives are usually composed of residents and directly control their own staff whereas estate management boards often have councillor representatives and frequently use local authority officials. TMOs enter into agreements with their local authorities specifying the nature of the responsibilities delegated to them. In 2001 there were 202 TMOs covering about 84,000 properties. Research into TMO activities has produced favourable results. Price Waterhouse (1995, p 120) concluded that tenant management cooperatives were 'very effective mechanisms for securing improved housing services, higher levels of tenant satisfaction and more economical running costs' and estate management boards had shown they could deliver 'a tenant-oriented service ... in the most difficult operational contexts'. Cairncross et al (2002, p 8) were similarly impressed stating that:

> TMOs are providing an effective service in terms of their own aims and objectives. In most cases, they are doing better than their host local authorities and compare favourably with the top 25% of local authorities ... the poor quality of the housing stock which some TMOs have taken over, makes their achievements in terms of performance all the more remarkable.

The stock transfer process has promoted interest in forms of organisations that give tenants more influence in the decisions made about their homes. The 'community gateway model' (Chartered Institute of Housing, 2002) builds in extensive tenant involvement into the transfer organisation with the objective of moving eventually to full tenant ownership. However, concerns from lending organisations about this model and the investment necessary to prepare tenants for collective ownership responsibilities have limited its take-up.

Given the success of TMOs and their fit with Tony Blair's promotion of social capital it is surprising that they have not been encouraged by New Labour – only 4% of existing TMOs were established in 2001, a decline from 14% in 1994. Rather than develop TMOs, which produce complications in the transfer of local authority stock to registered social landlords, New Labour introduced Tenant Participation Compacts. Beginning in April 2000 local councils had to start a process of agreeing an involvement framework for tenants directed towards the attainment of 'best value' in the delivery of housing services. The declared objective of the compacts was to 'help to bring the quality of participation across all councils up to the best and to ensure that all tenants have equal opportunity to participate' (DETR, 1999a, p 6) but there has been a noticeable attempt to incorporate tenants into the monitoring of local authority performance targets set by Whitehall.

Tenant involvement in local authority housing will always vary between authorities because tenants will desire diverse levels of input and local authorities will have different attitudes to tenant participation. However, the acid test of tenant involvement is the power to influence big decisions such as stock transfer. The guidance to local government on stock transfer requires local authorities to undertake an appraisal of the options available to meet the government's decent homes target. The guidance states that tenants should be actively involved in the options appraisal process and that no options appraisal will be approved by the Regional Government Office unless an extensive consultation exercise has been undertaken. However, should tenants decide to stay with their local authority, either at the option appraisal stage or in a ballot, the resources that would have been available via a stock transfer will not be forthcoming. Indeed, a consultation paper issued in June 2004 contained a paragraph proposing that councils in which tenants had decided to stay with their local authority should be withdrawn from the statistics on the 2010 decent homes target. This paragraph was later withdrawn (Macdonald, 2004).

Housing association tenants

In 2004 the Housing Corporation declared that 'resident involvement should be at the heart of housing associations' corporate strategy, decision making and ethos' and that 'every housing association will be required to draw up a resident involvement statement over the next year in partnership with residents' (Housing Corporation, 2004b). In the future 'involvement reviews' would be incorporated into the regulatory and inspection procedures of housing associations.

In the past, tenant participation has been a neglected dimension of the operations of registered social landlords. The Audit Commission (2004, p 4) noted that involvement 'is still often sidelined or done grudgingly' and there was a dearth of information on the extent of involvement and ambiguity about the purposes of such involvement. If the purpose of involvement is to improve service delivery and the social capital in the neighbourhood by the collective participation of consumers then only limited changes in the paternalist structures of registered social landlords are necessary. However, if the objective on tenant involvement is to improve the accountability of registered social landlords to their tenants – to close the 'democratic deficit' – then more fundamental reforms will be necessary. These reforms might include the creation of independent resident associations, access to high-quality advice and a majority of elected tenant representatives on management committees.

The financial institutions

Until the 1980s building societies were the major providers of house purchase finance. They differed from commercial banks in being 'mutual' – there were no shareholders – and their aim was to meet the reciprocal requirements of lenders and borrowers. Building societies had their origins in the 17th century but developed in the 19th century when working-class people agreed to pay into a fund to build houses. When sufficient finance had been raised to acquire a house, lots were drawn to determine which member should move into the new dwelling. Payments into the fund continued until every member of the society was able to own a house and then the society was terminated. In order to speed up the housing of its members some societies allowed people who did not require homes to join the association and paid interest on the investment. These societies were called 'permanent' and, at the start of the 20th century, had become the most common form of building society

By the 1970s building societies had become major financial institutions and the government worked with them to stabilise the housing market, often by supplying loans. However, their activities provoked criticism. It was alleged that their conservatism produced mortgage queues, their mutuality had become a myth and that unaccountable directors rather than savers and mortgage-holders controlled the movement (Boddy, 1980). The societies were accused of proliferating branch offices, being reluctant to lend in certain geographical areas and of operating a cartel in fixing the mortgage interest rate. In the late 1980s the Conservatives attempted to deal with some of these criticisms by exposing the societies to more competition from banks, specialist mortgage companies and other financial institutions.

The movement of the banks and specialist mortgage lenders into the mortgage market led to the breakdown of the building society cartel; by 1987 building societies were responsible for only 51% of net mortgage lending compared to 79% in 1980. The societies argued that if banks were to be allowed into their business, then societies should be granted more scope to diversify. The 1986 Building Societies Act enabled such diversification to develop. Societies were allowed to raise more funds from wholesale markets (that is, to borrow from institutions as well as individuals), to purchase land, to act as developers, to set up estate agencies and to offer cheque clearing facilities. In the 1990s the distinctions between building societies and banks was further blurred by many building societies abandoning their mutual status and paying dividends to shareholders.

Today the financial institutions involved in mortgage lending are brought together under the auspices of the Council for Mortgage Lenders. Mortgage lenders provide finance not only for individual homeownership but for stock transfer from local authorities to registered social landlords and for 'buy to let' schemes. New Labour has encouraged mortgage lenders to become involved in urban renewal initiatives – seven of the nine pathfinder market renewal organisations have mortgage lenders involved as 'stakeholders'.

Private landlords

The Labour Party's traditional hostility to private landlords reached its zenith in the mid-1970s when the Labour government started to use housing associations to buy out private landlords operating in the major cities – a programme that foundered on the public expenditure restraints of the late 1970s. In its opposition years, Labour's attitude towards private landlords gradually changed and, as New Labour, the Party embraced private landlords as an integral part of the housing system (see Box 3.6). This was reflected in the Housing Green Paper (DETR, 2000b, sections 5:1 and 5:2) that stated:

> A healthy private rented sector provides additional housing choices for people who do not want to, or are not ready to, buy their own homes. It is a particularly important resource for younger households. Through its flexibility and speed of access, it can also help to oil the wheels of the housing and labour markets…. We therefore want the sector to grow and prosper…. Landlords can be assured that we intend no change in the present structure of assured and assured shorthold tenancies, which is working well. Nor is there any question of our re-introducing rent controls in the deregulated market.

New Labour has promoted responsible private landlordism by encouraging the development of landlord forums and voluntary accreditation schemes whereby landlords are brought into mainstream provision in return for promoting acceptable standards. The private sector remained constant at 10%

Box 3.6: Private landlords: key facts

- Since 1991 the private landlord sector share of the housing market has increased from 10% to 11% and the absolute number of households renting from private landlords has increased by approximately 400,000 since 1991.
- In 2001 the median number of properties owned by landlords was four, down from nine in 1994.
- Nearly two thirds of dwellings in the private rented sector are owned by private individuals. 73% saw their property as an investment but only 9% viewed renting property as a full-time occupation. Only 7% of dwellings were owned by residential property companies.
- Landlords usually prefer tenants in full-time employment, especially young professionals. Lettings to tenants claiming Housing Benefit accounted for 18% of all lettings and nearly 75% of landlords who had let to tenants on Housing Benefit preferred not to.
- Only 15% of landlords who manage their property themselves are members of a trade/professional body and only 15% have been involved in a local authority landlord forum.
- In 2005, average private sector rents were £119 in England, ranging from £72.36 in the North East to £190.84 in London (National Housing Federation, 2005).
- Between 1993/94 and 2003/04 private landlord rents (after Housing Benefit) more than doubled compared to a 47% increase in the local authority sector and a 65% increase in the housing association sector.
- In 2001, 17% of dwellings in the private rented sector fell below the decent homes standard because of disrepair compared to 8% in the owner-occupied sector, 9% of local authority dwellings and 5% of registered social landlord houses.
- In 2001, the average rental return (net of running costs and excluding increases in capital value) on market value was 5.5% although the rising house prices in many areas would have provided landlords with substantially higher total returns.
- In 2002/03, 39% of private tenants were aged under 30 compared to 29% in 1988. Over the same time period the percentage of private tenants over 60 declined from 33% to 13%.
- About 40% of private landlord tenants have lived in their current accommodation for less than a year.

Main sources: ODPM (2004d, 2005a)

to 11% of the housing stock between 1997 and 2004 but larger institutional landlords were in decline, being replaced by smaller landlords acquiring properties under 'buy to let' schemes. In 2004 there were 526,000 outstanding loans on 'buy to let' dwellings, an 18-fold increase since 1998.

Although New Labour has adopted a 'light touch' in monitoring the private landlord sector it has started to take a more proactive approach in two sub-sectors: low-demand areas and houses in multiple occupation. In its Green Paper New Labour stated:

> There are, however, areas of declining housing demand, particularly in parts of our northern cities, where the large-scale operations of some unscrupulous landlords, often linked to criminal activities such as Housing Benefit fraud, drug-dealing and prostitution, are destabilising local communities, creating a range of social and economic problems, and seriously hampering efforts at regeneration. Not only can they make life very difficult for respectable tenants, but also they are increasingly offering homes to anti-social households, including some who have been excluded because of their misbehaviour from nearby social housing. This unholy alliance of bad landlords and bad tenants creates a complex and intractable set of problems.... (DETR, 2000b, sections 5:32 and 5:33)

The 2004 Housing Act granted powers to local authorities to license private landlords in low-demand areas but strictly limited their use. Licensing powers could be introduced only with the permission of the 'appropriate national authority' and only in conjunction with other measures likely to contribute to the improvement of the social and economic conditions in the area.

Devolution

In the past there have been differences between the housing policies pursued in England and Scotland. These differences were related to legal variations in landlord and tenant law, political affiliations and the relative autonomy of the Scottish Office, which, until 1999, held responsibility for Scotland's housing programmes. In 1999, housing was included in the areas of responsibility devolved to the Scottish Parliament. The Scottish Parliament has primary legislation powers and limited tax-raising capacity but Housing Benefit policy is reserved for Westminster. The Scottish Parliament and its executive arm, the Scottish Executive, receive finance from Westminster as 'the Scottish Block' according to a formula, known as the 'Barnett formula', based mainly on the population structure of Scotland compared to the UK. This formula is also used to distribute finance to Wales and Northern Ireland.

The National Assembly for Wales, established in 1999, was granted neither primary legislative powers nor the right to vary taxation. It was, however, entitled to vary secondary legislation and was given responsibility for supervising the Welsh Office, a task previously undertaken by the Secretary of State for Wales. Housing for Wales, the Welsh equivalent of the Housing

Corporation, was abolished and its responsibilities transferred to the Welsh Assembly.

Following the partition of Ireland in 1921, housing policy in Northern Ireland was steered by a devolved Parliament with Unionist control, and local authorities provided the bulk of the limited social housing supply. In the 1960s Northern Ireland had lower proportions of homeowners and social housing tenants and a higher proportion of private renters than the UK as a whole (Paris, 2001, p 14). The fairness of the housing system was a significant issue in the 1960s civil disturbances (Cameron, 1969) and the introduction of direct rule from Westminster was accompanied by the removal of housing powers from local government. A Northern Ireland Housing Executive was established responsible for the implementation of Westminster housing policies and the supply and administration of social housing. The Executive inherited a legacy of poor housing conditions with 19.6% of the dwelling stock unfit for human habitation – a rate three times that of England – and 26.2% lacking one or more of the basic amenities. Between 1971 and 2005, partially because there has been an assumption in favour of development in the planning system and partially because of extra public spending, the production of dwellings per 1,000 of the population has been higher than in the UK as a whole. However, the tenure pattern change – assisted by a Northern Ireland version of the Right to Buy – has been similar with a steep increase in homeowners and a decline in social housing. Growing waiting lists and homelessness acceptances prompted the House of Commons Northern Ireland Affairs Committee (2004, p 35) to conclude that 'if urgent action is not taken a crisis in the supply of social housing seems inevitable'. In 1998 the Northern Ireland Assembly was established as part of the Belfast Agreement. Under devolution the Department of Social Development is responsible for housing policy but the Assembly was suspended on 14 October 2002 with the Secretary of State for Northern Ireland assuming responsibility for the direction of the Northern Ireland Departments.

Table 3.7 sets out some basic statistics on housing in the constituent parts of the UK. Unfortunately, although significant variations in housing policy between England, Scotland, Wales and Northern Ireland are highlighted from time to time, space limitations have meant that it has not been possible to supply a detailed account of housing policies in Scotland, Wales and Northern Ireland. Students are referred to the books listed under 'Further reading' at the end of this chapter.

Table 3.7: *Housing in the UK, 2004*

	England	Scotland	Wales	Northern Ireland
Population (millions)	**49**	**5**	**2.9**	**1.7**
Tenure (%)				
Homeowners	71	65	73	70
Local authority/	11	20	14	19
Housing Executive				
Housing association	8	7	4	3
Private landlord	10	6	9	8
House prices (£s)	182,000	117,000	138,000	123,000
Unfitness (%)	4	1[a]	8.5	4.9
Overcrowding[b] (%)	2	3	3	3.8

Notes:

[a] In Scotland a 'tolerable standard' is used to measure housing conditions. This is lower than the fitness standard.

[b] Below the bedroom standard.

Sources: Adapted from Northern Ireland Housing Executive (2003); ONS (2005a)

Overview

- In its first term of office (1997-2001) New Labour made few changes to the housing policy set by the Conservatives.
- In 2002 mounting evidence of deterioration in the housing situation prompted the government to make a step change in its intervention in the housing market.
- Elected representatives now have more autonomy in determining Scotland's housing policy but devolution to Wales and Northern Ireland is limited.
- In England, the government manages the detailed implementation of its housing policy through targets and performance indicators.

Questions for discussion

1) Examine the main differences between housing associations and:
   (a) private landlords;
   (b) local authorities.
(2) How has New Labour encouraged 'responsible' private landlordism?
(3) In what ways does central government control the housing activities of local government and housing associations?
(4) What is a 'quasi-market'?

(5) In what ways has the regional dimension of housing policy become more important?

Further reading

Powell's (1999) *New Labour, New Welfare State* (1999) and *Evaluating New Labour's Welfare Reforms* **(2002)** contain accounts of New Labour's housing policies in the context of its overall approach to social policy.

Comprehensive accounts of housing policy in Scotland, Wales and Northern Ireland can be found in **Sim (2004)** *Housing and Public Policy in Post-devolution Scotland*, *Housing in Wales in an Era of Devolution* by **Smith et al (2000)** and *Housing in Northern Ireland – and Comparisons with the Republic of Ireland* edited by **Paris (2001)**. The **Scottish Executive's (2005)** *Homes for Scotland's People: A Scottish Housing Policy Statement* sets out future housing policies for Scotland.

The complicated system of housing finance is explained in *Housing Finance* by **Garnett and Perry (2005)**. **Kemp's (2004)** *Private Renting in Transition* examines New Labour's policies on the private rented sector.

Wilcox's *UK Housing Review 2005/06* supplies statistics on housing policy plus commentaries on policy outcomes.

Website resources

The ODPM's website at www.odpm.gov.uk contains information on New Labour's housing policies.

The Evaluation of English Housing Policy 1975-2000: Theme 5 Management Effectiveness (ODPM, 2005d), available at the ODPM's website, contains useful material on 'best value' and tenant participation.

Reviews of government policy can be found at the website of the Select Committee on the ODPM, accessible via the House of Commons home page at www.parliament.uk/about_commons/about_commons.cfm. This site also contains research papers and answers to written questions on housing policy.

The websites of:

- The National Housing Federation [www.housing.org.uk]
- Chartered Institute of Housing [www.cih.org.uk]
- The Housing Corporation [www.housing corp.gov.uk]
- Shelter [http://england.shelter.org.uk]

have commentaries on housing policy and links to other sites.

The following magazines are available online:

Inside Housing: www.insidehousing.co.uk. This site also gives access to a range of policy/research papers via 'Housemark'.

Property People: www.ppmagazine.co.uk

Environmental Health News: www.ehn-online.com/housing.shtml

Comparative housing policy

Summary

- Cross-national comparisons contribute to an understanding of continuity and change in housing policy and to an appreciation of the possible range of housing policies. However, there are obstacles to forming robust conclusions based on existing cross-national data.
- Since the 1980s housing policies appear to have been converging.
- Policy transfer is difficult to identify but there is some evidence that policies are transmitted between countries.

Why compare?

There are four principal reasons for engaging in comparative studies.

- Cross-national comparison offers the opportunity to identify possible global factors in housing policy development and thereby highlight the specific determinants of dissimilar national policies. As Doling (1997, p 23) says, 'Simply put, it can aid the better understanding of the social world'. Part of this understanding involves exploring broad structural trends, the role of policy transfer between countries and the interaction between the state, the market and civil society in particular countries. None the less, the identification of cross-national trends is bedevilled by the variability and complexity of potential policy interventions. Policy inputs are diverse ranging across intricate and constantly changing forms of direct subsidies, cheap loans and tax breaks given to producers – often applied at regional and local level – to complicated systems of consumer assistance in the form of tax concessions and means-tested allowances.

- An examination of housing policies in other countries can supply ideas for programme development in the UK by identifying what policies are in operation elsewhere and, perhaps, assessing their effectiveness in relationship to UK policies. As examples:
  - Bradshaw and Finch (2004) examined the impact in 22 countries of consumer housing subsidies – equivalent to Housing Benefit in the UK – on family income. They found that, compared to other countries, Housing Benefit made only a modest contribution to mitigating housing costs and, taking housing expenses into account, the ranking of the UK 'child support package' moved from third to eighth in the list of counties studied.
  - Scanlon and Whitehead (2004) identified major differences in the cost of private renting in the UK compared to Sweden and Germany, indicating the possible impact of a supply shortage in the UK.

However, comparing the effectiveness of policies across countries is problematic. There is a dearth of comparable information on housing policy outcomes with idiosyncratic and non-comparable measures – often related to specific and embedded national housing politics – used by different countries in the production of housing statistics. This results in the employment of somewhat crude indicators of between country differences simply because they are available. The lack of comparable information on housing costs led Bradshaw and Finch (2004) to use 20% of average income as a crude proxy for necessary household housing expenditure and Scanlon and Whitehead (2004) had no quality indicator. Even when comparable information is available its interpretation presents problems and there is a danger of imposing ethnocentric criteria when evaluating housing outcomes. One might, for example, attempt to compare housing standards in terms of the number of rooms per person but this might ignore extended family values and a climate that provides opportunities for a 'street culture' that reduces the need for living space. Tenure differences – frequently used in comparative studies – are also difficult to interpret due to variations in housing conditions *within* tenures.

- Comparative studies can undercut what we take for granted by demonstrating that a particular housing system is not natural and hence inevitable (Dickens et al, 1985, p 29). For example, although homeownership is often seen in the UK as a natural tenure that will expand with affluence (Saunders, 1990), there is no clear relationship between the wealth of a country and its proportion of homeowners. Rich countries such as Germany, Denmark and Switzerland have low homeownership rates whereas some poor countries, Bangladesh for example, have high rates.
- Housing is not a mandate of the European Union but the common elements of the Union's financial system have implications for UK housing policy; European Union competition policy, for example, places restraints on the amounts that member states can spend on subsidising social housing.

Moreover, the requirement that the European Union should work towards the removal of obstacles to the free movement of persons and the acute housing problems of many of the countries joining in 2004 may involve action by the European Union, if not in the form of a new housing mandate, then through the use of other mandates such as economic regeneration.

Housing policies: five national case studies

In 1990 Esping-Andersen identified three 'worlds of welfare capitalism' that he modified in 1999 to include a 'family' dimension in the analysis (see Box 4.1). Other authors (for example, Ferrera, 1996; Allen et al, 2004) have identified a fourth category – South European states regarded by Esping-Andersen as a sub-category of the Conservative/corporatist regime. Spain, Portugal, Greece and Italy are characterised by polarisation between well-protected workers and those with minimal entitlements, a strong reliance on family networks to provide welfare and fragmented welfare delivery systems. Although housing policy was not a factor in the construction of this four-dimensional typology and the classification ignores variations over time within welfare regimes, authors interested in comparative housing policy have found the taxonomy helpful (Barlow and Duncan, 1994; Doling, 1997). It will used in this chapter with specific countries taken as examples of particular welfare state types. A fifth category has been added to represent countries formerly dominated by communist ideology but whose economic structures have been in transition to market-based, capitalist systems. Available statistical information on the five countries plus the UK is presented in Table 4.1.

Germany

The reunification of Germany in 1990 brought together two very different housing systems. East German housing policy, following the basic tenets of communism, aimed at a sufficient housing supply and at an equitable distribution of dwellings among the population. In East Germany, 41% of the housing stock was owned by the state. It was let at very low rents and allocated according to need, the requirements for key workers in particular areas and as a reward for party loyalty. The cooperative sector (18%) and the private landlord sector were subject to rent control. Homeownership constituted about 25% of the housing stock, mainly a residue from former regimes.

Housing was awarded only low priority in the first national plans of the German Democratic Republic and many pre-war dwellings fell into disrepair. Later plans gave housing a higher priority but the attempt to rectify the earlier neglect as quickly as possible produced small and somewhat austere dwellings in prefabricated, high-density units. Prior to reunification housing was a source of discontent – the waiting list for accommodation was 470,000 and many young couples had to wait several years for a small flat. 18% of dwellings had

Box 4.1: The 'three worlds of welfare capitalism'

Liberal	Conservative/ corporatist	Social democratic
Characteristics		

Liberal

Characteristics

- A low degree of labour decommodification and a dominant role for the free market.
- Few social rights, a low level of benefits, little redistribution of wealth, social stigmatisation and a high level of private welfare.
- A strong institutionalised work culture with social insecurity used as an incentive to economic development.
- A high level of social stratification based on income.

Conservative/ corporatist

- A high level of labour decommodification (for breadwinners) and a dominant role for the family, conservative elites and religiously based democratic parties.
- Social rights tied to class and status and offering the most social protection to those having a stable job; a welfare system accessible by everybody and a medium level of wealth and income redistribution.
- A high degree of linkage between the different political institutions, actors and policies (corporate political structures).
- A relatively high level of social stratification based on social or occupational status.

Social democratic

- A high degree of labour decommodification and a marginal role for the family.
- Social rights based on the idea of 'citizenship'.
- A universal welfare system with a high level of income and wealth redistribution.
- A low level of social stratification.

Typical countries

US	Germany	Sweden
Australia	Austria	Denmark
Canada	France	The Netherlands
Ireland	Belgium	Norway
New Zealand	Japan	Finland
UK	Italy	

Source: Based on Esping-Andersen (1990, p 52; 1999, p 85)

Table 4.1: *Housing statistics: selected countries[a]*

	UK	Germany	Sweden	Czech Republic	US	Spain
Population (millions)	59.7	82.2	8.9	10.5	293	41.2
GDP per inhabitant (US$)	29,100	26,400	29,200	16,100	37,600	23,300
Persons per dwelling	2.3	2.1	2.1	2.8	2.5	3.2
Poverty rate (50% of median income)	11.4	9.8	5.3	4.3	17.1	11.5
Gini coefficient[b]	36.8	30	25	25.5	40.8	33
Tenure (%)						
Owner-occupied	69	41	40	48	68	84
Private rented	10	59[c]	23	7	30	14
Social rented	21	6[c]	21	24	1	2
Cooperatives/co-ownership	0	–[c]	16[d]	18	1	0
Central heating (%)	88	88	99	73	88	40
% of dwellings built pre-1919	20	16	11	na	8	13
% of dwellings built pre-1945	41	29	32	32	24[e]	34
Dwellings per 1,000 people[f]	452	434	483	427	428	528
New dwellings per 1,000 people	3	5.1	1.5	2.4	6.4	9.2
% living in overcrowded housing[g]	9	16	10	na	5.7	27

Notes:

[a] All data is for 2001 unless otherwise stated.

[b] The Gini coefficient is a measure of inequality: 0 = total equality, 100 = very unequal (latest available figures).

[c] The 'private' sector in Germany is owned by a diversity of agencies and some operate as 'non-profit' organisations or cooperatives. 6% of the total stock has been estimated as 'social', that is, subsidised and subject to rules on allocation.

[d] If the co-ownership sector is classified as home ownership, the owner-occupied sector increases to 55%.

[e] Pre-1949.

[f] 2002/03.

[g] More than one person per room.

Sources: Adapted from Scanlon (2004); United Nations Commission for Europe (2004)

no shower or bath, 24% of households did not have sole use of a lavatory and 53% had no modern heating system.

Constituted as the Federal Republic in 1949, West Germany implemented a 'social market' in housing. The state was to be involved in rectifying imbalances between supply and demand but with the overall objective of applying market principles whenever supply and demand reached equilibrium. Thus, in West

Germany, state involvement in the housing market has fluctuated according to the ways the supply/demand balance has been perceived. Moreover, its federal structure gave considerable scope for variation between the *Länder* and between the local authorities in the specifics of housing policy.

The serious housing shortage at the end of the Second World War – only 9.5 million habitable dwellings for 15.3 million households – prompted the government to subsidise housing construction and impose rent controls. Subsidies for rented accommodation were made available, albeit in different forms, to all kinds of suppliers in return for compliance with rent regulation, dwelling size and quality, the incomes of the tenants housed and tenant nominations from local government. This subsidy form produced a range of social housing suppliers. Non-profit organisations, some sponsored by trades unions or locally elected authorities and others set up in the form of cooperatives, offered accommodation at cost or subsidised rents. Commercial organisations, anticipating long-term profits from social letting with government subsidies, also entered the social market but were allowed to operate as full commercial landlords when the low-cost loans, paid in return for regulation compliance, had been repaid. In West Germany the term social housing came to describe a method of financing housing accompanied by regulations on use rather than – as in Britain until the mid-1970s – housing owned by local government.

These arrangements plus the generous tax treatment of the pure private landlord sector prompted a healthy supply of new dwellings and, in accordance with the social market philosophy, moves towards applying market principles were made whenever supply and demand seemed to be in balance. In the mid-1960s, rent controls were gradually phased out by allowing decontrol wherever the local housing deficit was estimated to be below 3%. In order to protect the poorest from the full impact of higher rents, a means-tested Housing Benefit was introduced. Rent control was reintroduced in the early 1980s but not on new dwellings and, over time, the rents of existing properties were allowed to increase towards new property rental values. In 1986 subsidies were withdrawn from organisations involved in social renting and, although these subsidies were reintroduced a few years later in response to pressure from the flow of immigrants and Census evidence of a housing shortage, the new subsidies were more selective and at a lower rate.

The housing system before reunification

At 43% homeownership was low in comparison to the UK. This can be explained, in part, by West Germany's initial concentration on building flats in the cities to overcome the acute housing shortage. Later, the availability of a large, diverse private rented sector and a less visible social housing system that did not stigmatise its residents, limited the growth of homeownership, despite state encouragement through a favourable tax regime (Kleinman, 1996, p 92).

In addition, the economy supplied low inflation and housing was not subject to the speculative booms characteristic of the UK. In West Germany owner-occupation came to be regarded as the tenure for the long-term 'home': expensive, built in the suburbs to high standards on land subject to tight planning restraints and occupied in later life after a long period of saving.

Cooperatives and companies owned by local authorities, the regional states, churches, trades unions or industrial companies owned about 22% of the stock. However, in accordance with the social market philosophy, as the low-interest loans received from the state were repaid, there was a tendency for such non-profit organisations to opt out of taking nominations from local authorities and for the municipal companies to become private. In 1990 about 36% of the housing stock belonged to the private landlord sector which supplied a diverse range of dwellings catering for a variety of mainstream housing requirements.

Reunification

Following German reunification in 1990 the East German housing system was subject to the 'big bang' of market forces. The state-owned housing stock was transferred to local authorities who, in return for debt reduction, were supposed to sell them, via communal housing companies, to private investors and tenants. The cooperatives retained their properties but, as an incentive to sell, were allowed to write off debt provided they sold a proportion of their stock. Rents were to be increased in steps to match West German levels with Housing Benefit helping poorer families to afford the increase. Tenants were given incentives to buy in the form of discounts on the market price of their accommodation and the Federal government allocated resources for the improvement of older dwellings and for new building. This attempt to rebuild the East German housing system on West German principles was hampered by ownership claims on property built before the formation of the German Democratic Republic and by the movement of over two million East Germans to the West. By the early 2000s, the former East Germany had a large housing surplus with one in seven properties unoccupied. To cope with this surplus an extensive demolition and improvement programme was established.

The movement of people to the former West Germany prompted the government to stimulate housing supply by a combination of tax incentives and direct subsidies. House building peaked at 8% of national income in the late 1990s but then went into steep decline as incentives were withdrawn in accordance with indicators of a balance between supply and demand. There has been a growing tendency for the most forms of non-profit housing organisations to convert to private status thereby producing a smaller social housing pool occupied by tenants with the lowest incomes.

Sweden

Sweden developed a comprehensive housing policy between 1942 and 1968 aimed at promoting a general improvement in living conditions for all its citizens rather than just for the poor. A system of housing allowances for low-income families and pensioners was introduced in 1948 and, to stimulate supply, long-term, low-interest loans for the portion of the capital requirement most difficult to finance on the normal credit market were offered. These housing loans were an important dimension of state housing production control with preferred suppliers – non-profit housing corporations often linked to municipal government – receiving higher loans than homeowners and private landlords. State loans to private landlords were accompanied by rent control, which, while ensuring that the rent of a new property was sufficient to meet capital and maintenance costs, was aimed at preventing the rents for older property – built at lower cost – rising to market levels. Between 1968 and 1978 specific rent control was gradually relaxed in the expectation that the availability of accommodation from 'cost-rent' housing corporations would dampen rent levels in the private landlord sector. Rents in the housing corporation sector were subject to negotiation between the National Tenants' Union and the National Federation of Cost-rental Housing Corporations mediated by a rental market committee. The rents for dwellings owned by the municipal non-profit housing companies were then used as a yardstick for privately owned rental housing.

Housing production declined in the early 1990s from 69,000 per year in 1990 to 11,900 in 1994 as a consequence of a major recession. In response to the growing influence of liberal market ideas, interest rate subsidies were phased out and 'non-profit' suppliers were subject to the same tax regime as profit rental suppliers. This raised housing costs with rents absorbing about 30% of average incomes. Means-tested housing allowances were increased to mitigate the impact on low-income households. In addition, access to mortgage finance was liberalised as a stimulus to homeownership. Since 2000, a developing housing shortage in some parts of the country plus a low-demand problem in other parts has led to renewed state involvement in housing but on a selective basis. Temporary investment grants are directed to specific places and specific groups whereas the National Board for Municipal Housing, set up in 2002, encouraged non-profit housing companies in low-demand areas to remove surplus housing either by demolition or recycling for other uses. Today there are four principal elements in the Swedish housing system.

Homeownership

This accounts for 40% of the housing stock. Owner-occupiers can deduct their mortgage interest costs from their tax liability at a rate of 30% but are subject to tax on the imputed rental income and a capital gains tax.

Tenant-ownership cooperatives

Members of tenant-ownership cooperatives own an individual share in the collective value of the properties. Usually members are responsible for the maintenance of their individual dwellings and can sell the 'right to occupy' their property at the market price although some cooperatives reserve the right to determine the sale price. In essence, tenant-ownership, which accounts for 16% of the housing stock, is a form of homeownership with the cooperative element used to manage blocks of flats.

Cost-rental housing corporations

Many of these have strong connections with locally elected authorities. They own about 21% of the housing stock and charge rents that, in aggregate, cover the historic costs of providing the houses. These costs are low because the stock was mainly built before the mid-1970s. Housing corporations do not let their properties only to low-income households.

Private renting

The private rented sector in Sweden has been in decline as its profitability has been reduced because the general rent level in the private sector is set in relationship to the general level of rent in the housing corporation sector.

Spain

Housing supply in Spain is characterised by a high proportion of owner-occupiers (84%), a small private landlord sector (14%) and a very small public sector (2%).

The destruction of houses during the Spanish Civil War prompted the Franco regime to create a new system of state assistance for the construction of 'protected' houses. Such 'protected' houses could not be sold and had a rent cap of 20% of the tenant's income. However, few 'protected' houses were built and the *Ley de Arrendamientos Urbanos*, imposing rent control and allowing the transfer of leases to family members, prevented investment in the private landlord sector. In the 1950s policy shifted to promoting homeownership to reflect the family values of the Catholic Church and to pacify a disaffected working class who were moving into the urban areas. 'Protected' houses – what in the UK would be called social housing – could be sold and the 1954 and 1957 Housing Acts offered financial incentives to construction firms and development companies to build for homeownership. The Acts divided state-aided dwellings for homeownership into two main groups: 'Group 1' dwellings of 50-200 square metres with no restriction on the sale price, and 'Group 2' dwellings, also of 50-200 square metres, but with a cap on the sale price and higher subsidies. The subsidy equalled about 15% to 30% of the price of a dwelling (Belsky and Retsinas, 2004) and was augmented by general tax concessions on the capital invested in owner-occupation and on the mortgage interest paid. Between 1961 and 1976, 4.2 million houses were constructed of which 2.9 million were state assisted in some way (Wynn, 1984) but, as the production of larger, unsubsidised dwellings gained momentum, the share of the subsidised units declined.

The 1976 Social Housing Act was an attempt to rectify the perceived problems of Franco's housing policies, that is, developers making profits from government subsidies and the lack of affordable accommodation for people with low incomes. All producer subsidies except for tax exemptions were eliminated and replaced by consumer subsidies in the form of reduced-interest loans based on income, house price and family size. In 1985, the Boyer Decree, in an attempt to revive the private landlord sector, ended rigid rent control by linking five-year rental contracts to increases in the retail price index at the end of the contract. However, the rent increases were insufficient to attract new investment and today the rental market is small and concentrated in the main cities (Ball, 2005). A limited scheme exists to help low-income families to pay their rent.

In the early 1990s the emphasis on consumer subsidies was underpinned by further reforms. The regional governments were allocated a target of the number of houses to enter the market at affordable prices and these 'regulated' houses attracted a loan rate at less than the market rate provided the income of the resident was below a specified threshold. Restrictions were placed on the sale price of the 'regulated' dwellings. Local government could also assist the building of affordable housing as it was entitled to a 15% share of the land for residential development that it could sell or use for affordable housing.

At 84%, homeownership in Spain is one of the highest in the world and, unlike Northern Europe, apartments as well as single-family houses tend to be owned (Hoekstra, 2005). About 20% of the urban population of Spain also own a second home in the countryside or on the coast. This high homeownership rate has been attributed to a cultural tradition of 'patrimony' – a specific stock of housing and land conserved within the extended family (Allen et al, 2004) and is regarded by some authors as a great success (Belsky and Retsinas, 2004). However, the emphasis on homeownership has contributed to an affordability problem. The number of persons per dwelling was higher in Spain than in any other European Union country before enlargement. A high percentage of people aged 30 live in the parental home – 44% of males and 30% of females, and the median age of leaving home is 26 for men and 23 for women compared to 22 and 20 respectively in the UK (Aassve et al, 2002). This indicates that access to independent accommodation is problematical – only about 10% of new construction is directly subsidised before sale to poorer households – and the age of leaving home in Spain is positively related to income (Aassve et al, 2002). However, it also reflects the different social meaning attributed to young people leaving home. As Allen et al (2004, p 44) comment:

> In southern Europe, leaving the parental home has a definitive character. More than half of those who leave their parental home in Spain start with owning their own home. These young people skip the stage of living alone or in cohabiting couples in rented housing prior to marriage and having children.

The Czech Republic

Before the Czech Republic was formed in 1993 housing policy in the former state of Czechoslovakia reflected communist thinking. Housing was provided and distributed, not by the market, but in response to 'needs', economic requirements and political affiliations. There were four main types of tenure: state, 'enterprise', cooperative and private. State housing – consisting of apartments nationalised in 1948-49 and dwellings constructed under the state-directed Complex Housing Construction Programme – accounted for 45% of dwellings in 1991. These 'panelak' estates were heavily subsidised, a large percentage consisted of prefabricated flats and management was provided by housing services companies on behalf of the state. In the 'enterprise' form of tenure, introduced in 1959, particular industrial companies held the right to allocate dwellings built with state finance. The purpose of this tenure was to attract labour to preferred regions and industries. The 'cooperative' was also set up in 1959: the state financed most of the costs but, in return for individual contributions of about 20% of scheme cost, prospective tenants could have quicker access to housing and, in some cases, better-quality homes. Individually self-built houses for homeownership were supported by state loans at a low interest rate and by housing allowances directed to workers in preferred industries.

Transitional housing policy

Following the removal of the communist regime and the formation of the Czech Republic as a separate state from Slovakia, housing was subject to a process of eliminating administrative allocation and establishing a more market-orientated system. Members of cooperatives were allowed to purchase their properties and houses nationalised under the communist regime were returned to their original owners. State stock was transferred to the municipalities and some municipalities embarked on a programme of selling dwellings to individual tenants, tenants who formed cooperatives and to real-estate development companies. However, there was no general 'right to buy' of state housing as occurred in some other 'transition' states, it being argued that a good supply of rented accommodation promoted labour mobility. Rents became deregulated on vacant possession but the law provided reasonable protection from eviction. Rents for sitting tenants remained regulated and, despite substantial increases after 1991, in 2002 they were below a 'market' rent and, in most municipalities, did not cover costs. Lux et al (2003) calculated that the 'subsidy' from living in a regulated dwelling at below the market price was about even across all income groups – a reflection of historical patterns in the initial acquisition of such regulated dwellings.

In 1993, to protect lower-income households from the impact of rent increases, the government introduced a system of housing allowances. Initially, the allowances were given to households in the rental sector for a maximum of two years with the household expected to move to cheaper accommodation within this period. In 1996, a new housing allowance system was introduced for households with a total income of less than 1.4 times the subsistence level. The support was available to households in all forms of housing but, in general, it covered less than 20% of total housing costs. In 1997, a time-limited special allowance was provided to households living in regulated rental housing provided that income did not exceed 1.6 times the subsistence level. About 7% of households receive a housing allowance (Lux, 2003a).

The belief in market efficiency led to the virtual ending of state subsidies for house building except to homeowners through various forms of tax breaks and 'contract saving for housing' which added premiums to savings made for the purchase of a house. The subsidy removal resulted in a sharp decline in house construction to only 14,482 in 1996. This failure of the market to boost housing supply produced a move towards greater state intervention. The shortage of accommodation for low-income families was to be overcome by new subsidies for municipal house building targeted at people with special needs, at single-member households with an income below 80% of average monthly income and at multiple-member households with an income of less than 150% of average monthly income. After 1996, housing construction increased to reach 27,292 in 2002 – still low in relation to the 1990 figure of 44,594 new dwellings. Older home renovation was stimulated by low-interest loans to municipalities and the 'panelak' estates have been provided with more amenities and decoration to counter their featureless appearance.

There are now four sectors in the housing market. At about 7% of the housing stock the private rented sector has been created mainly by restitution of property nationalised in 1948 to the 'rightful' owners. The municipal rented sector accounts for 24% of occupied dwellings but is decreasing as a consequence of sales to tenants. At about 18% of the stock the cooperative sector is decreasing as sales to individuals outstrip acquisitions from the municipal sector. At 50% the owner-occupied sector is expanding from new build (encouraged by the introduction of interest-free loans in 1997 and, later, low-interest loans for first-time buyers) and transfers from the municipal and cooperative sectors.

United States of America

In the US, Federal intervention in the housing system started in the 1930s when the economic depression severely impeded the functioning of the housing market. In 1931, 50% of all mortgages were in default and residential construction had declined by 95% since 1928. To deal with this situation the Federal Housing Administration (FHA) was created to insure private mortgages and thereby stimulate private construction. In 1938 the Federal National Mortgage Association was also established to purchase mortgages from lenders thereby freeing funds for new mortgages. In 1968 the Federal National Mortgage Association was privatised and, quaintly known as Fannie Mae, it continues to buy mortgages on the secondary market, pool them and then sell them to investors as mortgage-backed securities.

Under the 1937 National Housing Act, federally funded public housing could be built and managed by local housing authorities. Such public housing was linked to slum clearance schemes and occupancy was restricted to households with low incomes. As part of the 1944 Serviceman's Readjustment Act low-interest loans for house purchase were guaranteed for returning GIs. The 1949 Housing Act extended the scope of the 1937 Act and set a target of 135,000 low-income units per year for six years. However, by the end of the 1950s only 250,000 additional public housing dwellings had been erected.

Public housing continued to be built as part of urban renewal programmes in the 1960s and early 1970s under the 1966 Demonstration Cities and Metropolitan Development (Model Cities) Act and the 1974 Housing and Community Development Act. However, from the mid-1970s, public housing was gradually replaced by a number of producer subsidies aimed at stimulating private sector housing construction for particular groups such as older people and low-income and moderate-income families. Most of these producer subsidies were consolidated in the 1986 Tax Reform Act that authorised a Low Income Housing Tax Credit, distributed by the states to companies and investors in housing, and redeemable against Federal tax liability. It was targeted at the acquisition, rehabilitation or new construction of rented housing for lower-income households. In the 1980s and 1990s, Federal government intervention in the housing market was significantly reduced but many states entered the housing policy domain mainly by the sponsorship of Community Development Corporations and promotion of the Low Income Housing Tax Credit to stimulate housing production.

Consumer subsidies in the US have taken two main forms. Owner-occupiers have been able to offset their mortgage interest payments against their tax liability and, under section 8 of the 1974 Housing and Community Development Act, housing allowances were made available to low-income households renting at 'fair market rents'. In the 1980s this was replaced by a system of housing vouchers based not on an individually determined 'fair market rent' but on a 'payment standard' for rental housing set for each area. In

2005, housing vouchers were the major form of Federal rental assistance for low-income families, helping over two million households. Prospective tenants are issued with a voucher and, when accepted by a landlord offering accommodation of a set standard, they pay 30% of their income in rent. The remainder, up to the 'payment standard', is paid by the local housing authority subsidised by the Federal government. Housing vouchers are not an entitlement; there is limited funding and a long waiting list for potential recipients.

Homeownership

In 1981, 65.3% of households in the US were owner-occupiers. This percentage declined in the 1980s and early 1990s but, by 2004, had increased to 68.4%. Americans usually buy their properties on 30-year fixed-interest loans with tax relief on mortgage interest reducing outgoings by about 2% per year. There are marked ethnic variations in homeownership rates with only 44% of those classified as 'black' being homeowners. In an attempt to increase homeownership President Bush signed the American Dream Downpayment Act in 2003 offering Federal government assistance to selected first-time buyers to help finance the deposit on a home.

Private renting

Except in certain states rent control has played a minor part in the history of private renting in the US. Most North Americans pay the market rent for their privately rented accommodation with means-tested vouchers helping those with the lowest incomes. On average, private sector rents absorbed 26% of the income of renters in 2002 but this figure masks large variations with 50% of renters paying more than 30% and some households paying up to 60% (Joint Centre for Housing Studies of Harvard University, 2004).

Public housing

In the 1990s, public housing was subject to a process of erosion. Under the HOPE V1 programme, introduced in 1992, public housing complexes were to be demolished and replaced, in part, by new units of mixed-income housing. Public housing tenants were given a voucher, equivalent to the subsidies on their public housing, and allowed to cash in the vouchers on other forms of housing. Since 1992 more than 120,000 public housing units have been demolished but only 40,000 'mixed-income' units have been built and, by 2004, 49,000 residents had been relocated away from public housing. The average poverty rate of the new neighbourhood to which these 49,000 residents were relocated was 27% below that of their former neighbourhood (Berube, 2005, p 43).

The remaining 1.3 million public housing units represent just over 1% of the dwellings in the US. President Clinton's 1998 Quality Housing and Work Responsibility Act passed responsibility for public housing to 3,400 quasi-autonomous local Public Housing Agencies and encouraged them to create more balanced communities (see Chapter Eight) and establish greater social discipline. Such agencies were allowed to consider a prospective tenant's employment history when making allocation decisions and were required to set standards prohibiting people involved in 'antisocial behaviour' from acquiring a tenancy. Adult residents of public housing without work had to contribute no less than eight hours of work per month within the community in which they resided, or to participate on an ongoing basis in an economic self-sufficiency or job-training programme. Recipients of housing benefits could lose them if they did not fulfil the work requirements.

The convergence thesis

Comparative housing research has been strongly influenced by structural approaches. The social reformist approach has identified the 'logic of industrialisation' as the principal motor of housing change, and a strong element of functionalism has permeated the approach. Donnison (1967), for example, identified 'developmental stages' in housing policy from 'haphazard' to 'comprehensive', implying an evolution of housing systems towards a 'higher' order. According to Marxist theory it is the requirements of a capitalist economic system that determines housing policy with the state intervening in the market to restore profitability when capitalism is in crisis (Harloe, 1995). Both structural approach variants predict housing systems convergence. Schmidt (1989) attempted to test the convergence thesis by examining housing markets and housing policy in advanced industrialising countries from the 1970s to the mid-1980s. He found that the 'logic of industrialism' did not adequately explain housing trends in the countries under inspection – the specific national politics of housing policy were more important.

> The results show that contrary to convergence theory, and its associated thesis of a particular 'logic of industrialism', institutional factors loom large. Analysing the structure of the market, ideological factors are found to be of the greatest importance. (Schmidt, 1989, p 83).

However, an examination of the above five national case studies policies plus the UK experience indicates a tendency towards convergence in the 1980s and 1990s with 'recommodification' – a return to market principles in the distribution of housing – being the common factor. Such 'recommodification', although mediated through dissimilar housing regimes in different countries, has been reflected in the demise of public housing and rent control, more selective producer subsidies, an increase in the use of means-tested rent allowances and the growth of homeownership – a growth that some authors have linked to the development of an asset-based approach to social protection for old age in the context of state welfare retrenchment (Kemeny, 2005). This stripped-down, more selective approach to housing policy with the market dictating overall outcomes is the product of a number of factors: the abatement of mass housing shortages through the sustained house-building programmes in the 1960s and 1970s; the hegemony of neo-classical economic thinking within international financial organisations such as the World Bank; and the impact of 'globalisation'. According to the globalisation thesis 'we are now entering a new phase in which cross-border flows in goods and services, investment, finance and technology are creating a seamless world market where the law of one price will prevail' (Weiss, 1998, p 167). Although the immobility of housing limits the impact of globalisation, the influence of global forces on labour markets magnifies regional and local variations in economic conditions within countries via internal and international migration. This may have prompted a more selective, area-based policy response from national governments. Globalisation also magnifies risk – there was a large global increase in house prices between 1997 and 2004 (*The Economist*, 2005) with the possibility of a future slump – and, in a volatile housing market, globalisation promotes government deflection of this risk to homeowners (Doling and Ford, 2003, p 2).

Policy transfer

It is difficult to assess the extent of policy transfer between countries; few politicians, public officials or 'think tanks' are willing to admit to policy plagiarism! Nevertheless, it is possible to identify a number of examples of the influence of other countries' housing experience on UK policy and vice versa:

- In the 1960s the UK Conservative Party was attracted to the idea of a social market economy that had produced an 'economic miracle' in West Germany. The means-tested rent rebate and rent allowances introduced under the 1972 Housing Finance Act had a marked similarity to West Germany's 1965 rent allowances scheme. Both were designed to cushion a move towards market rents across all parts of the rented sector.
- The stock transfer policy from local government to housing associations reflects a move towards the long-established models of social housing in Sweden and Germany. Nevertheless, the 'unitary rental market', identified by Kemeny (1994) as characteristic of Germany and Sweden, whereby a variety of landlords – profit and non-profit – have been directed towards social purposes in return for state assistance and linking their rents to historic costs has not been a characteristic of UK housing policy. In the UK the

incomes of tenants in the social sector are lower in relationship to owner occupiers than in either Germany or Sweden: 42% in the UK, 64% in Germany and 57% in Sweden (Stephens, 2005a).
- The UK choice-based lettings scheme (see Chapter Seven) was based on the Delft lettings model developed in the Netherlands during the late 1980s.
- New Labour's proposal to link Housing Benefit payment to behaviour is similar to clauses in President Clinton's 1998 Quality Housing and Work Responsibility Act.
- The Right to Buy scheme in the UK provided a model for the privatisation of state housing in some of the countries in the transition from communism.

Overview

- Although comparative studies can contribute to an understanding of policy development and supply ideas for new housing policies they are limited by the lack of data suitable for comparative analysis.
- An examination of housing policies in different countries supplies some evidence on the relative contributions of global factors and specific national politics to the policy change process.
- Up to the mid-1980s the specific national politics of housing policy appear to have been more important than global factors but, since the mid-1980s, there is evidence that national housing policies are converging.

Questions for discussion

(1) Examine Table 4.1. What are the major differences between the countries included in the table?
(2) What are the principal problems involved in comparative studies of housing policy?
(3) What is meant by a 'unitary rental market'?
(4) On the basis of the information provided in Table 4.1, can any country be regarded as having the 'best' housing policy?

Suggest possible cross-national indicators for comparative studies of housing policy outcomes.

Further reading

Doling's (1997) *Comparative Housing Policy: Government and Housing in Advanced Industrialized Countries*, although out-of-date, is sound on theoretical approaches to comparative housing studies. **Kemeny and Lowe (1998)** examine different approaches to comparative housing research in 'Schools of comparative housing research: from convergence to divergence'. A comprehensive account of Spanish housing policy is available in **Allen et al (2004)** *Housing and Welfare in Southern Europe*. **Lux's (2003b)** *Housing Policy: An End or New Beginning* sets housing policy in the Czech Republic in the context of the experience of other 'transition' states. **Donner's (2002)** *Housing Policies in the European Union* gives a detailed account of the housing policies in European Union states before enlargement.

Website resources

The United Nations Economic Commission for Europe provides current figures on housing outcomes (www.unece.org/stats/data.htm) and data on housing policy in the member states of the European Union is available at www.unece.org/stats/trends2005/welcome.html. The latest edition of the *European Housing Market Review* can be found on the website of the Royal Institution of Chartered Surveyors at www.rics.org. The Joint Center for Housing Studies, based at Harvard University (www.jchs.harvard.edu) supplies comprehensive information on housing policy and its outcomes in the US.

five

Affordable housing

Summary

- Rented accommodation has been made more affordable by supply-side producer subsidies and means-tested housing allowances.
- In the past, homeownership support was provided by tax relief on mortgage interest, tax exemptions and home improvement grants.
- During the 1980s and 1990s there was a shift from producer subsidies to means-tested consumer allowances in the rented sector.
- Since the early 1990s the planning system has been used to secure more affordable housing.
- In recent years state support for homeownership has become very selective.
- New Labour has defined housing affordability in terms of the inability to gain access to housing at market prices.
- After 2002, New Labour began to intervene more actively in the housing market to increase housing supply with the long-term objective of making housing more affordable.

What is meant by affordable housing?

The notion of affordable housing has been interpreted in three ways:

- The 'safety net' interpretation is connected to the perception of housing as a basic necessity and with the concern that, if a high proportion of income has to be devoted to housing costs, then insufficient resources will be available for other essentials. This interpretation is sometimes called 'the residual income approach' and forms the basis for the rationale of Housing Benefit directed towards preventing post–rent incomes falling below the basic social assistance entitlement. However, Housing Benefit is not available to homeowners and this creates problems for working households who initially could obtain access to homeownership but, due to a fall in income relative to expenditure, experience an affordability problem.

- Because Housing Benefit is means tested and has a steep taper, concern has been expressed that reliance on the 'safety net' objective discourages work and imposes hardship on those with incomes just above Housing Benefit entitlement thresholds. Thus an alternative way to think about affordability is to consider a ratio of income to housing costs and to claim that the ratio should not exceed a specified figure. In the past this was sometimes informally set at 25% – a percentage that can be justified because, above this threshold, payment problems increase significantly (Bramley and Karley, 2005). The Office of the Deputy Prime Minister (ODPM) has not set a formal affordability benchmark but it has regarded subsidised and rent-pooled local authority and housing association houses as the main suppliers of affordable accommodation and described such provision as 'social housing'. This is a somewhat inappropriate term as it implies that all 'social' tenants are subsidised whereas many such tenants pay more than the loan, management and maintenance cost of their dwellings.

- The average age of the UK first-time buyer in 2001 was 34, up from 29 in 1974 and only 11% of first-time homebuyers were younger than 25, compared to 32% in the late 1980s. This developing problem of homeownership access has led to the term 'affordable' being used to draw attention to financial barriers to owner-occupation – regarded as the most desirable tenure. Homeownership affordability indicators have been devised to highlight the impact of housing market changes on potential first-time buyers.

With regard to new build, New Labour has defined affordable housing in terms of the inability to obtain access to housing at market prices and has relied on local government to supply more specific definitions. Circular 6/98, issued in connection with the use of planning agreements to secure affordable housing, stated that affordable housing was 'low cost market, and subsidised housing (irrespective of tenure, ownership – whether exclusive or shared – or financial arrangements) that will be available to people who cannot afford to rent or buy houses generally available on the open market' (DETR, 1998, p 2). Kate Barker's housing supply review (Barker, 2004) recommended that the government should establish a national housing affordability goal with regional variants. No official affordability targets were set in the government's five-year housing strategy (ODPM, 2005c) but the ODPM has produced an affordability measure that is now used in allocating resources for affordable housing to regions. An affordability problem is identified if lower-quartile house prices exceed lower-quartile earnings by an 8 to 1 ratio (Wilcox, 2005b).

Affordability in the 19th century

In the past, housing has been made more affordable mainly by the provision of a range of producer and consumer subsidies (see Box 5.1).

To the laissez-faire economist affordability is not an issue. Supply and demand will balance over time and overcrowding, homelessness and unfitness are either short-term problems, manifest while supply catches up with demand, or reflect consumer preferences to spend household income on goods and services other than housing. Laissez-faire thinking was influential in the 19th century but the externalities of poor housing gradually pushed affordability towards social problem status. If, as Chadwick (1842) had demonstrated, the lack of water supplies and sewerage to the dwellings of the working class generated health, moral and national efficiency problems affecting all classes then who was to pay for necessary amenities?

The payment of water and sewerage costs through the rates eased the affordability problem but there remained the issue of how to pay for the higher housing standards thought to be necessary for civilised living and character improvement. Lord Shaftesbury's 1851 Labouring Classes Lodging Houses Act gave local authorities the power to erect lodging houses but,

---

Box 5.1: Producer and consumer subsidies

Direct subsidies can be awarded to producers or consumers and can be means tested or 'universal'. When not subject to a direct income test the subsidy has often been linked to other selective criteria. Producer subsidies can take the form of capital grants or revenue assistance.

	Means tested	Not means tested
Consumer	• Housing Benefit • Improvement grants after 1989 • Disabled Facilities Grant • Energy Efficiency Grant • Mortgage Benefit (Income Support)	• Improvement grants before 1989 (subject to the value of the dwelling) • Assistance under the Key Worker Living Scheme (subject to area and job criteria) • Right to Buy discount • Other low-cost homeownership schemes
Producer	• Improvement grants for private landlords at certain times in the past	• Central government allowances made to local authority revenue accounts, eg Major Repairs Allowance • Social Housing Grant

according to the Act, the rents had not to be 'so low as to be an indirect means of giving relief to the poor' (that is, they could not be subsidised) and certain clauses allowed local ratepayers to delay any proposed scheme. Only Huddersfield and Birmingham used Lord Shaftesbury's law and, by the 1860s, only two answers to how to provide better housing were on offer. In eradicating the slums, reliance was placed on voluntary organisations whose benevolent investors limited their return on capital investment to 5%. Unfortunately the rents necessary to provide a 5% return and provide adequate homes according to the standards of the time were beyond the means of a large proportion of the working class. The charitable Peabody Trust, for example, offered austere but sanitary accommodation absorbing about 50% of the wages paid to many workers. This meant that unskilled labourers did not move into the properties – an outcome defended by 'filtering theory' with James Hole (1866) declaring that 'by increasing the number of first class houses for mechanics the vacated tenements increase the supply for the second and third classes and thus all classes are befitted' (quoted in Boddy and Gray, 1979, p 43). Octavia Hill adopted a different approach. Although she condemned any form of subsidy as undermining the independence of the working class she recognised that 'trickle down' did not work because of migration into cities and population increase. She set up an organisation to buy dilapidated properties, carry out urgent repairs and rent the dwellings to tenants able to pay rent for a reconditioned dwelling on a regular basis. Her tenants were not the artisans housed by the model dwellings companies but the poor. Nevertheless 'her flats could not be easily afforded by those earning less than a regular 16s to 18s' (Wohl, 1977, p 182) and hence the 'very poor' – about 16.5% of London's population – could not afford to live in her properties.

The Tudor Walters Committee, established to make recommendations on the standard of working-class dwellings to be erected after the First World War, highlighted the affordability issue. It recommended far higher benchmarks for the future – bathrooms, gardens and, in some cases, parlours – and accepted that state subsidies were necessary to achieve these standards. However, the Committee argued that the ultimate level of subsidy would depend on the relationship between the initial cost of the dwelling and the rental income derived from it over a 60-year period indicating that, in time, the dwellings would not require subsidy (Tudor Walters, 1918). The houses built under the 1919 Housing and Town Planning Act were of a high standard and, despite the subsidy, expensive to rent. Hence they were mainly occupied by skilled workers or by the middle class: indeed, some local authorities used a means test to select only high-income tenants! Speaking about one of the first council estates built in Liverpool, a former tenant remarked:

'It was posh, our next-door neighbour used to have tea on the grass, the lawn she used to call it. Some of them even had cars, even in them days, and yes, a number used to have cleaning ladies to do for them.' (quoted in McKenna, 1991, p 182)

Standards and affordability

Attempts were made to overcome the affordability problem in the 1920s by reducing the quality of council housing but, even with lower standards, many tenants still found it difficult to pay the rent and resorted to 'strategies that had served them in the old areas: the pawnshop, hire purchase, reducing expenditure on food, or taking in lodgers....' (Olecnowicz, 1997, p 7). This problem was compounded in the 1930s when local authorities, directed towards meeting the housing needs arising from slum clearance, were confronted by the slum dwellers' very low incomes. Further reductions in council house quality were made with the average council house cost declining from 77% of an owner-occupied house in 1934 to 50% in 1939. Branson and Heinemann (1973, p 211) state that 'For the most part the blocks built at this time were severely utilitarian in character.... Some of these blocks seemed to emphasise that they were rough places for rough people'. Yet, even with lower standards the affordability problem remained. The 1930 Housing Act contained a provision to allow local authorities to operate 'differential' rent schemes but few authorities adopted them either in the form of individual rent rebates or variable rents for 'compulsory' – re-housed from clearance areas – compared to 'voluntary' – re-housed from the waiting list – tenants. Council tenants with reasonable incomes strongly opposed such schemes. Moreover, many local authorities believed that concentrating the subsidies on the poor was a step towards housing support becoming the responsibility of the ratepayer because 'poor relief' could be interpreted as a public assistance matter, a traditional responsibility of local government.

From producer to consumer subsidies

Between 1945 and 1972 housing was made more affordable by rent control in the private landlord sector plus continued central and local rate subsidies in the council sector. Rent pooling – made possible by the 1935 Housing Act – with local authorities using the low cost of older homes to reduce the rents charged on new properties – helped to keep rents down. A few local authorities also ran rent rebate schemes.

The 1972 Housing Finance Act marked the first serious attempt to move from producer to consumer subsidies with the White Paper heralding the Act stating that the government's central policy was 'subsidising people, not bricks and mortar' (DoE, 1971 p 42). It introduced a national rent rebate for council tenants and a rent allowance scheme for tenants of other landlords that offered the opportunity for some low-income households to be able to afford to live in the better-quality local authority dwellings and for the tenants of private landlords to pay a rent sufficient to keep their houses in reasonable repair. The Act met considerable opposition from council house tenants with decent incomes who objected to paying 'fair rents' – above the historic costs of providing their dwellings – and giving any surplus to the Treasury. The return of a Labour government in 1974 meant that the 'fair rent' element of the 1972 Act was not implemented but the national rent rebate and rent allowance schemes were retained.

Housing Benefit

Between 1983 and 1990 rent rebates, rent allowances and the payment of rent through Supplementary Benefit – a scheme that had operated on different principles to rent rebates and rent allowances – were united in a Housing Benefit scheme administered by local government and directed by the Department of Social Security. Tighter eligibility criteria with students excluded from claiming and a steeper cut-out rate meant that the scheme became more a safety net than a measure to enhance general rent affordability (Stephens, 2005b). Under the 1988 Housing Act, designed to push all rents up to market, not 'fair' levels, the cost of Housing Benefit escalated and measures were introduced to contain expenditure. In 1996 'pre-tenancy determinations' were introduced whereby prospective tenants could apply for a determination of the eligible rent of a property for Housing Benefit purposes before the tenancy was agreed. It was argued that pre-tenancy determinations enabled prospective tenants to find out the maximum eligible rent for a particular property, thereby making it easier for them to shop around for a tenancy they could afford. In

Box 5.2: Housing Benefit

Housing Benefit is means tested. Eligibility is based on the difference between 'eligible rent' and a number of 'needs' allowances. If income is at or below the 'needs' allowances Housing Benefit will pay 100% of the 'eligible rent' but, for every £1 of income above the 'needs' allowances, Housing Benefit is reduced by 65 pence (the Housing Benefit 'taper'). For Housing Benefit purposes, the property must not be 'unreasonably large' and 'eligible rent' is limited to:

- for tenants of private landlords, the average rent in the area for the type of property in which a person lives as determined by the Rent Service (the 'reference' rent);
- for single people under 25, the rent of a single room with shared facilities.

People with capital above a set threshold are not eligible for Housing Benefit and entitlement deductions are made for non-dependants living in the household.

2005 Housing Benefit had the features outlined in Box 5.2 and was claimed by nearly four million households (see Table 5.1)

New Labour's Housing Green Paper listed a number of problems in the operation of Housing Benefit (DETR, 2000b, para 11.4):

- Delivery of Housing Benefit is complex, confusing and time consuming. Claimants are usually required to complete more than one claim form and attend more than one office if they want to claim Housing Benefit along with other social security benefits. Information Technology links between the different organisations are often poor and can be non-existent. In addition, when a rent officer determination is involved it can significantly add to the time it takes to assess a claim.
- The benefit rules are complex. Claimants don't understand them and often don't know what benefit rules apply to them and what support they might be entitled to.
- The performance of Local Authorities is inconsistent.... The Audit Commission suggests that only 56% of local authorities in England and Wales administer benefits efficiently.
- All this administrative hassle and delay can leave claimants with worrying rent arrears, or worse, risk of eviction – pensioners in particular can be worried unnecessarily about their housing at a time when they should be feeling secure in their homes – and landlords with cash flow problems and concerns about renting to Housing Benefit claimants.
- Housing Benefit fraud and error costs some £840m each year.
- For those of working age Housing Benefit can act as a barrier which deters people from getting into jobs. Many claimants simply do not know that they can still get help with their housing costs if they move into low paid work. Others are reluctant to risk taking up work – particularly where it is temporary or casual – because of the potential wait involved in re-claiming if the job ends.

Table 5.1: *Housing Benefit statistics: 2005*

Number of recipients (local authority tenants)	1,789,200
Number of recipients (registered social landlord tenants)	1,377,100
Number of recipients (private landlord tenants)	796,800
Average payment (local authority tenants)	£52.55
Average payment (registered social landlord tenants)	£61.74
Average payment (private landlord deregulated tenants)	£79.44
Number of payments affected by the reference rent rules	638,000
Number of payments affected by the single room rule	11,200

Source: DWP (2005a)

- Housing Benefit can be exploited by landlords. Some unscrupulous landlords charge high rents for poor quality housing paid for by Housing Benefit.
- Housing Benefit takes away responsibility from claimants. Housing Benefit gives tenants little interest in the rent – provided it does not exceed local limits it can be reimbursed in full, often directly to the landlord. This means that some tenants are not even aware of how much rent is being paid.

Three other points might have been added to this catalogue of troubles:

- Housing Benefit makes a contribution to the 'poverty trap', that is, the disincentive impact on work behaviour – not just on whether or not to enter the labour market but on the decision to work harder, longer and in a better job – due to its high taper rate (see Table 5.2). Although there is little empirical evidence on the actual impact of the taper, this potential disincentive impact raises the issue of the meaning of affordability in rented accommodation. Given the work disincentives involved in claiming Housing Benefit should not estimates of rent affordability ignore the availability of Housing Benefit? In the 1980s the Conservative proposals to shift from 'fair' to market rents in the not-for-profit sector prompted the National Federation of Housing Associations (now the National Housing Federation) to define and monitor affordability in the hope that this would encourage the government to maintain grant levels. The National Federation of Housing Associations' 'affordability test' stated that 'rents are affordable if the majority of working households taking up new tenancies are not caught in the poverty trap (because of dependency on Housing Benefit) or paying more than 25% of their income in rent' (National Federation of Housing Associations, 1995, p 4). In 2002, 62% of new housing association tenants failed the 'affordability test' (National Housing Federation, 2002). In 2001/02, 30.9% of the income of all housing association tenants and 26.2% of the income of local authority tenants was absorbed by rental costs before Housing Benefit (ODPM, 2005e, p 108).
- In 2002 the take-up rate was between 87% and 95%. This is a better rate than most means-tested benefits but between £600 million and £1,230 million of Housing Benefit entitlement is unclaimed.
- It has been alleged that the availability of Housing Benefit, which in some cases can pay all the rent, encourages people to 'up-market', that is, rent a property that offers more than their basic requirements. However, there is little research evidence to indicate that this is a problem (Kemp, 1992).

New Labour's response to these problems was to propose a new means-tested Housing Benefit, to be piloted in selected areas, normally paid directly to the tenant and based on a standard rent for a property of a particular size to be determined for each locality. The government claimed the reform would give 'a new deal for tenants' because:

Table 5.2: *Gross weekly earnings levels at which Housing Benefit entitlement ceases (£s)*

Household type	Weekly rent (£s)							
	30	**40**	**50**	**60**	**70**	**80**	**90**	**100**
Single person over 25	76.6	92.2	124.6	173.7	217.8	240.7	263.7	286.6
Couple over 25	83.7	104.8	145.9	197.2	248.5	295.4	318.4	341.3
Lone parent + 1 child under 19	67.2	82.4	101.8	141.4	192.7	244.0	295.2	346.5
Lone parent + 2 children under 19	67.0	82.4	101.7	141.3	192.6	243.9	295.1	346.4
Couple + 1 child under 19	83.7	104.8	145.6	196.9	248.3	299.5	350.7	387.8
Couple + 2 children under 19	83.6	104.8	145.5	196.8	248.1	299.4	350.6	401.9
Couple + 3 children under 19	83.6	104.7	145.4	196.7	248.0	299.3	350.5	401.8
Couple + 4 children under 19	83.6	104.6	145.3	196.6	247.9	299.2	350.4	401.7

Source: Adapted from Wilcox (2004)

> tenants who rent a property at below the standard allowance or who move to cheaper property in their local area, or who negotiate to keep the rent below the standard allowance, will be able to keep the difference – putting the decision in their hands. (DWP, 2002, p 4)

Initially the scheme was confined to nine 'pathfinder' local authorities and was to be extended nationwide to the private landlord sector subject to the experience of the 'pathfinders'. The early evidence from the 'pathfinders' indicates that tenants are more likely to fall into rent arrears in the new system (Kemp, 2006, p 28) and landlords have reported a 10% drop in lettings to Housing Benefit claimants (Roof, 2006, p 7). In his 2003 Budget statement, the Chancellor announced that the scheme would be extended to the social sector at some time in the future.

If implemented nationwide, the new system has the potential to simplify Housing Benefit thereby making it easier and quicker to claim. It would also give tenants personal responsibility for rent payment, minimise the visibility of Housing Benefit claimants to landlords and mimic the market by making rent increases more transparent. However, the scheme does nothing to alleviate the poverty trap; the experience of 'pre-tenancy determinations' indicates that few tenants will be able to shop around for lower rents and rent arrears are likely to become a bigger problem.

Estimating affordable housing requirements

New Labour assumes that social housing is affordable because rents are subsidised and pooled. In line with this affordability notion when estimating the need for social housing – sometimes called the 'sub-market' sector – academics have embraced methods that attempt to calculate the requirements that the housing market cannot meet. Holmans (1995), for example, has devised a model to predict the additional need for social housing based on the existing backlog of households who are likely to require help to access housing and future requirements generated by demographic and other factors. These calculations were updated and adjusted by Barker (2004) (see Box 5.3) but they assume that part of the backlog of need cannot be met by changes in the current distribution of housing (for example, overcrowded households moving to under-occupied housing) and that there is little substitutability between the 'market' and 'sub-market' sector according to price changes in the 'market' sector. If house prices increase significantly in the future more households will require 'sub-market' housing and, if prices remain static or decline, less 'sub-market' housing will be required. Bramley (2004) has estimated that, with a house price trend of zero, 12,000 households per year will be priced into the market sector illustrating how action on house prices can reduce state expenditure on social housing schemes. Holmans et al (2004) have calculated that 89,000 social housing units per year are needed compared to an average of 19,400 per annum produced between 1999/00 and 2003/04.

Promoting homeownership

The privileged position of homeownership in the UK has produced many schemes to make homeownership more affordable than its market price.

Tax relief on mortgage interest

Tax relief on mortgage interest was a major instrument of housing policy in the 1960s, 1970s and 1980s. Relief was given for the interest on the full amount of a loan of any size but, in 1975, when the average house price in the UK was £11,767, it was limited to the interest on £25,000 – raised to £30,000 in 1983. Until 1983 the allowable interest was deducted directly from taxable income, but, under the mortgage interest relief at source (MIRAS) scheme, the borrower paid the lender the interest less the standard rate tax relief. This concession was available to low-income households who did not pay tax. Failure to raise the threshold at which MIRAS ceased meant that its real value to the house purchaser declined and, in the late 1990s, taking advantage of the general fall in interest rates, it was phased out prior to its ending in April 2000. It was argued that the tax concession was unfair because it gave more assistance to high-rate taxpayers and those with the largest mortgages and that it artificially

Box 5.3: Households in need of sub-market housing: England

Households without self-contained accommodation

Households in temporary accommodation	94,000
Concealed families (eg young couples living with parents)	154,000
Households in shared dwellings	53,000
Would-be couples living apart	74,000
Single homeless people, hostel residents, etc	110,000
Adjustment for those saving to buy	–23,000
Subtotal	462,000

Owner-occupiers/private sector tenants needing social rented sector homes

Households applying for age or medical reasons	70,000
Households who cannot afford mortgage payments	20,000
Expiry of lease or inability to afford rent	30,000
Overcrowding	20,000
Subtotal	140,000

Local authority and registered social landlord tenants in unsuitable housing

Overcrowding	206,000
Households with children living above the ground floor	150,000
Overlap in categories	–10,000
Subtotal	346,000

Total	948,000

Additional need for social housing: England 2002-11 (per annum)

Net increase in households	28,000
Increase in vacant dwellings	1,000
Loss of re-lets due to Right to Buy	22,000
Reduction in private rental lettings to those on Housing Benefit	10,000
Replacement of losses (mainly through clearance)	5,000
Total	66,000

stimulated house prices by encouraging people to consume more accommodation than they required. In recent years fiscal policy has been used to dampen rather than to stimulate the housing market. The threshold at which Stamp Duty has to be paid was increased only in deprived areas and the Stamp

Duty rate was increased to 1% on properties worth between £60,000 (£150,000 in deprived areas) and £250,000, 3% on properties worth between £250,000 and £500,000 and 4% on those properties worth more than £500,000. These increases in Stamp Duty had little impact on house price inflation but they produced substantial revenue for the Treasury with a yield of £3.2 billion in 2002/03 compared to £625 million in 1996/97. The average Stamp Duty bill for a residential purchase increased from £570 in 1997/98 to £2,560 in 2003/04. Paradoxically, given the concern about the affordability of homeownership for first-time buyers, the average first-time buyer paid £1,000 in Stamp Duty in 2003, adding to the 'savings gap' preventing entry into homeownership (Housing Corporation, 2003, p 10). In response to this problem the threshold for Stamp Duty was increased to £120,000 in 2005.

Rent control

Rent control was perhaps the most effective low-cost homeownership scheme. Between 1915 and 1989, confronted by rent freezes, rent regulation and security of tenure for tenants, many private landlords sold their properties to sitting tenants often at substantial discounts on the vacant possession market price.

The Right to Buy

By 2005 the Right to Buy, introduced in 1980, had enabled over two million tenants to become homeowners. The number of dwellings sold under the Right to Buy has fluctuated each year (see Figure 5.1) and increased after 1998/99 in response to proposals to restrict entitlements and to rapidly rising house prices, especially in the North. In 2002/03 the Right to Buy produced £2.2 billion in capital receipts compared to £890 million in 1997/98. The impact of the Right to Buy is examined in Box 5.4.

In 1999 New Labour modified the Right to Buy by introducing regional variations in maximum discounts ranging from £22,000 to £38,000. Later, evidence was uncovered revealing that, in some areas, private companies were using cash incentives to encourage tenants to buy their homes (ODPM, 2003b). In return for a payment, residents were agreeing to move out of their homes so that the company could let them at market rents. Tenants then sold the homes to the company after three years so they could keep their discounts. To maintain the affordable housing pool and curtail the detected abuse the maximum discount on sales was reduced from £38,000 to £16,000 in local authority areas where affordable housing was very scarce. The 2004 Housing Act contained a number of clauses to restrict the Right to Buy, including the extension of both the initial qualification period and the time after sale when local authorities may require owners to repay some of their initial discount, to five years.

People who became tenants of non-charitable housing associations before

Box 5.4: The impact of the Right to Buy

- Although the case of a former council house in Fulham, bought for £50,000 in 2000 and on sale for £900,000 in 2005, is rare, there has been a significant increase in the assets of the overwhelming majority of households who have bought their homes. In the main these households had low levels of wealth.
- On purchase many owners invested in their properties.
- Although over two million homes have been sold since 1980, only 750,000 council and housing association homes have been built since then. When sitting tenants buy their houses the affordable housing stock available to new tenants is not restricted immediately, but, as existing tenants leave, the number of affordable rented properties available to let diminishes (see Figure 5.2).
- Proportionately more houses than flats have been sold and there have been more sales in rural areas.
- There has been a tendency for purchasers to be better-off and older with 76% of purchasers in employment compared to 35% of council tenants overall.
- According to Jones and Murie (1998, p 1):

The Right to Buy, alongside other policies, has contributed to increased concentration of low-income households in the social rented sector and in particular estates. When resold, former council houses are rarely the cheapest homes on the market and purchasers are often already home-owners. The evidence suggests that open market purchasers often move on after a short period and that the turnover of properties is high.

However, recent trends in Right to Buy sales may have mitigated its area impact.

- There is some evidence that the Right to Buy might have contributed to the decline of some low-demand areas by sales to private landlords who may let to undesirable tenants (Murie and Ferrari, 2003).
- The use of the capital receipts derived from council house sales has been restricted by central government in different ways at different times but the overall impact has been to benefit councils with good-condition stock and low housing needs (Reeves, 2005).

1988 retain the Right to Buy and tenants whose homes are transferred from local authorities to housing associations have a preserved Right to Buy. Other housing association tenants have restricted opportunities to purchase their homes at a discount between £9,000 and £16,000 under the 'Right to Acquire' – available to tenants of property built or improved with public money or transferred from a local authority after 1997 – and through 'voluntary purchase' schemes available at the discretion of the housing association. The 2001 Housing (Scotland) Act created a uniform Right to Buy for all social sector tenants

Figure 5.1: Right-to-buy sales and stock transfer: Britain (000s)

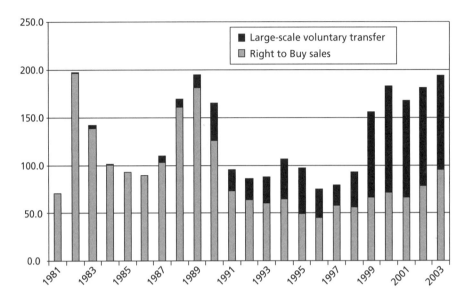

Source: Adapted from ONS (2005b)

Figure 5.2: Houses available for letting, 1992/93 to 2002/03 (000s)

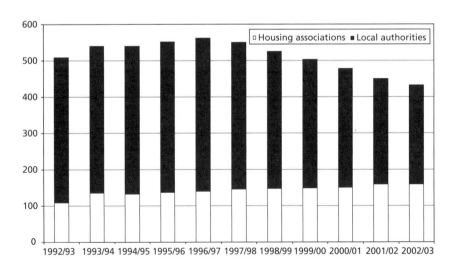

Source: Adapted from Wilcox (2004)

with a qualifying period of five years and a maximum discount level of £15,000. This scheme does not apply to current council tenants, who retain their existing rights. Charitable housing association tenants are exempt and the scheme will not be available to other housing association tenants for a period of 10 years.

Protecting homeowners from loss of income

Income Support pays 'reasonable' mortgage interest – up to 1% above the Bank of England base rate – but never any capital repayments. A claimant's assets must be less than £8,000, there is a mortgage ceiling of £100,000, unchanged since 1995, and assistance becomes available only 29 weeks after the original Income Support claim. Private mortgage payment protection insurance is available but the coverage of such insurance is limited.

Equity sharing

The Conservative Party introduced a number of novel but limited low-cost homeownership schemes. Equity sharing was the most enduring. Do It Yourself Shared Ownership (DIYSO) allowed the buyer to select a property on the open market whereas conventional shared ownership involved a housing association building or acquiring a property for sale. In both cases, the purchaser bought part of the equity in the property and paid a subsidised rent to a registered social landlord on the remainder of the equity. The proportion of the equity that purchasers bought was flexible, usually ranging from 25% to 75% and, over time, purchasers could 'staircase' by buying more or less of their property. In 2001, government support for DIYSO was withdrawn and replaced by Homebuy. Under this scheme the applicant pays 75% of the cost of a dwelling and 25% is paid by a registered social landlord. The 75% stake can be increased in one stage to the full equity. When the house is sold, the registered social landlord is paid the relevant share of the current value.

The Key Worker Scheme

This scheme was introduced in August 2004. It replaced the Starter Home Initiative and covers public sector workers such as nurses, teachers, police officers, social workers and fire officers. Via registered social landlords, it offers equity-sharing Homebuy schemes, shared ownership in newly built housing association property and what is called 'intermediate renting', where the rent is set at a level between that charged by social and private landlords. It is available in London, the South East and the East of England where the high housing costs have affected employers' ability to recruit and retain staff. Most of the resources have been used to promote open market purchases, which may have helped to push up house prices. The scheme has also been criticised because it is poorly targeted with beneficiaries having an average income of £33,000 and with existing homeowners, now requiring a bigger home because of family commitments, receiving no help (Maxwell, 2005).

The future of low-cost homeownership

In response to the Conservative proposal to extend a 'right to own' to housing association tenants on the same terms as the Right to Buy for council tenants, New Labour announced changes to the Homebuy scheme aimed at making a contribution to an additional one million homeowners by 2010. Three schemes will be available:

- Social Homebuy will allow social sector tenants, with the agreement of their landlord, to purchase a 25% or more share in their existing home at a discount equivalent to the Right to Acquire discount (£9,000 to 16,000). However, a rent of up to 3% will have to be paid on the unowned equity and, on subsequent sale, the social landlord will have the right to first refusal or to nominate the next buyer and to any increase in the value of its stake in the house. In order to encourage social landlords to participate in the scheme they would be allowed to use all the capital receipts generated by the sales.
- New Build Homebuy will be available to key workers, social tenants, those on the housing register and other priority first-time buyers. It would offer 25% or more equity but without a discount, and a rent of up to 3% would have to be paid on the unowned equity. As part of this scheme English Partnerships would use public land for house building but retain a stake in the value of the land. When taken up by tenants of social landlords this scheme may release social housing for homeless families and supplement the cash incentive schemes operated by some local authorities that make a payment to council tenants to vacate their dwellings.
- Open Market Homebuy will be available to the same groups as New Build Homebuy but participants in the scheme would be expected to buy a 75% share of an existing house and a rental charge would be made on the 25%, financed by an interest-free equity loan.

New Build and Open Market Homebuy are designed to meet the requirements of those in the 'intermediate' housing market, that is, those unlikely to be allocated a social housing tenancy and above Housing Benefit entitlement but unable to afford full homeownership. The government anticipated that over 100,000 households could be helped by all the Homebuy schemes that would be financed partially by the state and partially by mortgage lenders. Should house prices decline the equity loss would be taken by the government, then the mortgage lender, then the owner.

Planning gain and affordable housing

The 1971 Town and Country Planning Act enhanced the powers of local planning authorities to enter into agreements with developers whereby, in return for planning permission, the developer provided benefits to the local authority. The 'rural exceptions policy', introduced in 1989, allowed exceptional permissions for affordable housing on sites adjacent to rural settlements provided that the dwellings remained available to local, low-income residents.

In the early 1980s some local authorities started to promote affordable housing through the planning process under section 106 of the 1990 Town and Country Planning Act – the successor to the 1971 Act. Under section 106, developers could be asked to supply low-cost accommodation in return for planning permission and, if this low-cost accommodation was built on the same site as the market-price housing, then balanced communities might be created. However, although the number of affordable homes obtained through the planning process has been increasing, only a small number of affordable homes has been secured – about 2.2% of the total new dwellings completed between 1992 and 2000 (Carmona et al, 2003, p 145) with 16,380 units in 2003/04. Three quarters of these affordable units also had to rely on Social Housing Grant and many were supplied 'off-site' thereby making no contribution to balanced communities (see Chapter Nine). The main obstacles to the use of planning gain to secure affordable homes appear to have been:

- the problems involved in producing robust estimates of affordable housing requirements – such estimates are legally necessary for the implementation of a local policy on affordable housing;
- the ODPM's lukewarm attitude to the initiative: its impact has not been regularly monitored and there has been a 'lack of clear instruction offered by government on how the system should be used' (Carmona et al, 2003, p 143).
- the exclusion of small sites, producing the division of larger sites into smaller sites to evade the policy;
- the protracted negotiations with developers necessary to secure affordable housing (Monk et al, 2005; National Audit Office/Audit Commission, 2006).
- the requirement that planning policy should not be expressed in favour of a particular form of tenure;
- the reluctance of developers to support the idea of 'integrated communities', that is, affordable properties 'pepper-potted' with the more expensive dwellings. Suspicious of the impact of such 'social engineering' on the profitability of the market-price houses, many developers have insisted on separating the two housing types in different parts of the site.

Some commentators have a preference for a transparent development levy that could be used to subsidise affordable housing. The Barker Review (2004) recommended that the government should introduce a planning-gain supplement tied to the granting of planning permission. New Labour has expressed interest in introducing such a charge. Although this 'in cash' rather than 'in-kind' levy would be simpler to implement and the resources obtained would be more flexible to use, such a levy would make it more difficult to secure new developments with balanced communities.

Increasing housing supply

Despite sporadic declines, the UK has experienced a long-term upward trend in house prices and, between 1997 and 2004, prices spiralled by 125% whereas average incomes increased by 18%. Although, as a consequence of higher interest rates, house prices started to become more stable in 2005, potential first-time buyers have difficulty in securing a foothold on the homeownership ladder. The National House Builders Council's first-time buyer ability to pay index, which takes into account the need to raise a deposit and monthly mortgage payments, indicated that, in 2003, despite low interest rates, ability to pay was lower than at any time since the late 1980s (Vass, 2004). The deposit necessary for first-time buyers to secure a property had increased from 10% in 1997 to 25% in 2003 and, in London, 31% of first-time buyers relied on relatives to provide financial help.

The Cheltenham and Gloucester mortgage lender has constructed an affordability index based on the percentage of take-home pay needed to cover a mortgage on an average-price first-time home. This index increased from 29.12% in 1997 to 45% in late 2004 (Great Britain) for a single-income buyer and from 14.9% to 23% for joint-income buyers but, because of lower interest rates, the index is not as high as in the late 1980s (Cheltenham and Gloucester, 2005). Wilcox (2005b) examined the ratio of house prices in the lower quartile to the gross household incomes of 20- to 39-year-olds in different areas and, making the assumption that a single earner would be able to obtain a mortgage of 3.75 times their income and households with two or more earners 3.25 times their income, he calculated the proportion of the relevant group that would not be able to afford homeownership. This ranged from 59.6% in London to 27.1% in the North East but there were substantial inter-regional variations in affordability indicating the importance of travel to work areas in estimating the requirements for intervention in the housing market.

Concerns about the impact of high house prices on economic stability and growth and hence on meeting the conditions necessary for Britain to adopt the Euro led to the publication of the *Sustainable Communities: Building for the Future* (ODPM, 2003a) and the setting up of the Barker Review (see Box 5.5). Barker maintained that housing supply in the UK was only half as responsive to demand as in France and only one third as responsive as in the US. Reducing the real price trend in England to the European Union average would involve building between 70,000 and 120,000 additional private sector

Box 5.5: The Barker Review: summary

Analysis

- Household formation, on the basis of the 2001 Census, has been estimated at 179,000 households per annum but only 134,000 extra homes were built in 2002.
- In order to bring the real price trend in line with the European Union average, 70,000 to 120,000 private sector houses per annum will be required in addition to the houses anticipated by the *Sustainable Communities: Building for the Future* (ODPM, 2003a).
- To improve access to housing for those who cannot afford market prices, 48,000 social houses will be required each year – between 17,000 and 23,000 more than currently delivered.
- Land availability, restricted by the planning system, is the main constraint to increasing housing supply due to the following:
  - In some areas insufficient land is allocated for development and/or the rate of land release is not responsive to market conditions and rising house prices.
  - The cost of additional houses is felt at the local level whereas the benefits are often more diffuse.
  - There are obstacles to the development of land allocated for development.
  - The house-building industry faces a number of market and planning risks, which means that the industry is reluctant to invest in the long term.
- There is evidence that builders can maximise profits by holding back development thereby increasing prices, and the housing shortage means that the building industry lacks efficiency incentives.
- In the South East the ratio of agricultural to residential land price is 1:303.

Major recommendations

- Government should establish a market affordability target.
- Each region should set its own target to improve market affordability and this target should specify sub-regional targets.
- Local plans should be more realistic in their initial allocation of land and more flexible in bringing forward additional land for development. When allocating sufficient land to meet their targets, local authorities should allow for the proportion of sites that prove undevelopable. In addition a buffer of land should be available to respond to changes in demand, which should be released when predefined triggers signify that supply and demand are not in balance. These triggers could include:
  - worsening market affordability for newly forming households and/or lower-quartile earners;
  - local house price increases relative to the regional average;
  - an increasing premium in land prices for residential use over other areas;

> ‣ employment growth significantly outstripping housing growth;
> ‣ a rising number of housing transactions.
> • Government should use tax measures to extract some of the windfall gain that accrues to landowners from the sale of their land for residential development.
> • A proportion of the revenue generated from the granting of planning permission in local authorities should be given directly to local authorities.
> • Tax measures could be used to affect developer behaviour by altering the relative cost of certain development choices to better reflect the externalities, for example the encouragement of brownfield development.
>
> *Source:* Barker (2004)

houses each year. She placed the lion's share of the blame for the poor responsiveness of supply to demand in the UK on the planning system. Her first recommendation was that the government should establish national and regional affordability targets and take steps to increase supply whenever this target was not achieved.

Low-income households and homeownership

70% of households in England are now homeowners and hence the tenure covers a wide diversity of incomes. Burrows (2000) found that 7% of owner-occupiers with mortgages had incomes below the poverty line but, because of the size of the tenure, 50% of all those with incomes below the poverty line were homeowners. In 2002/03 over 3.3 million homeowners had total housing costs that represented more than 30% of their disposable income (Wilcox, 2005c, p 131) but there is no general system available to help low-income homeowners other than the Income Support available only to those without full-time work. This absence of general support for low-income homeowners in full-time work, plus the availability of Housing Benefit for people who rent, tends to push low-income households into the rented sector. It also contributes to inequality. The Gini coefficient in 2000/01 (see Chapter Four) *before* housing costs was 34 but increased to 38 *after* housing costs (Shephard, 2003). Although some of this difference can be attributed to methodological problems it also reflects the limitations of state support for homeownership.

Overview

- Until the introduction of a national system of rent rebates and rent allowances in 1972 – later to be called Housing Benefit – many households found it difficult to pay for the quality of housing deemed acceptable at the time.
- In the 1980s and 1990s there was a marked shift away from 'bricks and mortar' subsidies to means-tested consumer subsidies.
- In the past, homeownership has been stimulated by various forms of subsidies but today help in becoming a homeowner – other than the Right to Buy – is very limited.
- Since 2002 the government has intervened in the housing market to promote greater supply in the hope of making houses more affordable.

Questions for discussion

(1) What is meant by affordable housing?
(2) Why, in the 1930s, was there opposition to 'differential' rents?
(3) Assess the merits and limitations of Housing Benefit as a method of subsidising housing costs?
(4) How can the planning system promote affordable housing?
(5) Discuss the analysis of housing supply and demand contained in the Barker Report.

Further reading

Both the interim and final reports of **Barker's** review of housing supply – *Delivering Stability: Securing Our Future Housing Needs; Interim Report* **(2003)** and *Delivering Stability: Securing Our Future Housing Needs; Final Report, Recommendations* **(2004)** – are important.

Website resources

The planning section of the ODPM's website gives an account of the government's policies: www.odpm.gov.uk/index.asp?id=1143104

The Housing Corporation supplies descriptions of low-cost homeownership schemes at www.housingcorp.gov.uk

six

Homelessness

Summary

- The definition of homelessness is contested, with the available definitions linked to different explanations and forms of action.
- In England homelessness has been divided into two categories – rough sleeping and statutory homelessness.
- The 1977 Housing (Homeless Persons) Act placed obligations on local housing authorities to help homeless people but only those in 'priority need' and 'unintentionally' homeless received significant assistance.
- Becoming homeless is a process involving a number of interacting factors.
- New Labour has emphasised the personal rather than the structural causes of homelessness.
- Despite the success of some special initiatives, homelessness has increased over the last 30 years.

Why did homelessness become a social problem?

In England homelessness is officially divided into two categories – rough sleeping and statutory homelessness – a division reflecting a long tradition in attitudes towards homeless people. In the past people now called 'rough sleepers' – mainly men – have been regarded as a threat to social order; deemed as *being* a problem they have been subject to social discipline. People now called the 'statutory homeless'– containing a high proportion of households with children – have often been represented as *having* a problem and requiring assistance. None the less, concerns that such help would lead to jumping the housing queue and hinder self-reliance helped to produce low-standard, stigmatised forms of provision.

The Elizabethan Poor Law

The 1601 Act for the Relief of the Poor – a consolidation of earlier legislation – placed a duty on the churchwardens of every parish to appoint 'overseers of the poor'. The overseers' obligations included raising the 'weekly or otherwise (by taxation of every inhabitant ...) convenient stock of flax, hemp, wool, thread, iron, and other ware and stuff, to set the poor on work' (1601 Act for the Relief of the Poor, quoted in Bruce, 1973, p 39). The Elizabethan Poor Law was grounded in mercantilist economic theory. This asserted that, because the wealth in the world was finite, any increase in trade by one nation must be at the expense of its competitors. To maximise its wealth each state was exhorted to aim for a favourable balance of trade and, by accumulating wealth in precious metals, provide the resources for the defence of the realm. It was the duty of the sovereign to ensure the maintenance of the state's human capital – its 'loyal subjects'. The 1601 Act, by placing an obligation on each parish to set the poor to work, provided such 'loyal subjects' with an income for rent payment. It was aimed at preventing what was then called destitution – now subsumed under the term homelessness.

Settlement and Removal Laws

The cost of poor relief was met by levying a rate on property in a parish. This raised the issue of the 'rightful place' of any applicant for relief. Which parish had to pay? In an attempt to answer this question various Acts of Settlement and Removal were passed and, by the late 17th century, the basic principles governing parish support obligations had been established. A person acquired a settlement in a particular parish by occupying a property worth more than 10 pounds per year, by serving an apprenticeship in the parish, by marriage or by being hired for more than a year. A 'stranger' could be removed from a parish, without legal procedures, if discovered within 40 days of arrival.

'Rogues, vagabondes and sturdy beggars'

Apportioning the cost of relief was not the only objective of the settlement legislation. By imposing a parish obligation to supply a means of income for the destitute – provided people abided in their rightful place – it also promoted social stability. People who strayed from their rightful place were regarded as a social problem; labelled 'vagrants' they were subject to repressive legislation. In the 16th century the vagrancy laws were directed at the growing number of 'masterless men' who had taken to leaving their parish of birth in search of work and freedom from feudal ties. These migrants were regarded as a 'new and terrible problem' with the settled population living 'in terror of the tramp' (Humphreys, 1999, p 65). The 1597 Vagrancy Act (39 Eliz. c 3), deemed 'all wandering persons and common Labourers refusing to work for such reasonable wages commonly gyven in such partes where such persons do or shall happen to dwell or abide' to be 'rogues, vagabondes and sturdy beggars'. They were to be whipped, incarcerated in a 'house of correction' and then removed to their parish of origin.

Homelessness and laissez-faire economics

Although Adam Smith, the doyen of laissez-faire economics, condemned the settlement laws as a hindrance to labour mobility the growing influence of market theory led to only modest changes in the harshness of the vagrancy laws. The 1824 Vagrancy Act redefined vagrancy as a 'failure to maintain oneself' or as living as 'an unlicensed pedlar, a prostitute or a beggar'. Vagrants were divided into three groups according to their perceived character – 'idle and disorderly', 'rogues and vagabonds' and 'incorrigible rogues'. People 'sleeping out' were classified as 'idle and disorderly' but, following a second offence, they became 'incorrigible rogues' punishable by imprisonment or a public flogging (Humphreys, 1999).

Under the 1834 Poor Law Amendment Act unions of parishes were required to build workhouses where the conditions of the inmates were to not to be 'really or apparently so eligible as the situation of the independent labourer of the lowest class' (Poor Law Commissioners, 1834, p 228). Workhouses accommodated destitute people with a settlement in the area and, as part of the 'less eligibility' principle, married men were often separated from their spouses and children. The workhouses also contained 'vagrant' or 'casual' wards, popularly known as 'spikes'. Here, short-term accommodation and sustenance were available to 'tramps' in return for a work task – usually breaking stones for use on local roads. At the beginning of the 20th century it was estimated that between 30,000 and 80,000 people used the workhouse casual wards (Royal Commission on the Poor Laws and Relief of Poverty, 1909, p 1080) but, rather than rely on the workhouse, many people 'on the tramp' preferred to sleep rough or to use a Common Lodging House. Common Lodging Houses provided cheap accommodation on a nightly basis, variable in quality and price with the cheapest being the 'halfpenny hang' – sleeping hanging over a rope strung across a room. Booth (1902) estimated that there were 165,000 'homeless' in the UK – people he described as 'loafers, casuals and some criminals'.

During the inter-war period the workhouse casual wards (renamed Public Assistance Institutions in 1929), commercial Common Lodging Houses and provision made by charities such as the Salvation Army remained the major sources of accommodation for wandering people. They were described as being 'without a settled way of living', a phrase that illustrates how single homeless people were regarded as 'rootless' as well as 'homeless' – they lacked connections to mainstream society.

The 1948 National Assistance Act

This Act consolidated the distinction between single and family homelessness. Single homelessness was regarded as an employment and resettlement matter whereas family homelessness was viewed as a welfare issue. Under the Act, a National Assistance Board assumed overall responsibility for the workhouse casual wards. It had an obligation to 'make provision whereby persons without a settled living may be influenced to lead a more settled life' and a duty 'to provide and maintain centres for the provision of temporary board and lodgings for such persons' (1948 National Assistance Act, para 2.1).

Local authority public assistance committees, renamed welfare committees, became responsible for various forms of care, including residential provision for homeless people. The National Assistance Act imposed a duty on local authorities to provide 'temporary accommodation for persons in urgent need thereof, being need arising in circumstances that could not reasonably have been foreseen' (1948 National Assistance Act, para 2.2). This duty was designed for emergencies and was not seen as replacing local authority waiting lists in allocating houses. Homeless people with children could be offered assistance but the help was temporary and provided by a social work authority which, in county areas, was located at a different tier to the housing authority.

The 1977 Housing (Homeless Persons) Act

Local authorities interpreted their duties under the 1948 National Assistance Act in a restrictive, some would say mean-spirited, manner. To them, 'circumstances that could not reasonably have been foreseen' meant fire, flood or other natural disaster – other reasons were a signal that the applicant wanted to jump the long housing queue; 75% of all homelessness applications were rejected in Greater London (Holman et al, 1970). People without children had little hope of assistance and homeless people with children could be denied help because their 'habitual place of residence' was in another local authority. When local authorities offered a homeless family somewhere to live it was often a caravan or low-standard communal accommodation. The system had all the 'less eligibility' characteristics of the Poor Law from which it had descended, indeed, some of the communal accommodation was in former workhouses and many authorities did not allow a man to live with his wife and children. If, after spending time in temporary accommodation, the family could not obtain permanent housing, then the children might be taken into local authority care.

Cathy Come Home, first shown on television in 1966, told the story of how a young couple, Cathy and Reg, became homeless. Having been passed between authorities because of disputes about responsibility for them – echoes of the settlement laws – Cathy and her children had to live in a squalid dormitory to which Reg was not admitted. Eventually their relationship broke down and the local authority took the children into care. *Cathy Come Home* dramatised the experiences of thousands of homeless people in the 1950s and early 1960s and its broadcast converted family homelessness into a social problem – questions were asked in Parliament, a special Cabinet meeting was held and the housing charity *Shelter* was formed.

The government's immediate response to *Cathy Come Home* was to accelerate the housing programme and it was not until the mid-1970s that specific reform of the housing allocation system to assist homeless families was undertaken. Following a series of circulars urging local authorities to shift responsibility for homelessness from social services departments (the successors of welfare departments) to housing authorities and adopt a more liberal attitude to homelessness, the government supported a private member's Bill on homelessness. The private member, Stephen Ross, declared that the aim of his Bill was to introduce 'a new legislative framework to change the outdated concept that homelessness was a social work problem and to place it clearly in the sphere of housing' (Stephen Ross, 1977, quoted in Wilson, 2001, p 9). The 1977 Housing (Homeless Persons) Act still forms the basis of current homelessness legislation. It defined homelessness, set out a legislative structure under which local authorities should interpret their duties to homeless people and provided the basis for the compilation of homelessness statistics.

Rough sleepers

The 1977 Act did not include the majority of the people experiencing the most visible form of homelessness – sleeping rough. None the less, the developing tendency in the 1970s to treat homeless single people as victims of circumstance rather than as feckless threats to a society (Brennan, 1976) was reflected in changes in the vagrancy laws. Sleeping outdoors was no longer an offence unless it caused a nuisance and begging had to be 'persistent' to be unlawful (Humphreys, 1999, p 151).

In the early 1980s the number of people on the streets appeared to be increasing and they seemed younger than in the past. The government's response was to stop the payment of Housing Benefit to people under 18 and to reduce the amount paid to 18- to 25-year-olds. Margaret Thatcher believed that Housing Benefit was encouraging young people to leave home (Thatcher, 1993, p 603). In the event, these Housing Benefit restrictions did not have the anticipated impact and, by the late 1980s, considerable media attention had focused on the growth of 'cardboard cities' and begging, especially in central London. These homeless people were regarded as a threat to social order. Margaret Thatcher commented that 'Crowds of drunken, dirty, often abusive and sometimes violent men must not be allowed to turn central areas of the capital into no-go zones for ordinary citizens' (Thatcher, 1995, p 603). A new expression entered the discourse of homelessness – 'rough sleepers' – a term indicating that the sleepers were as coarse as their sleeping conditions. The voluntary sector responded to the identification of a young 'rough sleeper' problem by the creation of 'foyers' (see Box 6.1) and, in 1990, a Rough Sleepers Initiative was started. This consisted of a programme, costing £196 million over seven years, to contact rough sleepers in central London, allocate them to emergency hostel places and then offer more permanent, 'move-on' accommodation. In addition the police increased their activity, with the number of people arrested under the vagrancy legislation increasing from 192 in 1991 to 1,445 in 1992 (May et al, 2004). In 1995 the government claimed that the initiative was working and that 'the number of people sleeping rough in central London has dropped from over 1000 in 1989 to under 290 in November 1994' (DoE, 1995, p 37).

Box 6.1: Foyers

A programme linking hostel provision for young homeless single people to employment and training opportunities was started in 1991. The aim of these foyers was to break the 'no home, no job, no home' cycle. The idea was imported from France where 500 foyers offered an integrated system enabling young people to move around the country for employment or training with guaranteed accommodation. An examination of the first foyers in the UK by Quilgars and Anderson (1995) found that most young people thought the support services were useful; the approach reached young people who might not have used more formal employment services and that this was achieved mainly without making service use a residence condition. The foyer idea of linking accommodation, training and employment placement fitted well with New Labour's promotion of joined-up thinking and foyers multiplied in the late 1990s. By 2003 there were over 115 foyers with about 5,000 residents in units ranging from converted houses to large purpose-built accommodation for over 100 residents.

There has been a dearth of independent research on the impact of the expanded foyer provision especially from the user perspective. In 2000 a research report concluded:

- 'Available evidence suggests that Foyers and other schemes have some success in increasing their clients' self reliance, both in the labour and housing markets. However, many schemes had difficulty in providing information on client participation and achievements which made it impossible to come to definitive judgements on their effectiveness....
- Local needs analysis was often poor and sometimes appeared designed to justify a particular proposal rather than taking an open-minded look at what needs existed and how they could best be met....

- The relatively large size of Foyers may be linked to the wide range of services provided on-site, which was unlikely to be financially viable in smaller projects. A downside of this is that some large schemes were more prone to experience housing management problems including violent behaviour, vandalism and drug use, and had a more institutional atmosphere than some smaller schemes....
- Only half (53%) of schemes assessed the labour market needs of potential clients, and these were generally considered secondary to housing, social and other support needs....
- Recording of achievements was also generally poor and where such data was available the hard outputs and outcomes which were reported by schemes were generally disappointing. For example, only one in ten clients in full-time further education obtained a qualification while they were in the scheme, only half the participants in prevocational or basic skills training satisfactorily completed the course....'

Source: DETR (2000c, pp 1-6)

What is homelessness?

Definitions of homelessness are important because the meanings attached to the term influence estimates of the extent of the problem and the notions of causation attached to it. If homelessness is construed as rough sleeping then the small number of rough sleepers can be interpreted to be a result of their disturbed personal biographies. If a broader definition is accepted, including, for example, those in insecure and unfit accommodation, then the larger numbers involved may indicate a shortage of housing as the cause of homelessness. There is no internationally agreed definition of homelessness. Box 6.2 sets out some of the available national and international definitions.

The statutory definition

In order to place obligations on local authorities to assist homeless people, the framers of the 1977 Housing (Homeless Persons) Act had to define homelessness. Thus, at the time, the UK was unique in having a legislative definition of homelessness that carried consequences for action. The Act defined homelessness in terms of the absence of a legal right of the applicant – or any other person who normally resides with them as a member of their family or in circumstances in which it is reasonable for that person to reside with the applicant – to occupy a dwelling. In addition, a person who was legally entitled to occupy accommodation, but could not secure entry to it due to domestic violence or threats of domestic violence, was to be regarded as homeless. If a local authority accepted a person as homeless it was obligated to provide temporary accommodation while seeking to secure more permanent housing

Box 6.2: Definitions of homelessness

In the US the 1987 McKinney Homeless Assistance Act (section 11302) defines a homeless person as:

'(1) an individual who lacks a fixed, regular and adequate nighttime residence;
(2) an individual who has a primary nighttime residence that is:
   • a supervised or publicly operated shelter designed to provide temporary living accommodation;
   • an institution that provides a temporary residence for individuals intended to be institutionalized; or
   • a public or private place not designed for, or ordinarily used, as a regular sleeping accommodation for human beings.'

However, homeless persons, as defined by the Act, are not entitled to permanent accommodation – agencies may supply accommodation or other assistance and receive financial assistance from the Federal government.

There is no legal basis for a formal European Union policy on housing and therefore the European Union has not formulated a definition of homelessness. Different member states – if they bother to define homelessness at all – define it in different ways but usually as meaning 'rough sleeping'. The European Federation of National Organisations Working with the Homeless (FEANTSA) has attempted to promote a common understanding of homelessness across European states. It has set out four conceptual categories – 'roofless', 'houseless', 'insecure housing' and 'inadequate housing' containing 16 operational categories that can be utilised in monitoring progress in overcoming homelessness (FEANTSA, 2004, p 7). The sentiment that homelessness involves more than sleeping rough is echoed in the Council of Europe's definition, which, in addition to 'those without a roof over their head', includes people 'who live in a dwelling that cannot be considered adequate or socially acceptable' (Council of Europe, 1992, cited in Muñoz and Vázquez, 1999). The United Nations compiles figures on *house*lessness defined as:

• absolute houselessness: people sleeping rough or using public or private shelters;
• concealed houselessness: people temporarily housed with friends or family;
• at risk of houselessness: people at risk of losing their shelter by eviction or lease expiry with no other possibility of shelter in view.

for the homeless person and anyone who could be reasonably expected to live with them. The problem regarding which local authority was responsible for a homeless person was solved, in part, by placing an obligation to provide temporary accommodation on the local authority to which the application was made. This obligation continued until the conclusion of disputes about the homeless persons' 'local connection', if necessary, by an independent arbitrator.

If this homelessness definition had not been qualified during the Bill's passage through Parliament then the 1977 Act would have provided a route to accommodation available to all people without a legal right to occupy a dwelling. However, the local authorities claimed that such a duty to assist homeless people would overwhelm their housing services and some Members of Parliament asserted that people would manipulate their circumstances to benefit from the Act. One member alleged that women would become pregnant to acquire a house and then terminate their pregnancies after moving in (*Hansard*, 1977, col 1689). Thus, as the Bill passed through Parliament, a number of clauses were introduced to restrict local authority obligations. Only those in 'priority need' and 'unintentionally homeless' would be eligible for long-term assistance (see Box 6.3). Local authorities had an obligation to provide 28 days in temporary accommodation to households in priority need and intentionally homeless – all other homeless people were to be offered only advice and assistance.

The 1986 Housing and Planning Act

The homelessness definition in the 1977 Housing (Homeless Persons) Act created an anomaly. A person living in a good-quality property, but without a legal right to occupy, could be accepted as 'homeless' whereas someone with a legal right to occupy a derelict dwelling could not. Housing lawyers argued in the High Court – with some success – that, if a person left poor-quality accommodation, this was a 'reasonable' act and the person should be recognised as homeless. This 'lawyer-made' law received a setback in the 1985 when, in the case of *Pulhofer*, the House of Lords rejected the claim that a family living in very poor housing conditions could quit a property they were legally entitled to occupy and be accepted by the local authority as homeless. This decision was nullified in the 1986 Housing and Planning Act, which inserted a new clause into the definition of homeless. It stated that 'a person shall not be treated as having accommodation unless it is accommodation which it would be reasonable for him to continue to occupy' (1986 Housing and Planning Act, Part 1, section 14). This meant that local authorities were obliged to consider the quality of the accommodation occupied when determining a homelessness application and opened the possibility of unsatisfactory housing becoming a widespread reason for homelessness applications. However, the legislation allowed local authorities, in considering the 'reasonable to continue

Box 6.3: Priority need and intentional homelessness: 1977 Housing (Homeless Persons) Act as consolidated in the 1985 Housing Act

Priority need

(1) The following have a priority need for accommodation:
    (a) a pregnant woman or a person with whom a pregnant woman resides or might reasonably be expected to reside;
    (b) a person with whom dependent children reside or might reasonably be expected to reside;
    (c) a person who is vulnerable as a result of old age, mental illness or handicap or physical disability or other specific reason, or with whom such a person resides or might reasonably be expected to reside;
    (d) a person who is homeless or threatened with homelessness as a result of an emergency such as flood, fire or other disaster. (1985 Housing Act, section 59)

Intentional homelessness

(1) A person becomes homeless intentionally if he deliberately does or fails to do anything in consequence of which he ceases to occupy accommodation which is available for his occupation and which it would have been reasonable for him to continue to occupy.
(2) A person becomes threatened with homelessness intentionally if he deliberately does or fails to do anything the likely result of which is that he will be forced to leave accommodation which is available for his occupation and which it would have been reasonable for him to continue to occupy.
(3) For the purposes of subsection (1) or (2) an act or omission in good faith on the part of a person who was unaware of any relevant fact shall not be treated as deliberate. (1985 Housing Act, section 60)

to occupy' issue, to 'have regard to the general housing circumstances of its area' (1986 Housing and Planning Act, Part 1, section 14). Thus, if other people in the area had housing as bad as the applicant, a local authority could reject the application.

The 1996 Housing Act

Under this Act, passed in response to concerns that the 1977 Act was being used as a 'fast track' to social housing, local authorities were obliged to provide temporary accommodation only for up to two years and only when satisfied that other suitable accommodation was not available. The aim of this provision was to make it clear that local authorities did not have to arrange to supply 'settled' or 'permanent' accommodation to end their obligations under the homelessness legislation. The terms 'settled' and 'permanent' had not occurred in the 1977 Housing (Homeless Persons) Act but the Code of Guidance issued under the Act, to which all local authorities had to 'have regard to' in implementing the legislation, did use such words in establishing local authority obligations. Accordingly, most local authorities interpreted their obligations as involving the provision of a local authority or housing association property until, in the case of *R v London Borough of Brent ex parte Awua* (1995), the House of Lords established that this was unnecessary. The 1996 Housing Act reaffirmed this legal interpretation by stating that the obligations of the local authority were discharged when it was satisfied that other suitable accommodation – including a private landlord assured shorthold tenancy – was available in the area. In addition, the duty to provide accommodation for homeless people was separated from the allocation of local authority dwellings. In allocating tenancies local authorities had to offer 'reasonable preference' only in accordance with guidelines incorporated in the Act. Homelessness was not included as a need category for which 'reasonable preference' was to be given although homeless people might receive priority under other categories. The Act also stated that a person could not qualify as homeless if they had a legal right to occupy accommodation outside the UK.

Asylum seekers

The 1999 Immigration and Asylum Act completed a process, started in 1993, of excluding asylum seekers and other people subject to immigration control from receiving help via the homelessness legislation. With certain exceptions, asylum seekers could not qualify for the housing register and could not be allocated secure tenancies, or nominated for assured tenancies. The National Asylum Support Service, funded by the Home Office, became responsible for helping asylum seekers to find accommodation. It has pursued a 'no choice' dispersal policy, securing properties through arrangements with private sector landlords and local authorities with a 'difficult-to-let' problem. When accepted as a legitimate asylum seeker, with a temporary or permanent settlement right in the UK, refugees have the same entitlements to housing as other residents.

The 2002 Homelessness Act

New Labour's 1997 Manifesto promised to amend the 1996 Act and 'place a new duty on local authorities to protect those who are homeless through no fault of their own and are in priority need' (Labour Party, 1997, p 23). This pledge was partially redeemed in 1997 when 'households who are being accommodated by the main homelessness duty' was added to the list of need categories that local authorities were required to give reasonable preference in allocating dwellings. Significant change to the 1996 Housing Act had to wait until New Labour's second term. The 2002 Homelessness Act imposed a duty on local authorities to develop a homelessness strategy, abolished the two-year limit on the provision of temporary housing and disallowed an offer of an assured shorthold tenancy unless this was acceptable to the homeless person. The 2002 Priority Need Order extended the groups designated as 'in priority need' to cover:

- homeless 16- and 17-year-olds with the exception of those in care;
- care leavers aged 18, 19, and 20;
- those vulnerable as a result of time spent in care, the armed forces, prison or custody;
- those vulnerable as a result of having to leave home through violence or the threat of violence.

The definition of homelessness was changed to include circumstances where it was not reasonable for a person to continue to occupy accommodation if it was probable that this would lead to violence – not just domestic violence as in earlier legislation. This more liberal attitude to helping homeless people needs to be taken into account in analysing the statistics on statutory homelessness but, in accordance with New Labour's rights/obligation agenda, the 2002 Act added a behaviour condition to the rules governing the housing allocation. Section 160A stated:

> A local housing authority may decide that an applicant is to be treated as ineligible for an allocation of housing accommodation by them if they are satisfied that –
>
> (a) he, or a member of his household, has been guilty of unacceptable behaviour serious enough to make him unsuitable to be a tenant of the authority; and
> (b) in the circumstances at the time his application is considered, he is unsuitable to be a tenant of the authority by reason of that behaviour.

Scotland

Since devolution, the Scottish Executive has developed a distinctive approach to homelessness. The 2001 Housing (Scotland) Act requires local authorities to house homeless people, whether they are considered in priority need or not, while a homelessness claim is investigated. Moreover, if assessed as non-priority homeless, local authorities have to provide accommodation for a reasonable period. Under the 2003 Homelessness (Scotland) Act the distinction between priority and non-priority need will be phased out and, by 2012, all unintentionally homeless people will be entitled to a permanent home. Given this broader interpretation of homelessness it is not surprising that the number of applications for assistance increased from 47,000 in 2001/02 to 57,000 in 2003/04. Of more concern was the sharp increase in the number of households in temporary accommodation – up from 4,100 in 2001/02 to 6,500 in 2003/04 (Scottish Executive, 2005, para 2.31) – indicating a lack of long-term accommodation to meet the new statutory obligations.

Homelessness as 'rooflessness'

The 1977 Housing (Homeless Persons) Act provided the framework for the generation of homelessness statistics. Officially recorded homelessness increased rapidly in the 1980s and early 1990s – from 4,710 households in temporary accommodation in 1980 to 73,490 in 1992 – producing damaging headline figures for Conservative Party housing policy.

The publication of *Access to Local Authority and Housing Association Tenancies* (DoE, 1994) marked an attempt to redefine statutory homelessness and hence, in time, reduce the 'headline' homelessness figures. It recommended a homelessness definition as 'those who have no accommodation of any sort available for occupation' (DoE, 1994, p 4). Had this 'rooflessness' definition reached the statute book then the recorded incidence of homelessness would have fallen and the route to representing homelessness as a residual, personal problem would be open. The proposals met fierce resistance from housing professionals and the homeless definition in the 1977 Housing (Homeless Persons) Act was retained in the 1996 Housing Act. None the less, doubts remain about whether the statistics generated by the operations of the current law on homelessness reflect the true extent of the problem. In 2004 the Deputy Prime Minister commented:

> When I look at it, I see homeless people as people on the streets. I want to put this phrase into proper context. Obviously, I want to get people out of B&Bs and temporary accommodation and into council homes, but then you have to question if this is still classed as homelessness. (Prescott, as reported in *Housing Today*, 2004, p 7)

In *Sustainable Communities: Homes for All* (ODPM, 2005c) the Office of the Deputy Prime Minister (ODPM), noting that the vast majority of temporary accommodation for families is self-contained with cooking and bathing facilities, announced its intention to reclassify certain temporary units as permanent. This will reduce the official homelessness figures at least for a short time.

Home

The statutory homelessness definition can be labelled 'secondary' homelessness because it includes both people without shelter ('primary' homelessness) and people in temporary and insecure accommodation. However, the inclusion of 'home' in the term 'homelessness' suggests a broader definition – the Audit Commission referred to rough sleeping and statutory homelessness as 'only the tip of the iceberg' (Audit Commission, 2003, p 5). Because home is an emotional construct, agreement on a definition of 'homelessness' is unlikely but, as Waldron (1993) suggests, humans, as social beings, require a private and secure base in which to carry out necessary functions such as washing, sleeping, reproduction, socialising and so on, especially if the use of public space for the conduct of such functions is proscribed. Thus, the minimal requirements of a home might include privacy, personal space, sufficient room to store one's possessions, adequate heating and the security necessary for quiet enjoyment of one's personal life. In the past, Shelter claimed that homeless, 'in the true sense of the word' means 'living in conditions so bad that a civilised family life is impossible' (Shelter, 1969, p 4).

Counting homeless people

In 1994/95 the *Survey of English Housing* asked respondents if they had experienced homelessness in the last 10 years and, if so, had they applied to a local authority and been accepted as homeless? Homelessness had been experienced by 4.3% of the respondents whereas 3.3% had applied to the local authority and 2.5% had been accepted as homeless (Burrows, 1997). Most of this homelessness was short term indicating that the homelessness legislation was a route into the social housing sector but, given that the survey was restricted to heads of households, these figures indicate that the official statistics, generated by the operations of the homelessness legislation, underestimate the extent of the experience of homelessness.

Rough sleeping

Counting the people sleeping rough is difficult especially in rural areas. Many can be found easily – sleeping, for instance, in shop doorways or railway stations – but others make determined efforts to conceal their whereabouts and thereby avoid the public display of their personal circumstances and the possibility of arrest or being 'moved on'. Local 'street' knowledge is needed to discover rough sleepers – the rough sleepers count, made for the 1991 Census, found no rough sleepers in Birmingham but voluntary sector information indicated that up to 60 people were sleeping rough at the time (Adamczuk, 1992). 'Snapshot' counts estimate the number sleeping rough on a given night but the number of people who sleep rough in a particular year has been estimated to be 10 times higher (Shelter, 2004). In 2001, the government claimed that 730 people were sleeping rough in England on a given night compared to 1,850 in 1998. However, some outreach workers, who helped carry out the homelessness survey, asserted that homeless people sitting up were not included because they were not bedded down and charity representatives alleged that rough sleepers were moved to Bed & Breakfast (B&B) accommodation on the night of the count (BBC News Online, 2001). In England 508 people were found sleeping rough in 2004 (ODPM, 2005f, p 9).

Statutory homelessness

The homeless statistics generated by the homelessness legislation supply two measures of the extent of statutory homelessness (see Figures 6.1 and 6.2). The number of households accepted each year as unintentionally homeless and in priority need indicate the flow of people experiencing homelessness albeit often only for a short time. Trends in these figures need to be treated

Figure 6.1: Households in temporary accommodation: England

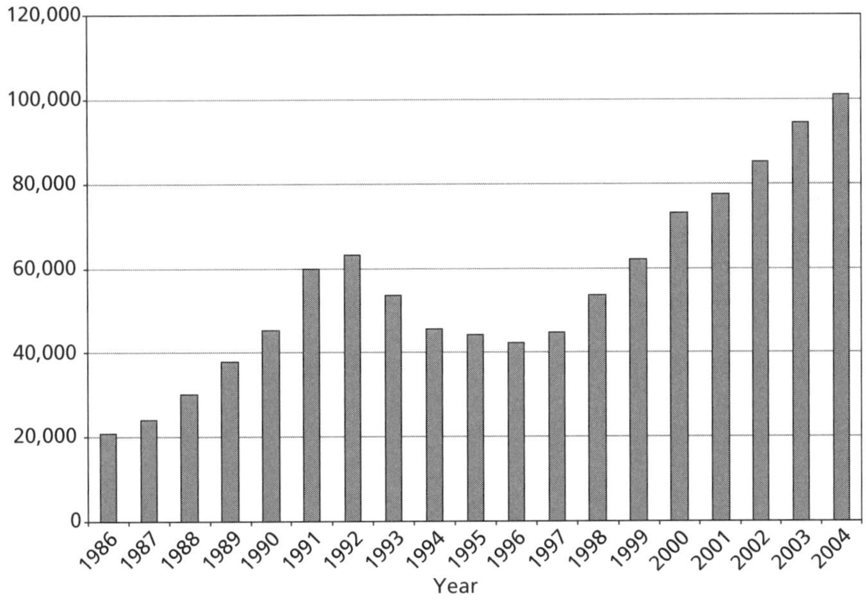

Note: These figures do not include those 'homeless at home' ie, those households accepted as homeless but who remain in their existing accommodation on a voluntary basis until more permanent accommodation can be secured. If 'homeless at home' households were included in the figures then, in 2004, an extra 23,280 households would have been added (Wilcox, 2004, p 185).

Source: Adapted from ODPM (2005a)

Figure 6.2: **Households accepted as homeless in priority need: England**

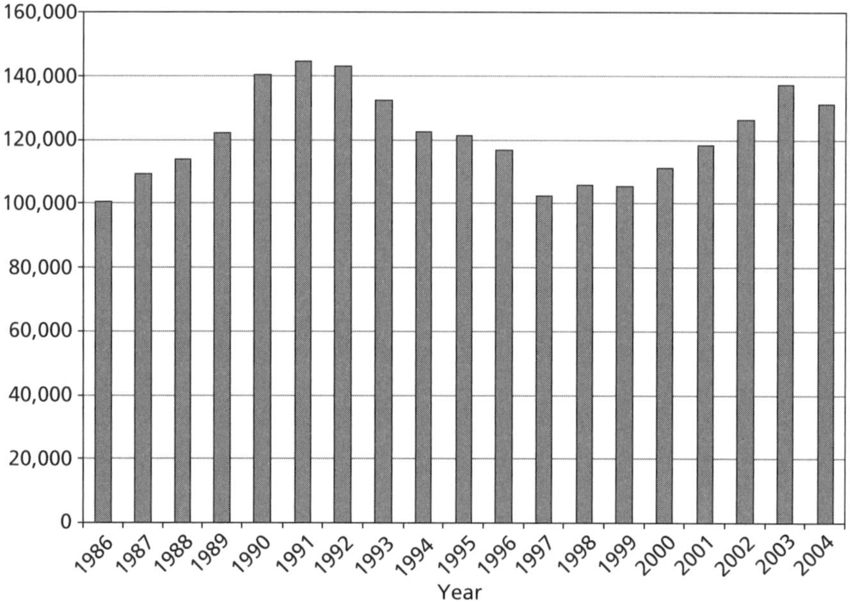

Sources: Adapted from Wilcox S (2003); ODPM (2005a)

with caution. Changes in legislation and regulations affect acceptances as does the attitudes of the 'street-level bureaucrats' who act as filters into the system. Whether or not an applicant is 'intentionally' homeless or 'vulnerable' is a matter of interpretation and there is a fine line between preventing homelessness and gate-keeping. A 2004 survey of homelessness officers by *Roof* magazine found that 66% said they were under pressure to interpret the legislation strictly in order to minimise acceptances (Rashleigh, 2004) and the percentage of households deemed intentionally homeless increased threefold between 2000 and 2004.

The number of households in temporary accommodation is a count of the households lacking secure, permanent accommodation on a given date. The figure more than doubled during New Labour's first two terms of office and in *Sustainable Communities: Homes for All* (ODPM, 2005c) a 50% reduction in the number of households in temporary accommodation was set as a target for 2010. This would be achieved by supplying more social housing, reclassifying the better-quality temporary accommodation as permanent, a review of the current arrangements for allocating social housing to see if better cooperation between local authorities and housing associations could reduce reliance on temporary accommodation, and better prevention. In 2005 a new 'best value' performance indicator was introduced aimed at measuring the success of local authorities in preventing homelessness. Local authorities were asked to record all interventions that have prevented homeless applicants from becoming officially accepted as homeless under the existing legislation.

There are a number of types of temporary accommodation (see Table 6.1). B&B hotels are the worst form of provision – they are a risk to health (Royal College of Physicians of London, 1994) and severely impede the education of children (Power et al, 1995). Although, as the ODPM (2005c, p 57) points out, 80,000 households in temporary accommodation have their own front doors and washing and cooking facilities, all forms of temporary accommodation are damaging. A survey of 2,000 homeless households found:

- over half said that their health or their family's health had suffered;
- more than half of the respondents had been in temporary accommodation for more than a year;
- children had missed an average of 55 days at school due to the disruption caused by homelessness and frequent moves between schools;
- nearly half of the parents described their children as 'often unhappy or depressed' (Mitchell et al, 2004).

In addition, one study found that only 29% of children in homeless families were attending school compared to 73% before they experienced homelessness (ODPM, 2005f, p 18).

'Hidden' homelessness

Crisis (2002) has estimated that there are 106,000 'hidden' single homeless people who have found shelter in B&B accommodation, hostels and squats or are sleeping on friends' floors. A broad definition of homelessness would include these 'hidden' homeless people and perhaps those living in unfit and overcrowded

Table 6.1: *Households in temporary accommodation arranged by local authorities, by type of accommodation: 1997-2004 (fourth quarter)*

	1997	**1998**	**1999**	**2000**	**2001**	**2002**	**2003**	**2004**
B&B hotels	4,520	7,240	8,000	9,870	11,860	13,240	8,420	6,450
Hostels	8,730	9,760	9,660	10,790	10,680	9,640	10,370	10,060
Private sector leasing	14,040	17,400	19,820	25,260	24,490	33,010	46,310	55,590
Other	17,580	19,390	24,700	27,160	30,480	29,250	29,520	28,920
Total	44,870	53,790	62,180	73,080	77,510	85,140	94,620	101,020

Source: Adapted from ODPM (2005a)

accommodation. However, as the Department of the Environment commented in 1974, 'too wide a definition of homelessness could tend to obscure the pressing needs of those who are literally without shelter, or are likely to lose in the immediate future what shelter they have' (DoE, 1974, para 6).

Rough sleeping: causes and prevention

A Social Exclusion Unit report (SEU, 1998a) assembled a range of statistics to demonstrate that many rough sleepers have disturbed personal biographies and histories of institutional life (see Table 6.2). New Labour's strategy to reduce rough sleeping reflected these statistics. An attempt was made to persuade the armed forces, local authorities and the Prison Service to consider more seriously the accommodation requirements of leaving institutionalised life. The 'personal pathology' portrayal of the causes of rough sleeping was reflected in the strategy of the Rough Sleepers Unit, set up in 1998. 'Coming In Out of the Cold' (DETR, 1999b), as the strategy was called, was developed and modified as the Rough Sleepers Unit attempted to achieve its target of a 66% reduction in rough sleeping by 2002. The plan was similar to the Conservatives' Rough Sleeper's Initiative in that three types of accommodation were offered:

Table 6.2: *Backgrounds of people sleeping rough (%)*

Forced to leave home (young homeless)	80
Step-parent	25
Experienced sexual abuse (young women)	40
Broken or disturbed home (homeless people over the age of 35)	50
In care as children	25-33
Served a prison sentence (older people sleeping rough)	50
Been in armed forces	25
Mental health problems	30-50
Serious alcohol problems	50
Misuse of drugs (all people sleeping rough)	20
Misuse of drugs (younger people sleeping rough)	39
Excluded from school or long-term non-attenders (teenage people sleeping rough)	75
Older rough sleepers are eight times more likely to have never married and, if married, are four times more likely to have been divorced	
One in three prisoners are not in permanent accommodation prior to imprisonment and one in 20 had been sleeping rough immediately prior to imprisonment. A third of prisoners lose their housing on imprisonment	

Sources: Adapted from SEU (1998b, 2002b)

- direct access hostels and shelters, the first port of call for many on leaving the streets and a focus for the assessment of people's needs;
- specialist hostels and special supported schemes, designed to meet specific and higher or multiple support needs; and
- permanent move-on accommodation into which people could move when they are ready to sustain a tenancy with support from a Tenancy Sustainment Team if necessary.

New Labour's initiative was extended beyond London – a process started under the Conservatives – and was targeted at the groups identified as the most vulnerable – people with a mental illness and a drug or alcohol problem. Expert outreach workers were appointed and additional specialised hostel accommodation was commissioned. Nevertheless, problems remained in securing access to mainstream services and there was a high rate (40% in London) of return to the streets (Burchardt, 2005). A survey of 155 homeless sector organisations found that the average waiting time to secure a mental health assessment was over five weeks and, in a survey of 119 London front-line support workers, 79% reported difficulties in getting a mental health assessment for their clients (Warnes et al 2003, p 120). Although rapid access to treatment is considered crucial to overcoming drug and alcohol problems 'according to homeless sector staff accessing drug and alcohol treatment is often difficult: services are few and there is often a long wait' (Warnes et al, 2003, p 122). Moreover there is evidence that hostel places are becoming 'bed blocked' by people unable to find somewhere to 'move on'. It has been estimated that in 2004 46% of the 6,000 emergency hostel places in London were taken up by residents who could not find 'move on' accommodation (*Inside Housing*, 2004).

New Labour's strategy to reduce rough sleeping placed great emphasis on getting homeless people off the streets into some form of shelter, day and night. The Social Exclusion Unit (SEU, 1998a, p 20) declared that 'the explicit intention of the policy is to deliver clear streets'. 'Coming in from the cold', it was argued, would break the rough sleeping 'lifestyle' and 'street culture' and enable opportunities for treatment, occupation and work to be offered. The voluntary sector was encouraged not to abet rough sleeping by supplying uncoordinated help to people living on the streets and the public was exhorted not to give cash to rough sleepers. Tony Blair's notion that help must be conditional on the fulfilment of obligations was reflected in the statement:

> Rough sleepers themselves have a responsibility to come in. Once we are satisfied that realistic alternatives are readily available we – and the public at large – are entitled to expect those working on the streets to seek to persuade people to take advantage of them. This includes the police who sometimes have not been able to use

their powers because of a lack of options to move rough sleepers on to. (DETR, 1999b, p 10)

After this declaration local authorities were reminded of their powers under the vagrancy legislation. In 2003 begging – often associated with rough sleeping – became a recordable offence and the Anti-Social Behaviour Action Plan (Home Office, 2003) introduced targeted action to reduce begging in 30 areas.

Statutory homelessness: causes and prevention

'Perverse incentives'

In the early 1990s the government attributed the growth in statutory homelessness to the 'perverse incentives' created by the 1977 Housing (Homeless Persons) Act. It was alleged that the direct route into secure social housing provided by the legislation led many people to engineer their circumstances to conform to its requirements. *Access to Local Authority and Housing Association Tenancies* claimed:

> By giving the local authority a greater responsibility towards those who can demonstrate 'homelessness' than towards anyone else in housing need, the current legislation creates a perverse incentive for people to have themselves accepted by a local authority as homeless. (DoE, 1994, p 4)

The idea of 'perverse incentives' was linked to the notion that the traditional family form was disintegrating. Nicholas Ridley, Secretary of State for the Environment in the late 1980s, commented: 'A young lady with a child is in 'priority housing need' – one without is not. It became a way of life for some to have one or more children by unknown men, in order to qualify for a council house' (Ridley, 1991, p 91).

Lack of empirical evidence makes it difficult to evaluate the 'perverse incentives' thesis. In high-demand areas, where the homelessness route was the only realistic track into social housing, the temptation to manipulate circumstances to conform to the homelessness legislation must have been strong. Yet the track was not especially fast – the average time spent in B&B accommodation was 22 months and, at the end of the track, the accommodation available was often of poor quality. Moreover, the reduction in statutory homelessness occurred well before the 1996 Housing Act – designed to close the 'fast track' – came into force. Statutory homelessness also increased between 1997 and 2002 when the 1996 legislation was in operation although its impact was modified by the discretion available to local authorities in interpreting the Act – many had opposed its objectives.

Personal troubles

The quarterly statistics on homelessness include a section headed: 'Recorded reasons for loss of last settled home for households accepted as unintentionally homeless and in priority need in England'. In 2004 the top two reasons were:

- parents, relatives or friends not being able or willing to provide accommodation: 37%;
- relationship breakdown: 20% – with domestic violence the cause in two thirds of relationship breakdown cases.

In 2002, a Homelessness Directorate was established in the ODPM, bringing together the Rough Sleepers Unit and the officials responsible for statutory homelessness. The Directorate's attention focused on reducing the number of people living in B&B accommodation. Its target was to ensure that, by March 2004, no homeless families with children would be living in B&B hotels except in an emergency and even then, for no more than six weeks. By December 2004, 820 homeless families with children were living in B&B accommodation and 100 had lived there for over six weeks. The Directorate also promised a new approach to statutory homelessness. Henceforth, the focus would be 'as much on the personal problems that homeless people face – such as family or relationship breakdown, domestic violence, debt, alcohol and drug misuse, and poor physical or mental health – as on the places they live' (Homelessness Directorate, 2003, p 7). In 2003/04, the Supported People programme (see Chapter Ten) provided £52 million to meet the requirements of homeless families with support needs and £299 million for the support needs of single people.

In early 2005, *Sustainable Communities: Homes for All* (ODPM, 2005c, p 57) announced that additional funding would be made available to support 'the further development of mediation services to resolve family and relationship problems' and an action plan that accompanied *Sustainable Communities: Homes for All* stated that stakeholders would be consulted 'on possible changes to homelessness legislation that encourage homelessness prevention' (ODPM, 2005c, p 42) indicating that engagement in services to resolve family and relationship problems may become a condition for acceptance as 'homeless' (Housing Quality Network, 2005, p 2). This was an endorsement of the 'personal trouble' explanation of family homelessness, dormant in centre-left thinking on family homelessness since *Cathy Come Home*. As Gaubatz (2001, p 6) commented, 'Although there is a diversity of views about family homelessness in Great Britain a dominant perspective can easily be identified. British academics, policymakers, advocates and even many service providers have too often defined family homelessness solely as a housing issue'. However, although the recorded reasons for homelessness indicate a high proportion of relationship problems requiring prevention via support they relate only to the immediate reasons for homelessness and do not specify why homeless families had to live with parents and friends before becoming statutory homeless. Moreover, research in London has indicated that, whereas family 'mediation' can help prevent young people becoming statutory homeless, it was far less successful in preventing homelessness when older people with children were staying with family and friends because of the pressures caused by overcrowding (Ormerod and Alexander, 2005). As the National Audit Office (2005) has recognised (see Figure 6.3) becoming homeless is a process – the outcome of

Figure 6.3: The process of becoming homeless

Family of two adults with three children buy a house		Spiralling debts force family to sell and move in with mother's parents		Mother's parents can no longer cope with children: mother approaches local authority for help		Family move into private landlord accommodation leased by the local authority	
1997	**1999**	**2000**	**2001**	**2002**	**2003**	**2004**	**2005**
	Father loses job		Marital problems related to debt and overcrowding lead to father leaving wife and family		Family placed in Bed and Breakfast accommodation		Family allocated a local authority house

Source: Adapted from National Audit Office (2005)

a 'pathway' – involving a number of factors interacting over time. Repeated homelessness would be an indication that family homelessness involves 'more than a roof' and that homeless families require help to improve their 'coping skills'. In 2004 the ODPM required local authorities to record the incidence of 'repeat homelessness' – only 3% of recorded homelessness was 'repeat'.

A housing shortage?

The 1996 Housing Act closed the alleged fast track into secure social housing but, since 1996, the incidence of statutory homelessness has increased. The highest statutory homelessness incidence is in London (2.6 per thousand households compared to an English average of 1.6 per thousand households) where house prices and rents are high. A study of homelessness acceptances by local authorities in Scotland between 1980 and 1998 found a long-run national statistical relationship between homelessness and the housing market and that local authorities with high house prices tended to have high levels of homelessness (Scottish Executive, 2002). In England, homelessness acceptances increased the fastest in the regions experiencing the highest house price rises.

The Barker Report on housing supply made a connection between homelessness and the housing shortage, stating that the pattern of statutory homelessness 'follows closely the worsening affordability of private housing during the late 1990s/early 2000s, suggesting that these households may include some of those priced out of the private sector and owner occupied market, as well as migrants and those with social problems' (Barker, 2003, p 34). The statistics on the flow of households becoming homeless and the number of households in temporary accommodation (see Figures 6.1 and 6.2) indicate that there is a bottleneck in securing homes for the households in temporary accommodation. Social housing has been the major source of accommodation for homeless families but the number of social housing lettings has declined significantly in recent years, a consequence of council house sales and a decline in new social housing production (see Figure 5.1, p 104). In addition, housing associations – in their desire to create more balanced communities – appear to have become less willing to accommodate homeless families than in the early 1990s, with the number of housing association lettings to homeless families declining from 28% in 1993/94 to 15% in 2002/03 (Wilcox, 2004, p 192). There is some evidence that 'choice-based' lettings (see Chapter Seven) is having an adverse impact on the housing opportunities of homeless people because they find it difficult to access the system (ODPM, 2004e). In addition, it appears that housing associations created by stock transfer from local government are less willing to accept homeless applicants than local authorities – in 2004, 20% of their lettings were to homeless people compared to 34% for local authorities (*Housing Today*, 2005).

Hidden homelessness

The lower the number of people classified as homeless the more likely it is that homelessness can be represented as a personal problem produced by the 'agency' of individual behaviour. Including the hidden homeless in the definition of homelessness makes it more difficult to represent homelessness as a personal trouble and helps to promote structural explanations of homelessness.

Although the targeted intervention of the various rough sleeping initiatives has reduced the incidence of rough sleeping in the UK since 1990 the general trend has been for homelessness to increase. Edgar et al (2002) detect similar trends in the European Union. They argue that structural economic trends have generated greater social exclusion increasing the risk of homelessness. Moreover, there has been a tendency for European states to move towards the 'commodification' of housing and this has limited their ability to prevent homelessness. Thus 'structural factors create the conditions within which vulnerability to homelessness is perpetuated and in which agency factors interact to determine the scale and nature of homelessness in different societies' (Edgar et al, 2002, p 129). Figure 6.4 sets out the various factors involved in the causes of homelessness.

Figure 6.4: Causes of homelessness

Economic factors	Housing supply	Housing demand
• Globalisation • Unemployment • Wage levels • Labour mobility • Stability of income	• Planning policy • Producer subsidies • Consumer subsidies	• Household formation • Consumer subsidies • Interest rates

STRUCTURAL
INDIVIDUAL

Personal problems	Participating events	Demographic characteristics
• Drug misuse • Alcohol problems • Institutional background • Mental illness	• Marriage or partnership breakdown • Failure of sharing arrangements • Eviction or end of assured tenancy • Mortgage or rent arrears	• Age • Gender • Ethnicity • Children

Overview

- Homelessness has been identified as a social problem because it has been seen as a threat to the social order and as unacceptable in an affluent, civilised society.
- Definitions of homelessness are related to notions of its causation.
- Specific assistance was given to homeless families under the 1977 Housing (Homeless Persons) Act but only in specified circumstances.
- 'Rough sleeping' has been identified as a social problem distinct from the problem of 'single homelessness'.
- Under New Labour statutory homelessness has increased whereas the recorded problem of rough sleeping has diminished.

Questions for discussion

(1) Why was 'vagrancy' regarded as a social problem?

(2) You have been asked to count the number of rough sleepers in a large city. What problems might you encounter in making the count?

(3) How did New Labour manage to reduce the number of people sleeping rough?

(4) What is meant by the term 'perverse incentive'?

(5) It has been said that defining homelessness is a political act. What do you think is meant by this statement?

(6) Why has homelessness been said to involve 'more than a roof'?

Further reading

Humphreys' (1999) *No Fixed Abode: A History of Responses to the Roofless and Rootless in Britain* (1999) is an interesting historical account of responses to homelessness.

Homelessness Factfile published by **Crisis (2003)** is a comprehensive source of information.

A special edition of the *Journal of Community and Applied Social Psychology* (2003, vol 13) contains a discussion of theoretical approaches to understanding homelessness.

Website resources

Each local authority must publish a Homelessness Strategy. Many of these are available online.

The ODPM's website has a section on homelessness at www.odpm.gov.uk/stellent/ groups/odpm_homelessness/documents/sectionhomepage/ odpm_homelessness_page.hcsp

The European Federation of National Organisations Working with the Homeless maintains a website that contains statistics and information on homelessness in Europe at www.feantsa.org

Homeless Pages at www.homelesspages.org.uk is a good source of information.

The Third Report of Session 2004-05 of the ODPM Select Committee on Homelessness (ODPM Select Committee, 2005a) is available at www.publications.parliament.uk/ pa/cm200405/cmselect/cmodpm/61/61i.pdf

seven

Decent homes

Summary

- The state has controlled housing standards by issuing building regulations governing new construction and by enforcing minimum standards on the condition of the existing housing stock.
- Until the early 1970s, demolition in clearance areas was the dominant method of dealing with property deemed 'unfit for human habitation'.
- From the late 1960s, improvement grants, aimed at preventing properties deteriorating into a state of unfitness – often allocated on an area basis – gradually replaced demolition as the principal mechanism of urban renewal.
- Since the 1980s, state aid to the private sector for repair and improvement has been offered on an increasingly selective basis.
- There has been a gradual change in the official standards by which housing quality is measured from the sanitary standards of the 19th century to the 'decent' standard of today.

The slum

The 1875 Public Health Act, which set out model by-laws for the construction of new homes, plus the subsequent mandatory local authority building regulations have ensured that most new houses have been decent according to the norms of the time. However, because dwellings deteriorate and standards change, successive governments have attempted to establish housing minimum standards and to ensure that the existing dwelling stock meets these requirements.

In the 19th century the term 'slum' was applied to an entire area as well as to a specific dwelling deemed unfit for human habitation. As Mellor (1977, p 67) explains, 'the slum was the locale of vice, crime, delinquency and disease, a disorderly gathering of people beyond society and without community'. Its surrogates were 'plague spot', 'rookery', 'mean streets', 'Abyss' and 'Labyrinth'.

From the 1830s, attempts were made to deal with the 'nuisance' caused by individual unfit dwellings and legislation sponsored by authorities in Liverpool and Manchester made it possible to close cellar dwellings (Wohl, 1983). The 1868 Artisans' and Labourers' Dwellings Act, known as the Torrens Act after the Member of Parliament who introduced it into Parliament, allowed local authorities to require owners to demolish unfit houses but imposed no obligations on the landlord to re-house the displaced tenants. Torrens' original Bill had included local authority powers not only to force the demolition of insanitary houses but to build and own dwellings but in its passage through Parliament the Bill was diluted (Wohl, 1977, p 86). In its final form, without the provisions for new building, the Act was concerned with the externalities of public health and social order – widening alleys and courts – rather than with the welfare of the people living in the slums.

The 1875 Artisans' and Labourers' Dwellings Improvement Act

This Act, known as the Cross Act, made provision for eradicating slum areas in a planned manner. Its aim was to allow – but not compel – public funds to be used to eliminate the threat to public welfare posed by the slums and to ensure that replacement housing was provided. The cost to the state would be minimised by selling the cleared site to philanthropic, 'model dwelling' housing associations and only if this proved ineffective could local authorities build houses. Unfortunately the Cross Act did little to improve the slum dwellers' welfare. The cost of demolition with landlord compensation at market value was far greater than the amount housing associations could pay for the cleared sites. The call on public funds soon outstripped the resources earmarked for clearance and the promise that the clearance task in London could be completed at a public cost of £2 million proved to be unfounded (Yelling, 1982). The idea at the heart of the initiative – using the enhanced value of the cleared site to finance future demolition – was abandoned and, throughout the late 19th and early 20th centuries, municipal clearance was limited. The Cross Act had placed a duty on local authorities to arrange for new dwellings to be built on or near the cleared site, sufficient to re-house all the displaced persons – reduced to 50% in 1882 – but this provision, like the obligations placed on railway companies to replace the accommodation lost in station and railroad construction, was usually ignored. Joseph Chamberlain's famous central Birmingham 'grand improvement' scheme, started in 1875 under the Cross Act, led to the creation of Corporation Street and a decline in the death rate from 53.2 to 21.3 per thousand of the population. But, by 1888, not one new house had been built on site to replace the slums (Mayne, 1993, p 57). One local newspaper commented:

New Birmingham recipe for lowering the death rate of an insanitary area. Pull down nearly all the houses and make the inhabitants live somewhere else. 'Tis an excellent plan and I'll tell you for why. Where there's no person living, no person can die. (cited in Watts, 1992, p 53)

When housing associations did build new properties they had to let them at rents well beyond what former slum inhabitants could afford and the answer to a query from the Royal Commission on the Housing of the Working Classes on how many people from the slums had benefited from a new home under improvement schemes was 'very few' (Royal Commission on the Housing of the Working Classes, 1885, p 54). Thus, although slum removal helped to achieve the 'sanitary' objective – the last cholera epidemic was in 1867 and the incidence of typhus was much reduced – the poor were forced to move into adjacent areas of overcrowded and low-quality housing.

The 1930s clearance drive

The slum issue was placed in abeyance after 1919 while efforts were made to rectify the national housing shortage caused by the virtual ending of house building during the First World War. The 1919 Housing and Town Planning Act established that compensation for an unfit house should be at site value only but, up to 1930, only 11,000 slum houses were demolished and replaced (Bowley, 1945, p 135). Local authorities had to meet 50% of the cost and there was strong opposition from tenants because they 'were terrified of having to pay too high rents' (Simon, 1933, p 36).

The minority 1929-31 Labour government started the major slum clearance drive of the 1930s. The 1930 Housing Act offered additional subsidies to local authorities for demolition and construction and in 1933, when the Conservatives abolished the subsidy available for 'general needs' housing, almost all local authority housing building was directed towards slum clearance. The minister responsible, Sir Edward Hilton-Young, declared that slum clearance was 'a public health problem ... not a first line problem of housing; it is a problem of ridding our social organism of radiating centres of depravity and disease'. Accordingly, subsidies were 'appropriate in this region as a measure for the protection and preservation of the public health' (Hilton-Young, 1932, quoted in Yelling, 1992, p 134).

During the 1930s, when over 250,000 houses were demolished or closed and over a million people were re-housed, attention focused on the difficulties in re-housing the people affected by the clearance drive. Lack of land within city boundaries caused problems but the main concern was the ability of the former slum inhabitants to pay for their improved living standards. A study of council tenants in Stockton re-housed from the slums demonstrated a rise in mortality connected with malnutrition (Ineichen, 1993) and an examination of a clearance area in Manchester revealed that only 31% of the people re-housed on the new estate remained there three years after the move. Travel to work costs from outlying estates were a problem but Yelling (1992, p 74) maintains that 'the principal cause of this was undoubtedly rent', with local authority rents twice the amount paid in the slum areas. Older property improvement was not totally ignored between the wars. The 1926 Housing (Rural Workers) Act gave local authorities the discretionary power to give improvement grants to private landlords and the 1930 Housing Act made provision for the declaration of improvement areas in urban districts with grants available to encourage repair.

The bulldozer returns

Slum clearance was abandoned in the years immediately after the Second World War as attention focused on making good the backlog of houses caused by the five-year cessation of house building and the large number of dwellings badly damaged or destroyed. Clearance returned to the political agenda in 1954. One million dwellings were demolished in Britain in the years 1954 to 1975 as part of a large-scale urban renewal exercise. Initially this clearance drive provoked little controversy – the most significant objection being its limited scale in relationship to the true magnitude of the problem – but in the early 1970s the rationale of clearance began to be questioned. The vast majority of the dwellings demolished in the 1950s and early 1960s were grossly unfit and the people living in them, as tenants rather than owners, were excluded from the formal mechanisms of appeal against a clearance decision. However, by the late 1960s, local authorities were beginning to deal with a different type of area in which not all the dwellings were seriously unfit and where there were more owner-occupiers – former tenants who had purchased their houses from their landlords. Objections to compulsory purchase orders became more frequent and community activists started to assist local people to devise rehabilitation schemes as alternatives to clearance. Social research began to reveal the hardships created by the protracted clearance procedures that could leave people living in blighted areas for many years. The loss of community spirit when people were re-housed to different areas was highlighted and attention was drawn to the increased living costs in the new estates, both in terms of rent – few authorities operated a rent rebate scheme at the time – and the increased expense of travelling to work from the new periphery estates. Some of the people from clearance areas found replacement accommodation in sub-standard private sector housing near to the clearance area because it was less expensive than a local authority house.

Clearance or improvement?

The 1949 Housing Act allowed local authorities to offer improvement grants of 50% of the cost of rehabilitation up to a specified limit but only 7,000 grants were issued between 1949 and 1953, mainly because local authorities, which had to bear a proportion of the cost, did not inform the public of their availability. The 1954 Housing Repairs and Rents Act increased the value of improvement grants and the 1959 House Purchase and Housing Act made it mandatory for local authorities to pay 'standard' grants for the installation of basic amenities such as a bath and an internal water closet. Additional discretionary grants were made available to assist owners to improve their dwellings to a standard necessary for a 30-year life. This dual strategy – unfit property clearance and improvement for 'sub-standard' dwellings – was continued in the 1960s but, against a background of financial constraint, the Labour government published a White Paper *Old Houses into New Homes*. This announced that 'within a total of public investment at about the level it has now reached, a greater share should go to the improvement of older houses' (Ministry of Housing and Local Government, 1968, p 4).

The 1969 Housing Act increased grant payments, introduced a special grant for the provision of basic amenities in multi-occupied dwellings, and made grants available for environmental measures in what were to be known as 'General Improvement Areas' (GIAs). Great reliance was placed on the 'halo' impact of area selectivity:

> The effort and resources devoted to improvement provides a much better return when directed to the up-grading of whole areas – the houses and the environment. People are more likely to find it worth their while to co-operate and to maintain their houses after improvement. (Ministry of Housing and Local Government, 1969, p 3)

In the early 1970s, higher grant rates were offered in certain regions and the number of grants approved soared from 108,938 in 1969 to 360,954 in 1973 as a consequence of Edward Heath's attempt to inject demand into the economy and use home improvement to limit the requirement for new council housing. Improvement grants helped to upgrade the private sector housing stock, but many people with low incomes left their homes as landlords encouraged tenants to move to enable sales to homeowners – a process to become known as 'gentrification'. The White Paper *Better Homes: The Next Priorities* (Ministry of Housing and Local Government, 1973) heralded a return to rationing by specific area selectivity. Its principles were adopted by the Labour Party and the 1974 Housing Act introduced the idea of the Housing Action Area (HAA) to complement the existing notion of the GIA. HAAs were to be areas of housing and social stress exhibiting some combination of a number of problems such as a high proportion of unfit houses, furnished tenancies and shared accommodation. In HAAs local authorities had powers to pay more generous grants, to compel private landlords to refurbish their properties and to acquire rented properties by compulsory purchase. Government circulars on the implementation of the legislation emphasised that local authorities now had a wide range of powers which provided the basis for a comprehensive, corporate and flexible local strategy to tackle the problem of unfit and sub-standard housing. Box 7.1 offers an assessment of urban renewal policies between 1954 and 1979.

Selectivity and home improvement

Margaret Thatcher's first government (1979-83) displayed a strong commitment to housing rehabilitation in the private sector. In the 1970s, clearance was automatically associated with council housing and hence private sector improvement was a mechanism for preventing more local authority building. This commitment to rehabilitation was accompanied by a shift in policy towards extending the availability of improvement grants regardless of location. However, following the General Election of 1983, reductions in public

Box 7.1: Urban renewal: 1954-79: an assessment

Reflection on the years of urban renewal produces a mixed response. If improvement is measured in terms of the physical condition of the housing stock then significant progress was made with the number of households in England without one or more basic amenities – a fixed bath or shower, a hot water supply and an inside WC – falling from over seven million in 1947 to 700,000 in 1981 (Holmans, 2000, p 479). However, with hindsight, errors can be identified. The clearance procedures, involving many different local authority departments, were complex and protracted with the result that too many people had to endure years of living in deplorable surroundings. Scant regard was paid to the views of the tenants involved in the redevelopment process and, although too much should not be made of the loss of working-class communities, damage to neighbourhood spirit did occur as was first demonstrated by Wilmott and Young (1960). Many of the mass housing schemes that replaced the slums were badly built and poorly designed. Little attention was given to the economic impact of clearance with numerous small workshops and businesses lost in the redevelopment process. The improvement grant system tended to favour those with the knowledge of its operation and the resources to meet their share of the cost. When the system became more selective in the late 1970s, resources for improvement diminished and HAAs foundered (Monck and Lomas, 1980) – a demonstration that selectivity is often used as an excuse for reductions in expenditure rather than as a mechanism to concentrate resources on those in greatest need.

expenditure were made and improvement grants were badly affected by these cuts – grants awarded went down from 229,000 in 1984 to 98,000 in 1989.

Selectivity

The Green Paper *Home Improvement: A New Approach* (DoE, 1985) revealed government thinking on the principles to be applied to unfit and sub-standard housing. It proposed to switch responsibility for the older private stock from the government to the owner stating that 'home ownership offers opportunities for individuals to alter and improve their homes as they wish; they must carry the primary responsibility for keeping their property in good repair' (DoE, 1985, p 7). In future, eligibility for improvement grants would be determined by two criteria: the fitness of the property and the income of the occupiers. In relationship to the fitness standard, the Green Paper declared that 'a policy of raising the minimum standard to match rising social expectations would be inappropriate' (DoE, 1985, p 10). The owner-occupier of any dwelling deemed unfit according to a fixed standard would be eligible for an improvement grant but only if household income was below a specified level. This income testing was justified by the quotation of evidence that a significant proportion of the grants available had been claimed by more affluent groups. The new grant would cover only the cost of making a dwelling fit – additional expenditure to give a house a 30-year life would be covered by an equity-sharing loan whereby the local authority would acquire a share in the value of the property.

No action was taken on the principles outlined in the 1985 Green Paper until the 1989 Local Government and Housing Act, and, in the interim, the idea of equity-sharing loans was abandoned. Under the Act a new benchmark for the assessment of unfitness was introduced, which became the basis for the award of means-tested renovation grants. Declarations of HAAs and GIAs were abolished but local authorities were allowed to introduce group repair schemes and designate renewal areas. Clearance area declaration was permitted only when a local authority had carried out a detailed cost/benefit appraisal of the options for the area.

The new urban renewal regime produced disappointing results mainly because insufficient resources were available to enable the system to operate effectively. The notion of a mandatory grant to households with a low income living in unfit property implies that such households have a right to the grant but central government failed to make the finance available to meet the demand especially in neighbourhoods where there was a combination of low income and a major unfitness problem. Local authorities responsible for such areas had to remain silent on the mandatory grant entitlement and to delay the payments to those who had applied, thus creating uncertainty and frustration among applicants. The 1996 Housing Grants, Construction and Regeneration

Act made all grants discretionary, except for the disabled facilities grant (see Chapter Ten).

New Labour and decent homes

The private sector

The 1996 English House Condition Survey exposed a disconcerting level of unfitness and disrepair in the privately owned housing stock. In the private rented sector 19.3% of the stock was unfit while 28.9% of private tenants lived in 'poor' housing. In the homeownership sector 10.9% lived in 'poor' housing and 6% of the stock was unfit. Despite the problem, New Labour retained the discretionary nature of private sector improvement grants established by the Conservatives. As a result, state expenditure on private sector improvement declined from £385.6 million in 1994 to £268.2 million in 2001 (Wilcox, 2003, p 107). Yet, despite this reduction in state expenditure, the 2001 English House Condition Survey revealed that the number of private sector unfit dwellings had fallen between 1996 and 2001 (see Table 7.1), a testimony to the impact of rising house prices on the availability of equity for home improvement and on homeowners' willingness to invest in their properties at a time of rapid house price inflation.

The 2001 English House Condition Survey introduced a new benchmark for accessing housing stock condition – the decent homes standard. This incorporated traditional housing condition indicators such as fitness and disrepair but added others such as thermal comfort and the presence of modern facilities. The decent homes standard was an aspirational threshold, to be achieved in the private sector at some unspecified future date whereas, under the 2004 Housing Act, the fitness standard became a minimum standard that may trigger specific managerial action to rectify the unfitness (see Box 7.2 and Box 7.3).

Table 7.1: *Unfit dwellings: England: 1996 and 2001 (%)*

	1996	2001
Private rented	19.3	10.3
Local authority	7.3	4.1
Owner-occupied	6.0	2.9
Housing association	5.2	3.0

Source: ODPM (2003c)

Box 7.2: Unfitness

When a local authority finds a property that it deems unfit for human habitation it is under a statutory duty to take the most appropriate course of action. Scotland has its own standard – the 'tolerable standard' – that is less stringent than the one used in England and Wales.

Until the 2004 Housing Act, the definition of unfitness under the 1989 Local Government and Housing Act was:

A dwelling is unfit if, in the opinion of the authority, it fails to meet one of the requirements set out in paragraphs (a) to (i) of s.604 (1) and, by reason of that failure, is not reasonably suitable for occupation. The requirements constitute the minimum deemed necessary for a dwelling house to be fit for human habitation. They are that a dwelling house should:

(a) be free from serious disrepair;
(b) be structurally stable;
(c) be free from dampness prejudicial to the health of the occupants;
(d) have adequate provision for lighting, heating and ventilation;
(e) have an adequate piped supply of wholesome water;
(f) have an effective system for the drainage of foul, waste and surface water;
(g) have a suitably located WC for exclusive use of the occupants;
(h) have a bath or shower and wash-hand basin, with hot and cold water; and
(i) have satisfactory facilities for the preparation and cooking of food including a sink with hot and cold water.

The 2004 Housing Act replaced this standard with the Housing Health and Safety Rating System (HHSRS). Property 'hazards' are assessed and given a score by a local authority environmental health officer. Assessment is a two-stage process based on the likelihood of an occurrence and the probable harm to the most vulnerable potential occupant that would result from the occurrence. If the assessment produces a high score – labelled category 1 – then the local authority has a duty to take action. Action can take the form of hazard awareness advice, improvement notices requiring repair and/or improvement, making a demolition order, declaring a clearance area or issuing a prohibition notice that prohibits the use of all or part of the dwelling to all occupants or to members of a vulnerable group. A lower assessment score – category 2 – gives local authorities the power but not the duty to take action.

Box 7.3: What is a 'decent' home?

To be defined as decent, a home must meet each of the following criteria:

- It is above the current statutory minimum housing standard.
- It is in a reasonable state of repair: dwellings failing on this point will be those where either:
  - one or more key building components are old and need replacing or major repair; or
  - two or more of the other building components are old and need replacing or major repair.
- It has reasonably modern facilities and services: dwellings failing on this point are those that lack three or more of the following:
  - a reasonably modern kitchen (20 years old or less);
  - a kitchen with adequate space and layout;
  - a reasonably modern bathroom (30 years old or less);
  - an appropriately located bathroom and WC;
  - adequate noise insulation (where external noise/neighbourhood noise is a problem);
  - adequate size and layout of common areas for blocks of flats.
- It provides a reasonable degree of thermal comfort.

Source: ODPM (2005g)

This definition has been criticised for ignoring factors that residents regard as important such as improving the quality of the environment and making areas safer (Audit Commission, 2005a, p 15) but it can be argued that these items are part of an urban regeneration agenda, to be achieved through other programmes.

The decent homes standard formed the basis of the ODPM's response to the Treasury demand for targets in return for resources. Initially the targets applied only to social housing and it appeared that New Labour had stepped away from involvement in the poor conditions in the private sector. A consultation document stated:

> We are committed to improving housing quality in all tenures, including the owner–occupied sector. None the less, it is only right that the responsibility for maintaining privately owned homes, which for many people is their most valuable asset, should rest first and foremost with the owner.... (DETR, 2001, paras 3.1, 3.2)

Table 7.2: *Decent and non-decent homes: 2001 and 1996*

	2001			1996		
	Decent	**Non-decent**	**All dwellings**	**Decent**	**Non-decent**	**All dwellings**
Number (000s)						
Owner-occupied	10,435	4,336	14,771	8,083	5,843	13,927
Private rented	1,108	1,083	2,191	735	1,263	1,998
Local authority	1,599	1,191	2,700	1,548	1,921	4,369
Registered social landlords	1,005	383	1,388	588	353	941
All tenures	14,147	6,993	21,050	10,954	9,380	21,235
%						
Owner-occupied	70.6	29.4	100	58.0	42.0	100
Private rented	50.6	49.4	100	38.8	63.2	100
Local authority	57.3	42.7	100	44.6	55.4	100
Registered social landlord	72.4	26.6	100	62.5	37.5	100
All tenures	66.9	33.1	100	53.9	40.1	100
% of non-decent homes in the 10% most deprived areas (2001)		40.8				

Source: Adapted from ODPM (2003d)

Box 7.4: Fuel poverty

The decent homes standard defines thermal comfort in terms of minimum levels of loft and cavity insulation and the presence of an efficient space heating system. In 2001 an estimated 8.4% (1.7 million) households in England were living in fuel poverty as a result of a combination of low incomes, fuel costs and poor home fuel efficiency. In 2001 the UK Fuel Poverty Strategy defined fuel poverty as households that need to spend more than 10% of their incomes on fuel use and committed the government and devolved authorities to ending fuel poverty in 'vulnerable' households – containing elderly, disabled, long-term sick and young people – by 2010 using such schemes as Warm Front, which provides grants for insulation and new heating systems.

The consultation document proposed that many of the detailed provisions governing the way local authorities facilitated private sector improvement should be removed and replaced with a broad power to provide financial and other assistance for home repair and improvement. Local authorities were encouraged to develop private sector housing renewal strategies with loan schemes forming a major element in such strategies. Given that renovation grants had already been made discretionary in 1996 these proposals to abolish the statutory requirements on the types of assistance offered by local authorities made sense. However, the changes meant that housing renovation would be competing for resources from the 'single capital pot' with other local capital expenditure proposals and the lack of specified national grant entitlement structure, plus the tone of the government's statements on personal responsibility for home improvement, meant that the new regime's likely impact would be to reduce the help available to low-income households.

Targeting vulnerable households

The suggestions in the consultation document were implemented by the 2002 Regulatory Reform (Housing Assistance) (England and Wales) Order (Controller of HMSO, 2002), which came into force in June 2002 but, perhaps in recognition of the concerns about reductions in the share of the local authority 'capital pot' spent on private sector home improvements, the decent homes target was extended by a promise made to cover privately owned homes (whether rented or owner-occupied) occupied by 'vulnerable' families. The target set was for 70% of vulnerable households living in private housing sector to have a decent home by 2010. The ODPM identified 'vulnerable' households as:

> those who are in receipt of certain means tested or disability related benefits. These benefits are: income support, pension credit, housing benefit, council tax benefit, income based job seekers allowance, attendance allowance, disability living allowance, industrial injuries, disablement benefit, and war disablement pension. Also included are recipients of either working tax credit or child tax credit where the assessed income by Inland Revenue for the purpose of those credits is less than £14,200. (ODPM Select Committee, 2004a, para 2.7)

In 2001 there were 1,151,000 such vulnerable households in non-decent homes who may be helped by local authorities through government-sponsored home improvement agencies. These agencies, often called 'staying put' or 'care and repair', assist vulnerable people to access financial sources such as local authority grants and equity loans and provide support in finding a reliable builder. An examination of the early impact of the 2002 Regulatory Reform

(Housing Assistance) (England and Wales) Order revealed that local authorities were finding it difficult to secure private sector loan finance for home improvement and that 'private sector housing renewal was a very low political priority locally' (Groves and Sankey, 2005, p 3). Between 2001 and 2003 the number of vulnerable households in non-decent homes declined to 1,056,000 but most of this improvement occurred by a reduction in the number of households lacking thermal comfort assisted by grants from the Department for Environment, Food and Rural Affairs that pre-dated the 2002 Regulatory Reform Order. Other causes of non-decency had increased (ODPM, 2005h, p 4).

The social sector

The Conservatives limited the resources available for the upkeep of local authority sector dwellings and, in 1997, New Labour inherited a backlog of repairs costing an estimated £10 billion. As part of the 2000 Spending Review a target of ensuring that all social housing should meet the decent homes standard by 2010 was set. Four resource channels were made available to local government to facilitate the achievement of this target:

- mainstream Housing Revenue Account resources supplemented by 'prudential borrowing';
- stock transfer to a registered social landlord thereby providing access to private finance that, unlike public finance, was not subject to the Treasury constraints of keeping the Public Sector Borrowing Requirement at a 'prudent' level;
- the Housing Private Finance Initiative, which, while retaining ownership of dwellings by the local authority, taps private finance. Under this initiative a private sector contractor supplies assets and services to the local authority in return for a performance-related payment. The Housing Private Finance Initiative has had only a limited impact, with less than 20 authorities using it and then only for individual estates rather than for whole-stock transfer (Perry, 2005, p 14);
- the Arms-Length Management Organisations (ALMO) Initiative, under which local authorities can access additional public sector resources if their housing service receives a two- or three-star rating from the Audit Commission and housing management is delivered through an arms-length organisation. An ALMO is a not-for-profit organisation run by an unpaid board of directors that includes councillors and tenant representatives but with no group having a controlling majority. The council continues to own the homes but the ALMO is responsible for housing stock management. ALMOs produce less tenant resistance than stock transfer to a registered social landlord and they have become important mechanisms for diversifying the range of social landlords. By 2005 49 ALMOs with 700,869 dwellings

had been set up. However, their future is uncertain because they hold only short-term contracts and the extra subsidy they receive will end when the decent homes standard has been achieved. Some commentators believe that ALMOs may be staging posts to ownership transfer (Murie and Nevin, 2001, p 40).

Three of these options allow local authorities to retain a degree of control over their housing stock but mainstream housing resources are restricted, with the Major Repairs Allowance (MRA) aimed at keeping stock in its current condition 'not at the backlog in repairs that are required to achieve the ten-year decent homes standard' (ODPM, 2004f). Given that 43% of the 2,790,000 council dwellings do not meet the 'decent' standard and the cost of achieving the standard can be as high as £405 million – the estimate for Southwark (House of Commons, 2005) – then large-scale stock transfer to landlords, unfettered by the constraints of the Public Sector Borrowing Requirement, will be necessary to meet the government's decent homes target.

Stock transfer began in the 1980s as a local initiative and initially was restricted to southern district councils interested in the financial gains accruing from stock transfer and in maintaining a social housing supply that was being depleted by the Right to Buy. In the 1990s, restrictions on repair and improvement finance for council houses prompted stock transfers in cities and industrial areas in the North and the Midlands mainly to housing associations specifically created for the purpose. The process was stimulated by the Estates Renewal Challenge Fund that provided 'gap funding' to meet the difference between the value of the properties and the cost of improvement thereby allowing run-down estates to be transferred. As Pawson (2004, p 15) comments, the transfer process 'is now very largely propelled by the need for all local authorities to achieve compliance with the government's Decent Homes Standard by 2010'.

The lack of a mechanism to enable tenants to remain as local authority tenants in improved properties generated disquiet among many backbench Labour Members of Parliament. The Parliamentary Committee that monitors the ODPM recommended that:

> A flexible policy and a level playing field are needed so that tenants and councillors can tailor solutions to suit local circumstances. In some cases, the optimal solution, as well as the one preferred by tenants, may well be that the local authority retain full ownership and management responsibilities. (ODPM Select Committee, 2004b, para 128)

The government responded to this criticism, not in terms of public expenditure constraints, but in terms of efficiency and tenant satisfaction. It stated:

The Government believes that separation provides a strong incentive to better performance; ensures a sharper focus on the two distinct housing functions; encourages councils to put more effort into their wider strategic housing responsibilities and guarantees that tenants have a greater role in the future management of their homes.... ALMO inspections to date have resulted in an average improvement of performance scores of 20 per cent.... There is evidence that separation improves the landlord service. Tenants of RSLs [registered social landlords] created through stock transfer have higher satisfaction scores with 79 per cent of tenants of transfer RSLs satisfied with their landlord compared with 74 per cent of council tenants. (Deputy Prime Minister, 2004, p 10)

This statement illustrates stock transfer's dual purpose. Additional resources for improvement to the physical condition of the housing stock – the number of non-decent homes declined from 1.6 million in 2001 to 1.4 million in 2004 (ODPM, 2005h, p 5) – are conditional on diversifying housing management in the hope of creating a more entrepreneurial management style.

Overview

- In the past, slum clearance was directed towards the removal of 'rookeries' and 'plague spots', regarded as a threat to the nation's moral and physical health.
- The demolition of property classified as 'unfit for human habitation' was virtually abandoned in the late 1970s but clearance has returned to the political agenda in a different form as part of the housing market renewal initiative (see Chapter Nine).
- From the 1980s both the Conservative and Labour Parties have regarded private sector maintenance and improvement as the owner's responsibility; state assistance for improvements has been targeted and reduced.
- New Labour has concentrated on delivering the decent home standard in the social housing sector primarily through stock transfer from the local authority sector to registered social landlords.

Questions for discussion

(1) Why was 'the slum' regarded as a 'nuisance' in the 19th century?
(2) What problems did slum clearance create for the people who lived in the slums?
(3) What were regarded as the advantages of area-based improvement?

(4)   How has the ODPM justified stock transfer from local authorities to registered social landlords?

Further reading

Jones (1976) provides an interesting account of the impact of slum clearance in London in the 19th century. The Housing Green Paper **(DETR, 2000b)** sets out the rationale of New Labour's urban renewal strategy and its stock transfer policy.

Website resources

The housing policy website of the ODPM is a source of useful information: www.odpm.gov.uk/index.asp?id=1150232

The Chartered Institute of Environmental Health's website (www.cieh.org/) contains informed commentaries on private sector housing renewal policy.

eight

Overcrowded and multi-occupied dwellings

Summary

- Overcrowding was identified as a social problem in the mid-19th century because of its links to crime, immorality and disease.
- A robust overcrowding measure became available in the 1891 Census but specific action to tackle overcrowding – other than in multi-occupied properties – did not occur until the 1935 Housing Act.
- The 1935 Housing Act's overcrowding definition has been the basis for statutory action but other measures of overcrowding are available.
- Since the early 1970s overcrowding has been substantially reduced and it has been estimated that in England there are only 20,000 statutory overcrowded households. However, on other definitions, the number of overcrowded households is considerably higher.
- Houses in multiple occupation provide low-cost housing options for some of the most vulnerable groups, including social security claimants, those on low incomes, students and asylum seekers. They are regulated by local authorities under the 2004 Housing Act.

Whereas homelessness is a visible symptom of a housing shortage, overcrowding is a concealed response. This invisibility and the lack of an authoritative, up-to-date definition of the condition have combined to make overcrowding a neglected issue. In 21st century Britain overcrowding is not fully regarded as a social problem.

The externalities of overcrowding

Overcrowding was recognised as a social problem in the mid-19th century because of its association with disease, depravity and social disorder. Edwin Chadwick, a firm believer that disease spreads by breathing foul air – the 'miasmic' theory – regarded densely populated areas and crammed buildings as major causes of illness. He claimed that crowded districts produced concentrations of putrefying waste that were difficult to remove. However, Chadwick ignored evidence that overcrowded dwellings had a direct connection to health independent of its impact on sewage disposal (Wohl, 1977). He was more concerned about how 'the want of separate apartments' influenced the 'morals of the population' (Chadwick, 1842, p 190). Numerous witnesses to his sanitary investigation testified to 'young men and women promiscuously sleeping in the same apartment' (Chadwick, 1842, p 191). This concern about the link between immorality and overcrowding was an enduring concern in the 19th century. Lord Shaftesbury, in his evidence to the 1885 Royal Commission on Housing, claimed that a family sharing a room often meant a family sharing a bed. He went on to comment:

> ... a friend of mine ... going down one of the back courts, saw on the pavement two children of tender years, of 10 or 11 years old, endeavouring to have sexual connection on the pathway. He ran and seized the lad, and pulled him off, and the only remark of the lad was, 'Why do you take hold of me? There are a dozen of them at it down there'. You must perceive that that could not arise from sexual tendencies, and that it must have been bred by imitation of what they saw. (Lord Shaftesbury, 1885, quoted in Jones, 1976, p 224)

Despite this anxiety about the impact of overcrowding on the physical and moral fibre of the nation, robust action would have interfered with property rights and, without specific action to re-house the overcrowded inhabitants, would have exacerbated the destitution problem. Accordingly, local authority powers to control overcrowding were minimal and, until the 1875 Public Health Act, did not apply to dwellings occupied by a single family. They were applied sparingly except to Common Lodging Houses and, in Scotland, to tenements where the 'block living' in this housing type was seen as a threat to public order. The model by-laws issued by the Local Government Board specifying thresholds at which local authorities might take action were expressed in terms of cubic feet of air per person. Adults were allowed 300 cubic feet in a sleeping room and children 150 cubic feet, compared to the 600 cubic feet allowed in army barracks (Bowmaker, 1900). In some areas the by-laws were enforced by night visits from police officers and sanitary inspectors to check that the number of people living in a dwelling conformed to the statutory requirements as set out on a plaque attached to the building.

The 1935 Housing Act

Towards the end of the 19th century, pressure from the labour movement concerning a 'housing famine' prompted more robust attempts to measure the extent of overcrowding. The 1891 Census contained questions about the number of rooms in a dwelling and the number of inhabitants. On a definition of overcrowding as more than two people per room, but excluding people living in houses with more than four rooms and with a somewhat vague definition of a room, 11.2% of the population was found to be living in overcrowded dwellings. This declined to 8.2% in 1911 but the national average in England concealed a range from 36% in Jarrow to 0.5% in Bedford. The increase in house construction and the lower birth rates of the 1920s helped to alleviate the problem but, in the 1930s, a serious level of overcrowding remained. The 1931 Census recorded seven million people living at densities of more than 1.5 persons per room and 397,000 households at more than two persons per room. The Moyne Committee, established in 1933, made a number of references to overcrowding and its findings convinced officials that overcrowding was a more serious menace to health than unfitness. Overcrowding presented a troublesome issue for the Conservatives because the magnitude of the problem indicated that mass housing might be required in the suburbs. Hilton-Young, the minister responsible for health and housing, argued that overcrowding could be dealt with by 'rehousing on the overcrowded and slum sites in flats', thereby presenting it as an inner-city redevelopment matter rather than a general housing problem that might interfere with the operations of private enterprise in the suburbs (Yelling, 1992, p 105).

The 1935 Housing Act set out a framework for tackling overcrowding. A duty was imposed on local authorities to survey the houses in their districts to ascertain the extent of overcrowding according to a statutory definition (see Box 8.1) and to determine how many new dwellings were necessary to overcome the problem. When satisfied that the new dwellings would be forthcoming the minister could trigger legislation permitting local authorities to make overcrowding illegal and to allow any landlord to regain possession of a property if it became overcrowded (thereby portraying overcrowding as created by the tenants rather than the landlord). The Act offered subsidies to assist new building but these subsidies were limited to specific central areas and were related to building flats. The major attack on overcrowding was scheduled to follow the completion of the task of eradicating the slums but the outbreak of the Second World War prevented significant action.

Box 8.1: Overcrowding: 1935 Housing Act definition

The overcrowding definition in the 1935 Housing Act was designed to ensure that any overcrowding identified by local authorities could be dealt with in a reasonable timescale. Two standards were specified. The first standard related to 'sexual overcrowding' and was contravened when 'the number of persons sleeping in a dwelling and the number of rooms available as sleeping accommodation is such that two persons of opposite sexes who are not living together as husband and wife must sleep in the same room. For this purpose:

(a) children under the age of ten shall be left out of account; and
(b) a room is available as sleeping accommodation if it is of a type normally used in the locality either as a bedroom or as a living room' [This meant that large kitchens could be included as living and sleeping rooms.]

The second standard compared the number of rooms and the floor area of these rooms with the number of persons permitted to live in the accommodation.

Number of rooms	Maximum number of persons
1	2
2	3
3	5
4	7.5
5	10

An additional two persons were permitted for every room in excess of five and the numbers permitted were scaled down if any room was less than 110 square feet. No account was taken of children under one and a child under 10 was reckoned as one half of a person.

On this definition it was estimated that 341,000 people were living in overcrowded conditions but a slightly less austere definition – excluding living rooms and large kitchens as sleeping accommodation – increased the number to 853,119 (Bowley, 1945, pp 160-1).

After the Second World War no specific initiative was directed towards reducing overcrowding – the problem was regarded as one element of the overall housing shortage to be overcome by building more homes. The 1957 Housing Act, in establishing the duties of local authorities when allocating council houses, stated that they should give reasonable preference to 'persons who are occupying insanitary or overcrowded houses, have large families or are living under unsatisfactory housing conditions' (1957 Housing Act, section 113). The definition of overcrowding given in the 1957 Act was identical to that in the

1935 Housing Act and 'was, even in 1935, a very limited one' (Cullingworth, 1969, p 7). Indeed the very term 'overcrowding' suggested that 'crowding' was normal.

The extent of overcrowding

Estimates of the extent of overcrowding are related to the criteria used to measure its incidence. There are a number of available measures but all are subject to under-reporting. Illegal migrants are more likely to live in overcrowded dwellings and, because statutory overcrowding is a ground for eviction, many people living in overcrowded conditions will not want to draw attention to their circumstances.

The statutory standard

This standard is identical to the one in the 1935 Housing Act. Many local authorities use it to allocate re-housing points and to assess whether the housing conditions of a family applying for accommodation under the homelessness legislation are bad enough for the household to be designated as homeless. The families of individuals seeking immigration visas are frequently required to produce information regarding the suitability of their intended accommodation and the statutory overcrowding standard is often employed to determine if the accommodation available is suitable for the proposed immigrant. Few local authorities use the 1935 Act to reduce overcrowding as evicting overcrowded people may produce a re-housing obligation in areas where social housing is scarce.

This statutory standard is very low: as Ormandy (1991, p 9) has observed, 'the average two storeyed, terraced house (with three bedrooms, two living rooms and a kitchen) could be occupied by the equivalent of 10 persons without being overcrowded – and that could mean six adults and eight children aged between one year and 10 years'. The parliamentary committee that oversees the work of the Office of the Deputy Prime Minister (ODPM) recommended that the statutory standard should be upgraded but this was initially rejected on the argument that such a change would lead 'to increased demand for housing, to the detriment of other people whose living conditions may be worse; and would make it more difficult for authorities to juggle their priorities' (ODPM, 2003d). However, the 2004 Housing Act contained provisions to allow the Deputy Prime Minister to amend the definition of overcrowding through regulations.

The bedroom standard

This occupation density indicator was developed by the Government Social Survey in the 1960s for use in social surveys. It incorporates assumptions about the sharing of bedrooms that would now be widely considered to be at the margin of acceptability. Indeed, for the purposes of determining whether accommodation is too large under the Housing Benefit regulations, one more bedroom than the standard is allowed and persons aged 16 and over – rather than aged over 21 – are allowed a separate bedroom.

A standard number of bedrooms required is calculated for each household in accordance with its age/sex/marital status composition and the relationship of household members to one another. A separate bedroom is required for each married or cohabiting couple, for any other person aged 21 or over, for each pair of adolescents aged 10 to 20 of the same sex, and for each pair of children under 10. Any unpaired person aged 10 to 20 is paired, if possible, with a child under 10 of the same sex, or, if that is not possible, he or she is counted as requiring a separate bedroom as is any unpaired child under 10. This standard is then compared with the actual number of bedrooms (including bedsits) available for the sole use of the household. If a household has fewer bedrooms than implied by the standard then it is deemed to be overcrowded and a shortfall of more than two rooms is described as 'severe' overcrowding. As even a bedsit will meet the bedroom standard for a single person household or for a married/cohabiting couple, single person and couple households cannot be overcrowded according to the bedroom standard. Shelter has adopted the bedroom standard as the norm for assessing overcrowding on the grounds that the statutory standard is too stringent and the 'occupancy rating' is too generous (see Table 8.1, Table 8.2 and Box 8.2).

2001 Census standards

The 2001 Census used what is called the 'occupancy rating' to measure the extent of overcrowding. This relates the actual number of rooms required by members of a household to the number of rooms available. It is more generous than the 'bedroom standard' because all households are assumed to require two common rooms (excluding bathrooms) plus a specified number of bedrooms calculated from the number and ages of the household members

Table 8:1: *Overcrowding and under-occupation (the bedroom standard): Britain: 1971-2003/04 (%)*

	1971	1981	1991	2001/02	2003/04
1 or more below standard	7	5	3	2	2
Equal to standard	34	33	29	26	25
1 above standard	38	39	38	38	38
2 or more above standard	21	23	30	34	35

Source: ONS (2005b)

Box 8.2: Overcrowding: the bedroom standard

Using the bedroom standard, Shelter's researchers found that:

- There were 510,000 overcrowded households (2.4% of total households) in England.
- 48,000 households (0.2% of total households) were severely overcrowded.
- Newham (15%), Tower Hamlets (14%) and Hackney (10%) had the highest rates of overcrowding.
- Households consisting of lone parents (9%) and couples with dependent children (5.4%) were more overcrowded than households without children.
- 6.3% of children were living in overcrowded conditions.
- There was more overcrowding in the local authority sector (5.6%) than in the housing association sector (4.3%), the owner-occupied sector (1.4%) or the private rented sector (3.8%).
- Black and minority ethnic households (11.1%) were more likely to be overcrowded than white households (1.8%),

Source: Reynolds et al (2004)

and the relationships between them. Any person over 16 is deemed to require a separate bedroom if not part of a couple. Thus, for example, a family of four (two parents and two children aged 10 and 16) with two bedrooms and two common rooms would have an occupancy rating of −1 and be classified as 'overcrowded'. Unfortunately 'occupancy ratings' are available only for the 2001 Census. The 'room' standard is also used. This simply divides the number of people in the household by the number of rooms (excluding bathrooms, lavatories, halls, landings and storage spaces). More than one person per room is deemed overcrowded whereas more than 1.5 persons per room is considered as severely overcrowded.

Overcrowding: its impact

The lack of a contemporary, authoritative threshold for the measurement of overcrowding means that it is difficult to draw robust conclusions on the impact of overcrowding because the benchmark whereby a property is deemed to be overcrowded varies between studies. There are also various forms of 'selection effects' that should be taken into account in examining the relationship between overcrowding and health: people with poor health, for example, may be forced to live in overcrowded houses, so overcrowding may not be the cause of their poor health. Moreover, it is difficult to disentangle the effects of overcrowding from other housing conditions such as dampness and lack of basic amenities.

Table 8.2: *Overcrowding: households with one or more rooms below the 'occupancy' standard: 2001 (%)*

England and Wales	7.4
London	10.8
Tower Hamlets	27.6
Most overcrowded ward in Tower Hamlets	38.7
North West	5.4
Oldham	7.3
Most overcrowded ward in Oldham	23.3

Source: Adapted from ODPM (2004g).

A literature review on the impact of overcrowding carried out on behalf on the ODPM concluded that:

- Overall there was a weak relationship between overcrowding and aspects of health of both children and adults but a robust relationship between meningitis, tuberculosis and overcrowding.
- Overcrowding in childhood affects adult health.
- There is mixed evidence on the relationship between overcrowding and mental health.
- There is limited evidence on overcrowding, childhood development, growth and education.
- No studies were found that specifically drew out the differential effects of overcrowding on the education of people from different minority ethnic backgrounds.
- There is little in the way of evidence to conclusively demonstrate an impact of overcrowding (ODPM, 2004h).

This literature review was more a condemnation of the limitations of existing research than a testimony to the weakness of the relationship between overcrowding and health and education. As the review stated, '... the kind of evidence required to demonstrate that 'A causes B' is not necessarily available. To do this would require a large-scale longitudinal study that compared two groups of households – one group where overcrowding has been alleviated with a group where overcrowding remained' (ODPM, 2004h, p 7). Given the importance of the issue it is surprising that the ODPM has not commissioned such as study. Applying less rigorous standards to the evidence than demanded by the ODPM's researchers indicates:

- a widening gap in infant mortality rates between areas with high and low levels of overcrowding (Congdon et al, 2001);
- a significant association between overcrowding and poor respiratory health (Mann et al, 1992);

- a direct connection between social deprivation and psychiatric illness with overcrowding significantly associated with mental health (Harrison et al, 1998);
- Bangladeshi households in Tower Hamlets reported a range of problems associated with overcrowding including lack of privacy, disturbed sleep and conflict in the use of rooms (Kempson, 1999);
- a significant association between overcrowding and children's mental health (Evans et al, 2001);
- a very strong relationship between overcrowding and school performance (Goux and Maurin, 2003);
- an association between home accidents and overcrowding (Alwash and McCarthy, 1988).

Houses in multiple occupation

Who lives in houses in multiple occupation?

Houses in multiple occupation (HMOs) provide affordable housing options for some of the most vulnerable groups including social security claimants or those on low incomes, students and asylum seekers. The 2001 English House Condition Survey found that there were 640,000 private rented HMOs in England. According to the ODPM:

> The most common problems associated with multiple occupancy relate to poor fire safety standards, overcrowding, inadequate facilities and poor or unscrupulous management.... In all houses converted into bedsits, the annual risk of death per person is 1 in 50,000 (six times higher than in comparable single occupancy houses).... In the case of bedsit houses comprising three or more storeys the risk is 1 in 18,600 (sixteen times higher). (ODPM, 2003e, p 1)

Regulating houses in multiple occupation

Local authority powers to regulate HMOs evolved from the 1851 Act for the Regulation and Inspection of Common Lodging Houses. In the early part of the 19th century, Common Lodging Houses provided cheap accommodation, usually in the form of straw mattresses rented on a nightly basis in a communal room. These 'doss-houses', as they were sometimes known, were regarded as breeding grounds for crime and immorality. Overcrowding occurred on a massive scale. In 1851 the Police Commissioner for Leeds found 'in one small area 222 lodging houses in which lived 2,500 people, averaging two and a half persons per bed' (quoted in Hodgkinson, 1980, p 10). Although Lord

Shaftesbury recognised the connection between regulating overcrowding and the need to build new dwellings – his Act for the Regulation and Inspection of Common Lodging Houses was accompanied by his 1851 Labouring Classes Lodging Houses Act – this was not the dominant view. Many believed that the attitudes of the poor caused overcrowding because they preferred to spend their incomes on drink rather than on more spacious accommodation. Thus the action taken to overcome the problem consisted of regulations issued under the 1851 Act allowing the police and sanitary authorities to set standards and control the number of people occupying a dwelling. Although largely ignored in the growing Northern industrial towns, the Act was enforced in London where, because of fear of prostitution, women were not allowed to use Common Lodging Houses. Dickens (1888, p 24) commented:

> Every establishment of this kind throughout the metropolis is now under direct and continual police supervision; every room being inspected and measured before occupation, a placard being hung up in each stating the number of beds for which it is licensed, calculated upon the basis of a minimum allowance of space for each person. Every bed, moreover, has to be furnished weekly with a complete supply of fresh linen, whilst careful provision is made for the ventilation of the rooms, the windows of which are also thrown open throughout the house at 10am.

Over time Common Lodging Houses evolved into what are known today as boarding houses and the lower end of the Bed and Breakfast (B&B) sector. By the 1990s, B&B hotels had an important housing role. Local authorities used them to house people classified as homeless under the 1977 Housing (Homeless Persons) Act and the payment of 'board and lodgings' allowances led many people without permanent accommodation to use such hotels. Carter (1997) studied the extent and nature of this 'self-placement' and found that about 75,000 individuals were claiming benefits and using such hotels as semi-permanent accommodation. People with drug, alcohol or mental health problems, ex-prisoners, care leavers, young people and refugees were over-represented in London B&B hotels.

Before the 2004 Housing Act became law, local authorities had powers relating to the fitness of premises for the number of occupants and to enforce regulations requiring the person managing a HMO to observe specified standards of management. The 1997 Housing (Fire Safety in Houses in Multiple Occupation) Order placed an additional duty on local authorities to ensure that fire safety measures were adequate in all HMOs of three storeys or above. Under powers granted by the 1985 and 1996 Housing Acts, local authorities could also introduce registration schemes for HMOs. When used, such registration schemes placed a duty on a specified person, usually the landlord or owner, to register the property. Registration periods lasted five years. Schemes were based on model regulations issued by the Secretary of State in 1997 and were of two main types:

- notification schemes that simply required certain details about each property – number of rooms, amenities, works, and so on – to be registered, to help the local authority find out more about the HMOs in its area;
- schemes containing control provisions that could be used to prevent multiple occupation of a house unless it was registered, or if the number occupying the property exceeded the registered number. Contravention or failure to comply with a provision of a registration scheme was an offence.

The 2004 Housing Act

Although local authorities had the power to introduce licensing schemes for HMOs it was not compulsory for them to do so. New Labour's 1997 Manifesto promised to introduce a mandatory licensing scheme for HMOs. This pledge was redeemed in Scotland in 2000 and the 2004 Housing Act placed a duty on local authorities in England and Wales to ensure that prescribed HMOs in their areas are licensed and gave local authorities discretionary additional powers in respect to other HMOs. As Kemp (2004) has observed, the provisions of the 2004 Housing Act represented a trade-off between property condition, affordability and homelessness. If local authorities enforce higher standards then rents may increase, making accommodation less affordable and more people vulnerable to homelessness.

The 2004 Housing Act will be implemented in phases. It defines HMOs in broad terms covering houses, hostels, self-contained flats or other relevant buildings occupied by persons who do not form a single household and who share facilities. Buildings owned by local housing authorities or registered social landlords, and certain buildings occupied by students, are exempt from the definition.

The prescribed HMOs are subject to regulations issued by 'appropriate national authority' but the explanatory notes to the Bill when it was introduced to Parliament stated that it was intended to prescribe HMOs of three storeys and above in which at least five people live – an intention that eliminates many high-risk properties from compulsory licensing. Local authorities will be able to grant or refuse a licence based on:

- whether the property is reasonably suitable for occupation by the number of persons or households specified in the application;
- whether the proposed licence holder is a 'fit and proper' person;
- whether the proposed manager of the HMO or an agent or employee of that person is a 'fit and proper' person;
- whether the proposed management arrangements are satisfactory.

The most important sanction available to authorities will be the refusal or revocation of a licence. This will prevent the landlord from letting a property unless the authority is satisfied that suitable alternative management has been put in place. Landlords letting property in breach of the licensing provisions will commit an offence punishable by a fine of up to £20,000.

The discretionary powers of local authorities relate to HMOs not covered by the prescriptions on mandatory licensing. Local authorities must gain the approval of the 'appropriate national authority' in specifying the types of property to which discretionary licensing will apply.

Overview

- The 'externalities' of 'sweated properties', especially in Common Lodging Houses, helped to make overcrowding a social problem in the 19th century.
- Today overcrowding is a neglected problem and the statutory definition of the problem is very limited.
- Multi-occupied dwellings are an important source of accommodation for low-income households and government regulation of such properties is a compromise between the enforcement of minimum standards and the retention of a supply of cheap accommodation.

Questions for discussion

(1) What were the 'externalities' of overcrowding?
(2) Is the definition of overcrowding in the 1935 Housing Act an adequate basis for tackling the overcrowding problem today?
(3) Examine the relationship between overcrowding and health.
(4) What are the powers of local government to regulate houses in multiple occupation?

Further reading

Yelling's (1992) *Slums and Redevelopment: Policy and Practice in England, 1918-45, with particular reference to London* contains a comprehensive account of the 1935 Housing Act.

Ineichen's (1993) *Homes and Health: How Housing and Health Interact* and **ODPM's (2004h)** *The Impact of Overcrowding on Health and Education: A Review of Evidence and Literature* examine the impact of overcrowding.

Website resources

The Victorian Times website (www.victoriantimes.org) contains the *Report of Her Majesty's Commissioners for Inquiring into the Working Classes* (1885).

Statistics on overcrowding can be found on the ODPM's website. See *Overcrowding in England: The National and Regional Picture* at www.odpm.gov.uk/stellent/groups/odpm_housing/documents/page/odpm_house_028621-02.hcsp#P28_5034

Low demand

Summary

- Low demand was first recognised in the late 1970s as a 'difficult-to-let' local authority housing problem to be tackled by tenant involvement in neighbourhood housing management and estate design improvements.
- During the 1990s a more holistic approach to the problem was developed combining physical renewal and economic initiatives.
- New Labour identified an 'unpopular housing' issue in certain areas across all tenures. Initially it concentrated on improving human and social capital as solutions to the problems in deprived neighbourhoods.
- The establishment of the Market Renewal Fund in 2002 marked a partial acknowledgement that low demand was related to structural factors as well as to deficiencies in human and social capital.
- Creating the conditions necessary for the development of balanced communities and reducing antisocial behaviour have come to be recognised as potential solutions to the low-demand problem.

Priority estates

Diminishing demand first received central attention in 1974 when the Department of the Environment (DoE) carried out a survey of post-war 'difficult-to-let' dwellings and found 62,000 properties to be in low demand. In 1981 an investigation into the problem was published by the DoE. Glennerster and Turner (1993, p 3) summarised its conclusion as:

> …the team concluded that the 'hard to let' label was a misnomer. What they were really observing was merely the most unattractive end of the public housing market. They were the tip of a much larger problem of poor housing management.

In response to the identified council estate management problem the DoE set up the Priority Estates Project (PEP). At first, PEP focused on centralised, fragmented administration as the most important cause of 'problem estates' and promoted local estate management as the solution. Existing housing administrative structures were deemed to be incapable of providing 'flexible, adaptable, renting styles and systems' and 'estates deteriorated rapidly as a consequence of the remote, town-hall-based administrative system and the low level of direct services' (Power, 1993, p 202). Later, PEP coupled management decentralisation with tenant participation by promoting Estate Management Boards to engage tenants in the running of their estates. Evaluations of PEP's impact demonstrated modest achievement. The opportunities for tenant involvement and the 'on-the-spot' presence of housing managers produced improvements in some indicators of achievement (Glennerster and Turner, 1993). Yet, decentralised management was more expensive and, despite the investment in physical improvements in many estates, the projects were 'swimming against the tide', their impact thwarted by the 'growing social disadvantages' that created 'intense management pressures' (Power and Tunstall, 1995, p 6).

Architectural determinism

In contrast to the management/participatory approach of Anne Power, Alice Coleman (1985) placed emphasis on bad design. Adopting the basic premises of Oscar Newman (1973) concerning lack of 'defensible space' – characterised by a dearth of surveillance and the presence of numerous escape routes – Coleman claimed that many of the problems of unpopular estates could be eradicated by amending their design. Her argument was grounded in a study of 4,099 blocks containing 106,520 dwellings and 4,172 houses. Five indicators of social malaise – litter, graffiti, urine and faeces, vandalism and children in care – were correlated with 15 design features, and significant relationships were identified. Dwellings per entrance, dwellings per block, storeys per block, overhead walkways and spatial organisation registered the highest relationships to social malaise. Coleman linked such design faults to the 'utopianism' of Ebenezer Howard's (1902) garden cities and the 'radiant city' promoted by Le Corbusier (1927). Such 'utopian planners' had attempted to create community spirit through the imposition of an architectural style but had failed to recognise the 'territorial imperative', inbuilt through human evolution, that 'has led us to produce a shelter with its adjoining piece of territory and to impress it with distinctive marks of identity' (Coleman, 1985, p 18).

Estate Action

Both the poor design and poor management hypotheses on the causes of 'problem' estates received official support in the 1980s and early 1990s.

Following some informal steering of resources for physical improvement to local authorities adopting the PEP model, the Estate Action Initiative, introduced in 1986, provided funds for spending in specific locations according to the needs of the area and the viability of the action proposed by the local authority. Management decentralisation was an essential ingredient of a successful Estate Action bid. In addition, an element of stock transfer and building or refurbishment for homeownership was necessary. The idea that 'mixed tenure' enhanced social stability was gaining ground although the extent of the resulting mix varied significantly between Estate Action neighbourhoods (Tunstall, 2003). Compliance with central demands produced substantial capital resources for physical refurbishment. An evaluation of six early Estate Action schemes concluded that 'all the EAs [Estate Actions] were effective in achieving regeneration' but 'there was little evidence of estate-based financial management …, little success in involving residents in estate management with residents often expressing only limited interest' and 'only minimal reductions in crime and incivilities' (DoE, 1996, p 1).

In addition to Estate Action, £50 million was set aside for the Design Improvement Controlled Experiment (DICE) through which the number of flats with a common entrance was reduced, walkways demolished and cul-de-sacs converted into roads. Despite its methodological flaws – in particular her 'desultory' attempt to test for social factors (Hillier, 1986, p 39) – Alice Coleman's work had impressed Margaret Thatcher. 'I went further', she said, 'than the DoE in believing that the design of estates was crucial to their success and to reducing the amount of crime. I was a great admirer of the work of Professor Alice Coleman and I had made her an adviser to the DoE, to their dismay' (Thatcher, 1993, p 605). An evaluation of DICE (DoE, 1997, p 5) noted that all the individual schemes achieved some benefits but 'compared to the early Estate Action schemes (the most relevant policy alternative) the evaluation suggests that DICE was not a more successful regeneration initiative (nor, at best, does it appear to be less successful)'.

During the late 1980s there were signs that the DoE was beginning to recognise an economic dimension to 'problem' estates. Guidance on Estate Action bids started to emphasise the inclusion of job creation measures and, via City Challenge and the Single Regeneration Budget, created in 1994, specific measures aimed at council estates had to form part of a comprehensive and integrated package aimed at the economic and social revitalisation of an area.

Unpopular housing

The idea that 'problem estates' were caused by utopian planning and local government bureaucratic incompetence fitted well with New Right ideology. In the early 1990s, this causal notion received a setback when Page (1993) identified similar problems in the housing association sector – chosen by the

Conservatives to be the inheritor of local authority housing in part because of their alleged superior management ability. Page noted that, as housing associations had become the major providers of new social housing, they were under pressure to house homeless people and produce more dwellings from each pound of government subsidy. The result was the production of larger housing estates often by housing association partnerships formed to take advantage of the scale economies available from volume builders. He identified the emergence of 'social malaise' on these estates and a developing low-demand problem. Later, a study of the fortunes of large estates built by consortia of housing associations in the early 1990s confirmed Page's predictions. They were encountering difficult management problems and the percentage of people feeling unsafe on the street was 45% compared to the national figure of 24% (Manzi and Smith Bowers, 2004). In addition, some housing associations were finding their new estates 'difficult to let'. Media interest focused on the issue with Dr Henry Russell Court, a 50-dwelling flat development in Newcastle-upon-Tyne, attracting particular attention. Built in 1996 at a cost of £2 million it was demolished three years later due to lack of demand.

New Labour and unpopular housing

The notion that unpopular housing was not just a local authority issue was taken up by New Labour in *Bringing Britain Together: A National Strategy for Neighbourhood Renewal*. This stated:

> Poor neighbourhoods are not a pure housing problem. They are not all the same kind of design, they don't all consist of rented or council housing, and they are not all in towns and cities. (SEU Unit, 1998b, para 1.2)

The report was a comprehensive assessment of unpopular housing across all tenures in the context of neighbourhood deprivation. It identified 1,370 deprived neighbourhoods ranging from 50 to 5,000 households with 44 local authorities having the highest concentrations of deprived neighbourhoods. In the absence of robust neighbourhood statistics, the characteristics of these 44 local authorities were compared to the rest of England, the limitations of previous policies identified and principles for future policy set out (see Box 9.1).

New Labour declared that 'no-one should be seriously disadvantaged by where they live' (Social Exclusion Unit, 2001, p 3) and its diagnosis of 'deprived neighbourhoods' placed emphasis on deficits in human and social capital (see Box 9.2). Deficiencies in human capital would be rectified by area-based initiatives such as Sure Start – aimed at pre-school children and their parents in deprived areas – plus other 'action zones' covering health, education and employment. Social capital would be augmented by a new initiative, the New

Box 9:1 *Bringing Britain Together: A National Strategy for Neighbourhood Renewal*: summary

A comparison of the 44 authorities with the highest concentrations of deprivation with the rest of England

The 44 authorities had:

- nearly two thirds more unemployment;
- almost one and a half times the proportion of lone-parent households;
- one and a half times the underage pregnancy rate;
- almost a third of children growing up in families on Income Support (against less than a quarter in the rest of England);
- 37% of 16-year-olds without a single GCSE at Grades A-C (against 30% for the rest of England);
- more than twice as many nursery/primary and more than twice as many secondary schools on special measures;
- a quarter more adults with poor literacy or numeracy;
- mortality ratios 30% higher, adjusting for age and sex;
- one and a half times the level of vacant housing elsewhere;
- two to three times the levels of poor housing, vandalism and dereliction;
- more young people, with child densities a fifth higher;
- nearly four times the proportion of minority ethnic residents;
- high crime rates: 40% of all crime occurs in just 10% of areas and there is a strong correlation between crime and local conditions.

The limitations of previous initiatives to overcome deprivation

- There had been too many initiatives governed by too many centrally imposed rules on resource distribution.
- Programmes had not been 'joined up' and there had been a lack of local cooperation.
- Insufficient consideration had been given to links beyond the neighbourhood.
- Community commitment had not been harnessed.
- What works had been neglected.

Future policy: guiding principles

- Investing in people, not just buildings.
- Involving communities, not parachuting in solutions.
- Developing integrated approaches with clear leadership.
- Ensuring mainstream policies really work for the poorest neighbourhoods.
- Making a long-term commitment with sustained political priority.

Deal for Communities (see Box 9.3). In addition, the idea of 'permeability' – sometimes called 'linking social capital' – received attention. Attempts would be made to connect deprived neighbourhoods to wider area networks by, for example, better transport links.

There is a shortage of robust information on the outcomes of New Deal for Communities. The official programme evaluation identified a number of

Box 9.2: Human and social capital

Human capital refers to the education, skills, health status and social skills that an individual possesses that can be utilised to provide a future income and contribute to the public interest.

In *Bowling Alone: The Collapse and Revival of American Community* (2001) Robert Putman defines social capital in terms of the collective value of all social networks and the inclinations that arise from these networks to do things for each other. The World Bank (2000) has made a distinction between 'bonding' social capital, 'bridging' social capital and 'linking' social capital.

'Bonding' social capital relates to the ties that connect family members, neighbours, close friends and business associates. 'Bridging' social capital relates to the weaker horizonal bonds between people with different ethnic and occupational backgrounds whereas 'linking' social capital consists of vertical ties between poorer people and organisations such as banks, local government and employers. This classification draws attention to limitations of 'social capital' as an analytical concept: the different forms of social capital may be contradictory, for example enhancing bonding capital may limit bridging capital.

Box 9.3: New Deal for Communities

New Deal for Communities was launched in 1998 and, by 1999, 39 'pathfinder partnerships' had been identified to benefit from £2 billion invested over 10 years. The programme was aimed at tackling high levels of crime; educational under-achievement; poor health; inadequate housing and a poor physical environment in an intensive and coordinated way. According to the Neighbourhood Renewal Unit of the ODPM (Neighbourhood Renewal Unit, 2005, p 1) the guiding principles of the programme are:

- long-term commitment to deliver real change with communities at the heart of this, in partnership with key agencies;
- community involvement and ownership;
- joined-up thinking and solutions with action based on evidence about what works.

concerns about its operation. These included the cost of community engagement in terms of 'burn-out of key local community players; intra-community tensions; the demands placed on the time and resources of NDC [New Deal for Communities] employees and agencies' and a dearth of links between 'needs and aspirations' and 'appropriate projects and outcomes' (ODPM, 2003f, p 1). None the less, the evaluation argued that the lasting benefits of community engagement and agency partnerships may be worth the initial cost of promoting joined-up working and community involvement. Some imaginative schemes had been promoted but the extensive public involvement at the heart of the initiative – believed to be necessary to promote the development of social capital – seems to have promoted delay and disillusionment in many areas and the action proposed seemed to have been directed to meet the needs of the current inhabitants rather than to create a neighbourhood of choice for the future (Cole et al, 2003). An unofficial review of New Deal for Communities claimed that:

> Ten of the 39 New Deal partnerships have run into trouble, with residents, staff and communities feeling exhausted, disaffected and betrayed…. Many NDC partnerships entering their fourth year are only just embarking on their housing strategy or recruiting registered social landlords, and have not committed any spending to 'live' projects. (Knutt, 2003, p 3)

Evidence from household surveys conducted in 2002 and 2004 revealed some positives – fear of crime had been reduced, satisfaction with education had improved and the percentage of those who felt their health had got better had increased. On the other hand, economic inactivity had remained static and the percentage of people believing that their housing had improved showed only a modest increase, with a decline in London (ODPM, 2005i). Since 1999 Power and Willmot have been interviewing 200 families living in four of the most deprived urban areas in England, two of which have been subject to the New Deal for Communities programme. The reactions to the programme have been mixed with many people appreciating the practical help on offer but with harsh criticisms of 'funding, in-fighting and misinformation which wastes community time and produces slow or no results' (Power and Willmot, 2005, p 287).

The Neighbourhood Renewal Fund

In 2002 New Deal for Communities was supplemented by a Neighbourhood Renewal Fund, the outcome of the findings of 18 central interdepartmental teams established following the publication of the Social Exclusion Unit's 1998 report. The Neighbourhood Renewal Fund was targeted on the 88 most deprived local authorities for use by local 'pathfinders' in promoting 'joined-up' action by mainstream services whose earlier attempts to improve deprived neighbourhoods had been perceived as a 'fragmented effort' (ODPM, 2005j, para 4.97). The various forms of local intervention would be synchronised by Local Strategic Partnerships and day-to-day service provision would be coordinated by neighbourhood managers – an extension of the idea of local housing management. The aim was to bend mainstream provision to achieve 'floor' (absolute) and 'convergence' (relative) targets by 'joined-up' thinking from mainstream services. Such targets included increases in employment rates, reductions in burglaries and to reduce the gap in life expectancy between the national average and the fifth of areas with the lowest life expectancy.

Early evaluations of the impact of the Neighbourhood Renewal Fund have been positive with the 'pathfinders' making 'good progress in developing their capacity to engage with partners and deliver their programmes'. However, 'to date the positive changes being made to services are relatively modest in scale.... Pathfinders have also not made as much progress in the joining up of services between providers, as they have in working with individual providers.... The 'bending' of resources (the re-allocation of mainstream resources to a Pathfinder neighbourhood) was also less frequent and more commonly associated with additional police resources' (ODPM, 2004j, paras 3 and 14).

Low housing demand

Just as the Conservatives had shifted focus from the specific pathologies of 'problem estates' to a broader economic perspective, New Labour's initial concentration on the lack of 'joined-up' thinking and deficiencies in social and human capital was also revised. The *Report by the Unpopular Housing Action Team* (DETR, 1999c) identified 928,000 dwellings as 'unpopular':

- 11.5% of local authority housing stock; about 377,000 dwellings concentrated in the North East, North West, and Yorkshire and Humberside;
- 8% of housing association stock; 89,500 dwellings;
- 3% of properties in the private sector; 461,500 dwellings;

Among the reasons given for unpopular housing were the relative economic decline and out-migration from certain regions and that first-time buyers were by-passing particular areas. Signs of low demand in the private sector included low and falling house prices, a high population turnover and abandoned properties and, in the social rented sector, a low waiting list, frequent refusal of tenancy offers, a high tenant turnover and a high void rate.

A survey of the opinions of local authority officials and an analysis of local authority waiting lists and vacancy rates indicated that a sharper downward drift in the demand for local authority accommodation in the North and parts of the Midlands had started in 1994 whereas demand in the South had been on the increase (Bramley and Pawson, 2002). The relative scale of private sector low demand was more limited than in the social sector but similar trends were identifiable. Bramley et al, (2004, p 72) stated:

> ... figures from English local authorities' annual statistical returns show that private sector vacancies across the North of England rose by 16% between 1997 and 2000, whilst the comparable figure for London fell by a similar proportion. Perhaps more significantly, long-term private sector vacancies in the North of England rose steadily after 1997.

This geographical distribution of low demand was linked to structural economic trends in the economy. Turok and Edge (1999) examined employment trends between 1981 and 1996 in the 20 largest British cities and found that these cities had lost half a million – mainly manufacturing – jobs whereas the rest of the country gained 1.7 million. Job losses had resulted in population decline: between 1981 and 2001 Manchester and Newcastle lost 7% of their populations but, in the Northern regions, the housing stock increased by over 350,000. Lupton (2003, p 72) examined overall job change in 12 deprived areas between 1991 and 1998 and found that only two had a jobs gain higher than the average for England and Wales – one in London and the other in an area benefiting from a new motorway extension.

Low demand is a complex problem and has to be understood in the context of particular local housing markets and specific social environments – a high resident turnover in an area and consequent high vacancies, for example, may reflect an area's role as a 'gateway' into a city and hence may not be regarded as a problem. Bramley et al (2000, p 11) made a distinction between absolute low demand 'where housing is difficult to let or sell because there are not enough households in the area looking for homes' and relatively unpopular housing 'which is difficult to let or sell because it is of a type, or in a particular type of neighbourhood, which has specific problems which make it very unpopular relative to other housing available'. Thus, within the overall framework of low demand, particular, often highly localised factors, affect its incidence. Properties left vacant attract drug dealers and users and act as a base for other forms of antisocial behaviour. People with the resources to acquire other homes leave the area, leaving more vacant properties. The spiral of neighbourhood deterioration can accelerate through sales to private landlords interested in the returns to be made from Housing Benefit rather than in the behaviour of their tenants, and the general availability of housing can mean that tenants can behave badly without fear of eviction (Bramley et al, 2004, p 85).

Tackling low demand

A number of policies have been introduced to counter the low-demand problem.

- In 2002 a Market Renewal Fund was established to which nine 'pathfinder' agencies had access. These pathfinders covered about 60% of the identified low-demand stock and were set the task of, by 2010, closing the gap by a third between the level of vacancies and house values in pathfinder areas compared to the regional average. The broad programme objective was for pathfinder strategic plans to 'entail radical and sustained action to replace obsolete housing with modern sustainable accommodation, through demolition and new building or refurbishment' (ODPM, 2003a, p 5). The areas selected cut across local authority boundaries and pathfinders were expected to establish partnerships involving all stakeholders and develop strategic plans for whole housing markets based on detailed local studies that would reconnect pathfinder areas to nearby functioning housing markets. Selective demolition, environmental and structural improvements, new-build and schemes such as home exchanges – allowing residents to transfer their mortgage from a house with negative equity to a nearby dwelling whose value reflects the mortgage debt – were among the fund's potential uses. Initially it was anticipated that, in the long term, 400,000 demolitions may be necessary.
- Having identified that new building in the North was exceeding new household formation the government started to reduce the release of greenfield housing sites in the North West and the North East to limit new supply in areas close to low-demand districts. According to Lupton and Power (2002), this would reduce the social segregation caused by people with choice leaving inner cities.
- The resources available for new social housing in regions experiencing low demand were reduced.
- The 2004 Housing Act allowed local authorities to license private landlords in selected areas.

No sooner had the pathfinder market renewal agencies started their work there was an increase in house prices in many districts previously designated as low-demand areas. This was reflected in social housing demand with the vacancy rate for council housing declining from, for example, 4.7% in the North West in 2001 to 3.4% in 2004 (ODPM, 2005a) Between early 2002 and early 2005 lower-quartile prices in pathfinder areas almost doubled and the ODPM stated in evidence to the ODPM Select Committee (2005b) that 'the numbers of houses reported as being in low demand in the North and Midlands has fallen from almost a million in 2002 to around 850,000 in 2004'. Part of this reduction can be attributed to speculative purchases in the pathfinder areas in the hope of benefiting from future gains or at least the compensation arrangements for demolition (Shelter, 2004) but the jump in house prices also affected areas without pathfinder status. House price inflation had rippled out of the South into the North especially into areas experiencing the shoots of economic revival. People wanting to secure a foothold on the owner-occupation ladder could no longer bypass the cheapest homes on the market. House price inflation was fuelled by buy-to-let landlords interested in securing investment returns higher than those offered by the stock market. First-time buyers and 'buy-to-let' landlords were identified as two major drivers in the price increase of terraced houses in Rochdale by 36% in 2003/04 – the other factor being increasing demand from the Asian community who had a particular local attachment to the area (CSR Partnership, 2004, p 16). Although this market surge was variable in its impact – in some areas prices remained very low – it helped to prompt many local residents in pathfinder areas to press for refurbishment rather than demolition and the ODPM Select Committee (2005b, p 14) concluded that:

> if there is strong evidence that the rise in housing demand is sustained and not just the result of an artificial boost to the market due to speculative activity, the Pathfinders should review their demolition programmes as a matter of urgency and concentrate on neighbourhood management and housing refurbishment.

In response to such concerns the initial emphasis on demolition has been modified in favour of refurbishment but a reduction in low demand in a volatile housing market does not negate the need for initiatives such as the Market Renewal Fund. The Audit Commission (2005b, p 111) maintained that 'there remains a substantial gap between house prices in pathfinder areas and regional averages that cannot be explained by the smaller average size of houses in pathfinder areas' and the pathfinder areas contain housing types and layouts – maisonettes, old terraced houses, for example – that are unlikely to be in long-term demand if other choices are available. A flexible response from pathfinders is necessary although this is difficult to achieve because the compulsory purchase procedures necessary for demolition are complex and time-consuming.

Balanced communities

In the 1950s, council estates were inhabited mainly by the manual working class with at least one household member in employment plus a significant section of the lower middle class. In 1953 the income of council tenants was close to the median (Bentham, 1986) but, perhaps beginning with the 1950s slum clearance drive, there has been a marked change in the social composition of local authority estates that gathered momentum in the 1970s and 1980s

Table 9.1: *The residualisation of local authority housing in Britain*

	1972	2000
Income of local authority household heads as percentage of the income of homebuyers	56	30
	1981	**2001**
% of local authority tenants in full-time work	43	23

Source: Adapted from Wilcox (2004)

(see Table 9.1). This change – often called 'residualisation' – has also been reflected in the composition of the registered social landlord sector. Had social housing been dispersed throughout the community then this 'residualisation' may not have been problematical but the concentration of social housing in particular localities has produced difficulties. Local authority housing is not a uniformly desirable commodity and numerous studies have documented how the formal and informal procedures for allocating council housing have led to those people with the most pressing housing needs and with the lowest incomes receiving the least desirable properties. Jones (1988, p 96) summarises the process:

> The result of this process of complex bargaining is to establish a clear hierarchy wherein offers of good quality property are most often made to those most able to 'operate' the system whether by political influence, by possessing a bargaining counter, or by articulacy and social acceptability. Conversely, property perceived by the allocations staff as poor quality will be offered to those least able to refuse, least articulate and least able to enlist effective support.

The impact of this bargaining process has been compounded by centrally determined void reduction targets that have put pressure on allocation officials to offer the least desirable dwellings to the most desperate people thereby avoiding numerous refusals and long-term empty houses (Morrison, 2000). The residential sorting mechanism in the owner-occupied sector is more straightforward. In the virtual absence of state assistance to low-income homeowners then the market, which is strongly influenced by location, dictates that the lowest-quality homes will be occupied by those with the lowest incomes.

Unbalanced communities: why it matters

- The degree of residential segregation by income is a convincing manifestation of social exclusion per se. It is simply wrong for people with low incomes to be concentrated in certain areas. There is evidence of increased polarisation with the proportion of people having to move to make every area similar in economic composition rising by over one third between 1971 and 2001 (Dorling and Rees, 2004). In 2004, 1.5% of neighbourhoods in England had deprivation scores far greater than their regional averages (Berube, 2005, p 36).

• The Social Exclusion Unit (SEU, 2000, p 4) has stated that 'communities function best when they contain a broad social mix', a point developed by Berube (2005, p 3):

> Government can achieve greater success in delivering on key public services outcomes (e.g. crime, health, education) in mixed communities versus deprived communities. That is, it may be easier for Government to improve school performance, or reduce health inequalities, if people are more socially and economically integrated.

• If it is New Labour's policy to concentrate on the *combined* impact of health, education, housing, and employment opportunities by area-based strategies then it is logical to mitigate the impact of this amalgam by attempting to reduce the opportunities for these factors to compound at the neighbourhood level.

• Spatial concentrations of people with low incomes can make a neighbourhood unattractive to investors and employers, leading to less work and higher prices due to lack of competition.

• Although one should be aware of the 'ecological fallacy', committed when the characteristics of an area are held to convey information about individuals in these areas – an area with a high incidence of crime and poverty does not necessarily mean that the poor people in the area are committing the crimes – there is some evidence that it is worse to be poor in a poor area than in one that is socially mixed. Isolating neighbourhood impacts is difficult (Durlauf, 2004) and the British evidence on the compounding impact of concentrated poverty is sparse and inconsistent. Experiments in selling each alternative vacant house on estates have produced increases in property values, higher demand, more tenant satisfaction and gains in area reputation plus reductions in stigma, turnover and voids (Watkinson, 2004). Other evaluations of introducing a greater social mix into existing communities are less optimistic. A literature review of the impacts of housing diversification in the UK and the Netherlands showed 'ambivalent results that necessitate modest expectations' (Kleinhans, 2004, p 368). Atkinson and Kintrea (2000) found that building houses for homeowners on council estates in Scotland made little difference to the renters' social networks although there was a decline in the stigma arising from living in the area. Bolster et al, using longitudinal data from the British Household Panel Survey to examine the impact of neighbourhood on adult income, found 'no evidence of a negative relationship between neighbourhood and subsequent income growth. This is true for one-year, five-year and ten-year changes' (Bolster et al, 2004, p 2). The Prime Minister's Strategy Unit (2005) itemised some 'area effects' in the UK (see Box 9.4) but the most comprehensive evidence on neighbourhood impacts comes from the US (see Box 9.5).

• Research by Meen et al (2005) revealed that deprivation has to fall to a certain threshold before the local housing market begins to accelerate and highly skilled people and private sector capital are attracted to the area. This finding indicates that specific policies to promote a 'social mix' might produce a multiplier effect.

Creating balanced communities

Under New Labour there have been three initiatives aimed at producing more balanced communities.

'Choice-based' lettings

Creating balanced communities is only a potential by-product of this initiative. It is mainly directed at changing the image of local authority housing by rebranding housing applicants as active consumers with more choice in the location and type of their house and building a sense of community by providing greater scope for 'extended families' to live near each other (Young and Lemos, 1997). In 1999 42% of tenants stated that they had 'no choice at all' when housed in the social housing sector (ODPM, 2005e). New Labour started to encourage 'choice-based' lettings in 2001 when it provided the finance to support 27 pilot schemes and set a target that all local authority areas would have adopted the approach by 2010. Rather than allocate particular

---

Box 9.4: Area effects

• People living in deprived areas are less likely to exit poverty than those living away from concentrations of deprivation.

• Living in deprived areas can help perpetuate worklessness as there are fewer employed contacts through which individuals can find work. Finding work through personal contacts is the most common route into employment.

• Educational attainment is affected by neighbourhood characteristics. Concentrations of deprivation in an area affect the mix of children in a school; children from low socioeconomic groups tend to benefit from a more mixed school intake.

• The likelihood of using drugs is raised by living in an area where they are more readily available. 65% of heroin users say friends are all users.

Source: Prime Minister's Strategy Unit (2005, p 35)

Box 9.5: The impact of concentrated poverty: evidence from the US

- Under the Gautreaux programme, established in Chicago in 1976, people could move from inner-city public housing projects to the suburbs supported by a housing allowance covering part of their housing costs. Rubinowitz and Rosenbaum (2001) examined the suburban movers' fortunes compared to those who stayed in the city. Of the suburban movers 75% were working compared to 41% of those who stayed in the city and 40% of the movers' children past the age of 17 were enrolled in a college compared to 24% of the city children.
- Studies of the housing voucher programme that helps families relocate from high-poverty areas to low-poverty areas (see Chapter Four) have demonstrated success in improving health, reductions in juvenile offending, improved educational achievement and higher rates of employment (Katz, 2004).
- A study by the US Department of Education found that poor students in schools with high numbers of poor students were at greater risk of lower achievement than poor students in schools with low numbers of poor students (Century Foundation Task Force on the Common School, 2002).
- Kling et al (2005), using data from a demonstration project that assigned housing vouchers by lottery to public housing tenants, found that allocation to lower poverty areas reduced arrests among female and male youth for violent crime but, in the case of males, problem behaviour and property crime increased in the long term.

dwellings via a points scheme, 'choice-based' lettings initiatives advertise vacancies and invite expressions of interest for properties from prospective tenants who are supplied with information on the popularity of particular types and locations of property. Rejecting an offer does not bring penalties as is sometimes the case in traditional allocation schemes. People with pressing housing problems such as those in temporary accommodation are often given priority by time-limited 'priority cards' or by a banding system. The scheme places emphasis on consumers choosing a home rather than on bureaucratic property allocation. A number of possible gains from 'choice-based' lettings were identified including the possibility that new groups of customers, who might not have considered social housing as an option because of its association with 'need', might be identified. This identification of new customer groups opens up the possibility to create more balanced communities.

Whereas an early evaluation of 'choice-based' lettings discovered an increase in demand in almost all the pilot areas and an increase in interest from working households in several pilots (ODPM, 2004e), as yet, there is no evidence of a positive impact on the creation of balanced communities. Indeed, Barnard and Pettigrew (2004, p 6) noted that 'the introduction of choice-based letting systems has not led applicants to be more willing to move to areas they considered 'rough' or unsafe', a finding that confirms other research findings (Atkinson and Kintrea, 2001).

The Market Renewal Fund

As described earlier, this fund enables local authorities to upgrade existing properties, demolish others and replace them with new dwellings. As Berube (2005, p 46) has stated, 'Though not acknowledged explicitly, the housing market renewal pathfinders have a unique chance to re-envision concentrations of poverty as more economically integrated communities'. More affluent people may move into the area to live in the new houses and existing inhabitants will not have to move out of the district to improve their housing circumstances. In 2005 the Chancellor announced a new initiative aimed specifically at creating balanced communities in existing council estates. He declared that 'overcoming ... 'area' effects will require the transformation of neighbourhoods from mono-tenure social housing estates into communities containing a much broader socio-economic mix of households' (HM Treasury, 2005a, p 147). Nine demonstration projects were established to discover how a mix of housing types and tenures could be achieved.

New balanced communities

Section 106 of the 1990 Town and Country Planning Act allows local authorities to insist that a proportion of affordable homes is supplied in any new development. Thus, as a condition of planning approval developers can be steered into creating balanced communities often via partnerships with housing associations. If enthusiastically implemented then, over time, areas will become more balanced in their social composition and reductions in the availability of affordable homes – generated by creating mixed communities in existing council estates – will be mitigated. However, few affordable homes have been provided by the section 106 mechanism (see Chapter Five) and the policy's impact has been modified by permission to provide the affordable housing 'off site' (Monk et al, 2005).

Some research evidence indicates that engineered attempts to promote balanced communities have achieved only modest success with little interaction between the market-price inhabitants and the affordable-housing residents (Jupp, 1999; Atkinson and Kintrea, 2001; Ruming et al, 2004). However, the 'balanced' estates scrutinised had little time to develop community spirit – the evaluation of the Gautreaux programme in the US revealed initial tensions that settled down over time. Moreover, in many neighbourhoods, the affordable housing was concentrated in a particular part of the development rather than intermingled with the 'market-price' housing. It also needs to be remembered that there may be very little interaction between people on exclusively market-price estates and that benefits may accrue from better performance in primary schools, the availability of amenities prompted by the general area affluence and by a reduction in stigma. The Scottish experience of 'gro grants', available to developers in the 1990s to supply quality homes in low-cost areas, indicates positive gains from more balanced communities such as the absence of 'postcode' discrimination (Minton, 2002). Allen et al (2005) examined the long-term impact of three purposely planned mixed tenure estates. These are rare in England and the researchers had difficulty in locating the three estates that formed the basis of their study. Although the limited social range of the people living in these mature estates, the amenity quality and the physical environment restricted the applicability of the researchers' findings they concluded that owners and renters occupied 'distinctive social worlds and opportunities for social interaction were limited – co-operation between neighbours tended to take place on practical rather than personal issues' (Allen et al, 2005, p 3). Nevertheless, there were strong cross-tenure friendships between children, a lack of social prejudice about tenure and the mixed tenure enabled young people and those who had experienced marital breakdown to stay in the area.

Antisocial behaviour

Tenure-related action

Surveys of housing managers and tenants on what makes certain areas 'difficult to let' and 'difficult to live in' have demonstrated a consensus on an important factor – the presence of antisocial behaviour in the area. As far back as 1974, a Housing Development Directorate survey (Wilson and Burbridge, 1978) revealed that what is now called antisocial behaviour was cited by managers and tenants as a cause of houses being hard to let more often than any other reason and, in 2001, tenant surveys (SEU, 2002b) revealed that the most important sources of dissatisfaction were the poor reputation of the area, crime and antisocial behaviour. A review of the research evidence concluded:

> Anti-social behaviour destroys quality of life and contributes to fear of crime. It can result in people not going out or stopping their children playing outside. For black and ethnic minority groups the impact of racially motivated attacks can be seen as an attack on the whole community.... The impact on deprived neighbourhoods is particularly profound, as anti-social behaviour can rapidly tip struggling neighbourhoods into decline. (SEU, 2002b, p 5)

The incidence of antisocial behaviour is unevenly distributed between different types of area with people living in council estates and low-income areas most likely to identify high levels of antisocial behaviour (see Table 9.2). If anti-social behaviour is equated with crime then there is a striking concentration in

Table 9.2: *Experience of antisocial behaviour by type of area: England and Wales: 2001/02 (%)*

Type of area	Noisy neighbours/ loud parties	Teenagers hanging around the streets	Rubbish/litter lying around	Vandalism/graffiti/deliberate damage to property	People attacked/harassed because of race/colour	People using/ dealing drugs	People drunk/ rowdy in public
Inner city	18	45	50	53	20	49	31
Urban	11	36	34	37	9	33	24
Rural	4	16	16	18	3	16	12
Council estate	16	48	47	52	12	47	29
Non-council estate	9	28	28	30	8	27	20

Source: Adapted from Home Office (2002)

its incidence. When areas are grouped into ten deciles according to crime rates, the areas with the highest rates of crime, when compared to the second highest decile, had victimisation rates 'four times higher for personal crime and twice the rate for property crime' (Burney, 2005, p 22). As would be expected, there is a strong association between perceptions of the extent of antisocial behaviour and the enjoyment of living in an area (Thorpe and Wood, 2004).

Local authorities have long held the power to evict a tenant involved in antisocial behaviour but this required the victims to give evidence in court, and judges, concerned with civil liberties, were reluctant to grant the necessary possession orders. The 1996 Housing Act extended the grounds for possession for nuisance or annoyance, stating that the perpetrator of antisocial behaviour could be a visitor to a household, and established that the antisocial behaviour could be in a locality as well as being directed to a specific household. It allowed evidence from observers not targeted by the perpetrator to supply the basis of an application for possession and created 'introductory' tenancies for council house tenants and 'starter' tenancies in the housing association sector lasting for 12 months. If at any time before this 12-month period ended the tenant misbehaved the social landlord could evict the tenant via simpler procedures than possible under a secure tenancy. The 1996 Housing Act also enhanced the powers of social landlords to use injunctions against antisocial tenants. A court injunction prohibits specified forms of behaviour and may be accompanied by powers of arrest for an injunction breach.

Anti-Social Behaviour Orders

The 1998 Crime and Disorder Act introduced the Anti-Social Behaviour Order (ASBO) allowing the police or the local authority to seek court civil orders to control the antisocial behaviour of anyone aged 10 or over if actual or threatened violence was involved. An ASBO prohibited action likely to lead to a criminal act and enforcement was to be by prosecution for the *criminal* offence of failure, without reasonable excuse, to comply with the order. Acceptable Behaviour Contracts were also introduced. These were voluntary agreements made between people involved in antisocial behaviour and the local police, the housing department, the registered social landlord, or the antisocial person's school. The 2003 Anti-Social Behaviour Act strengthened the powers of the police and local authorities to combat antisocial behaviour by removing the violence requirement – except when a power of arrest is attached to the ASBO – and permitting 'dispersal areas' where 'dispersal orders' could be made to move on, or remove back home, two or more people under 16 hanging around without supervision. It also gave registered social landlords the same powers as local authorities to prohibit antisocial behaviour and all social landlords obtained the power to demote tenancies to legal forms giving less security of tenure and removing the Right to Buy. Social housing landlords were required to publish a statement of their policies on antisocial behaviour by December 2004. Initially, it was proposed that the 2003 Anti-Social Behaviour Act should include a clause to withdraw Housing Benefit from antisocial tenants but this was not included in the legislation.

At first ASBOs were used sparingly but, by 2004, 3,826 orders had been issued and their use was gaining momentum. 42% of ASBOs had been breached and 55% of those who breached the orders received immediate custody on the first or later breach. Although ASBOs are controversial, with accusations that the government has created a mechanism to bypass civil liberties, the limited research on their effectiveness is optimistic. Campbell's review of their impact (2002, p 97) concluded:

> The overall opinion of ASBOs amongst those who have actually used them is generally positive…. It is widely accepted that, when used effectively, ASBOs are a useful tool to deal with anti-social behaviour and can deal effectively with particular groups, such as juveniles and private tenants. ASBOs were rarely described as difficult to obtain…. The outcomes of ASBOs were also regarded by the majority of those interviewed as positive, with a marked reduction in anti-social behaviour within the communities targeted and a perception that there had been a rise in the community's 'quality of life'.

Table 9.3: *Trends in antisocial behaviour: % of residents who thought an issue was a serious problem*

	1999/2000	2001/02	2002/03
Vandalism and hooliganism	8	11	12
Graffiti	4	6	6
Crime	12	15	15
Neighbours	3	3	4
Racial harassment	1	1	1

Source: Adapted from ODPM (2005e)

Although it is too early to evaluate the impact of ASBOs, as yet, they have had little impact on the overall incidence of antisocial behaviour (see Table 9.3).

Neighbourhood and structure

Low demand has many causes and, under New Labour, a remedy has been put in place for almost every cause. Sure Start, Health Action Zones, Excellence in Cities and so on are aimed at developing 'human' capital, New Deal for Communities fosters social capital, the Market Renewal Fund builds up physical capital, antisocial behaviour initiatives promote social order and the Neighbourhood Renewal Fund is aimed at coordinating these initiatives (and others) at the local level. The combined impact of all these initiatives needs to be considered in relationship to New Labour's declared objective that by 2021 no one should be seriously disadvantaged by where they live. Unfortunately there is a dearth of baseline neighbourhood information on which to assess the impact of the totality of New Labour's initiatives. Thus, in its review of the progress made by its initiatives, the government had to use a limited dataset based on local authority areas rather than on neighbourhoods (see Table 9.4).

One of the problems of New Labour's approach is that it consists of separate, centrally determined funding streams – over 70 area-based initiatives were identified by the Prime Minister's Strategy Unit (2005) – with little scope to transfer resources between each stream according to the priorities of local people.

In New Labour's programmes, neighbourhood as the cause of low demand has been emphasised to the relative neglect of the metropolitan area. Low-demand neighbourhoods require bridges to job opportunities across their potential 'travel to work' area by better public transport and improved access to informal and formal job networks that come from balanced communities (Lund, 1999; Fitzpatrick, 2004). The bigger picture of regional imbalances has also been underplayed in New Labour's response to low demand. As Lupton (2003, p 11) states, 'Critically all these programmes were local – not explicitly linked to broader local authority or regional regeneration strategies, and not

Table 9.4: *The gap between deprived areas and the England average: 1997–2003*

	Gap between deprived areas and England average[a]
Employment	−0.3
Teenage conceptions	−1.0
Female life expectancy	+0.1
Male life expectancy	+0.1
Vehicle crime	−1.3
Robberies	−0.1
Burglaries	−2.2
Key Stage 2: Level 4 Maths	−3.3
Key Stage 2: Level 4 English	−2.2
GCSEs	−1.8

Note: [a] – indicates a reduction, + an increase.

Source: Adapted from ODPM (2005j)

accompanied by any interventionalist regional economic policy which effectively finished in 1979 with the Conservatives abolition of regional economic planning boards'. New Labour has regarded London and its hinterland as a magnet attracting resources to the UK in a global economy and, as the ODPM Select Committee (2003, pp 22, 52) has claimed, the government has 'refused to constrain the growth of the South East' and 'has not yet sufficiently developed the links between its policies on regional economic growth and neighbourhood renewal'. The government has asserted that population growth in the South is due to internal factors and international migration, not the movement from the North, and has claimed that differences in economic growth within regions is as great as differences between regions. However, the impact of regional differences is significant, for example, the employment rate for young men with no qualifications living in council housing in the South East increased by 7% between 1993 and 2002 whereas it decreased by 7% in the northern conurbations (Faggio and Nickell, 2003).

Overview

- The labels attached to the problem now called low demand have changed since the 1970s as the focus in causal explanations has shifted from poor management, poor design and lack of tenant involvement towards economic change, 'unbalanced' communities and antisocial behaviour.
- There have been a number of policy initiatives since the 1970s to tackle the low-demand problem but, as yet, none have been sustained over the time-scale necessary to make a sustained impact and the problem of 'joining up' the initiatives at the local level remains.
- In the past, resident views of their problems and the structural economic and social factors influencing the incidence of low demand have been underplayed in policy initiatives.

Questions for discussion

(1) How have different social constructions of the low–demand problem influenced policy initiatives?

(2) What evidence is there to support the idea that it is worse to be poor in a poor area than in one that is socially mixed?

(3) Compare and contrast the Estate Action Initiative and New Deal for Communities.

(4) What is social capital?

Further reading

Lupton's (2003) *Poverty Street: The Dynamics of Neighbourhood Decline and Renewal* assesses the impact of government policies on the people living in 12 of the most disadvantaged areas in England and Wales.

Website resources

Many of the documents outlining New Labour's approach to neighbourhood renewal are online at the Social Exclusion Unit's website (www.socialexclusion.gov.uk).

The Joseph Rowntree Foundation's website (www.jrf.org.uk) contains the findings of a number of research projects on unpopular housing. Katz's (2004) interesting analysis of the situation in the US can also be found at this site as can Berube's (2005) analysis of Britain's approach to creating mixed-income communities.

The Audit Commission Housing Inspectorate Market Renewal Team acts as a 'critical friend' to, and scrutiniser of, market renewal pathfinders. Its website can be found at www.audit-commission.gov.uk

ten

Housing and social justice

Summary

- The ideas of social exclusion and social justice differ in that social exclusion refers to deficits in the human and social capital necessary to compete within the structures of a particular society whereas social justice is concerned with the fairness of these structures.
- There are long-established class relationships built into patterns of current access to housing that, in the past, have been mediated through tenure.
- Racial discrimination of various types has influenced the access of minority ethnic groups to good-quality housing.
- Gender differences in housing outcomes have reflected the dominance of the patriarchal family model.
- Disabled people have encountered barriers to independent living in integrated communities.

What is social justice?

Social justice is what philosophers call a 'contested' concept because there is no agreement about its meaning. At a basic level, social justice is concerned with the fairness of the processes involved in the distribution of goods and services within a particular society. There are two broad approaches to assessing the outcomes of these processes. Current time–slice theorists view the existing social product as a collective cake to be divided according to fair principles. In *A Theory of Justice*, John Rawls – 'arguably the most important political philosopher of the twentieth century' (Farrelly, 2004, p 3) – maintains that rational people, behind a 'veil of ignorance' about their future life chances, will agree to be part of a society so arranged that social and economic inequalities are permitted only if they are 'to the greatest benefit of the least advantaged' (Rawls, 1971, p 102). Thus, for Rawls, inequalities are just if they lead to an improvement in the position of the 'least advantaged' over and above what they would have obtained from an equal division of resources. In contrast, entitlement theorists examine the historical processes by which a particular social distribution has occurred. Robert Nozick, for example, argues that a social distribution is just if it came about by fair procedures, that is, by creation of an object, barter between free agents or as a gift. If people attain resources by these legitimate means they are entitled to keep them (Nozick, 1974) but, if resources have not been so acquired, reparations are necessary.

Social justice and social exclusion

The Commission on Social Justice, set up by John Smith when he was leader of the Labour Party, conceptualised social justice in terms of a hierarchy of four ideas:

> First, the belief that the foundation of a free society is the equal worth of all citizens, expressed most basically in political and civil liberties, equal rights before the law, and so on. Second, the argument that everyone is entitled, as a right of citizenship, to be able to meet their basic needs for income, shelter and other necessities.... Third, self-respect and equal citizenship demand more than the meeting of basic needs: they demand opportunities and life chances.... Finally, to achieve the first three conditions of justice, we must recognise that although not all inequalities are unjust (a qualified doctor should be paid more than a medical student), unjust inequalities should be reduced and where possible eliminated. (Commission on Social Justice, 1994, pp 17-18)

The second and third social justice dimensions identified by the Commission on Social Justice are related to what has come to be known as social exclusion – they are concerned with the distribution of the human and social capital necessary for an inclusive society based on equal opportunities to become unequal in a market economy. The finance to promote social inclusion can be supplied through collective resources without necessarily requiring the specific causal agents of an unequal society to pay for their past and current contributions to the exclusionary process. In contrast, social justice is about structured, unjust inequalities.

Why is social justice in housing important?

If the idea of social justice is used to identify what is problematic then differences in housing wealth, if unfairly structured through historical processes or if such inequalities cannot be justified as helping the least advantaged, are a social problem. Such inequality also exposes some people to greater risk of housing hardship than others and helps to perpetuate divisions in economic and social power that, through the impact of poor housing conditions on health and education, impairs the ability of some groups to compete in a market economy. In London, for example, a third of first-time buyers relied on relatives for help and, as Thomas and Dorling (2004, p 30) point out, high differentials in house prices and the impact of inheritance means that 'for the children of the poor there will be large parts of the country to which they cannot consider moving in the future even if they should wish to'.

Social class

Examining the relationship between social class and housing is complicated by different interpretations of the idea of class. Marx thought in terms of a two-class model: a bourgeoisie that owned the means of production and a proletariat without access to capital. In contrast, Max Weber (1864-1920) claimed that class referred to a market situation with a class existing when a number of people shared a specific causal component of their life chances represented exclusively by economic interests in the possession of goods and opportunities for income (Weber, 1924). In not designating *ownership* of the means of production as the decisive factor in social stratification, Weber opened the way to identifying a more differentiated stratification system. Weber's notion of class was widely adopted in the 1960s and became the basis for the compilation of the official statistics on the subject. Classification into five or six categories based on occupation became the norm and it was commonplace to find tables in housing textbooks linking housing conditions to class accompanied by commentaries based on the assumption that, because class was a determining force created by the structure of society, then any link between housing standards and class was unjustified. However, it is not sufficient to assume that the operations of the capitalist system – mediated through the housing system – are unfair. Such unfairness has to be demonstrated by exploring, on an historical basis, the ways in which the operations of the housing market have perpetuated unjustifiable inequalities. Thus this chapter is based on Nozick's notion of justice – it examines whether or not current housing outcomes have been created by historically fair procedures.

Tenure

The evidence (Daunton, 1983; Dennis, 1984) indicates that by the end of the 19th century the percentage of homeowners varied from 60% in some parts of South Wales to 5.9% in York, indicating that the owner-occupation/renting divide did not totally replicate social class divisions. The difference in tenure between the artisan elite and the middle class seems to have been as much a response to individual choice and local factors, support for self-help movements and industrial prosperity for example, as to differences in social class position.

By the late 1930s, tenure had acquired an identifiable relationship to class. Suburban homeownership was led by social classes I and II and the estates constructed by local authorities 'for the working class' became the residential areas for social classes III and IV although there is evidence that a significant section of the skilled working class were becoming homeowners (Speight, 2000). Private landlordism started to evolve into a residual domain of classes V and VI. In the post-war years local authority housing came to be occupied by skilled and semi-skilled workers. A metamorphosis in the class composition of the various housing tenures began in the 1950s, gathered momentum throughout the 1970s and snowballed in the 1980s. The composition of the owner-occupied sector diversified through the inclusion of more people from classes III and IV, whereas local authority estates became more the territory of classes V and VI and the economically inactive. Until its modest revival in the 1990s, private renting continued to decline, becoming the tenure of young, geographically mobile groups, and older people who continued to live in the house they had first settled in. Box 10.1 examines the implications of tenure divisions for social justice.

Box 10.1: Tenure and social justice

In 2004, 6.2 million people in England owned their property outright – an increase of 2 million since 1981 – and 8.3 million were still buying with a mortgage. Between 1945 and 2005, despite marked downturns in real terms in the mid-1970s and early 1990s, house prices increased at more than twice the rate of inflation. By 2003, households in England had 'positive' equity – house value minus mortgage – averaging £81,000 (Vass and Pannell, 2004). According to Thomas and Dorling (2004, p 10), between 1971 and 2002 housing wealth as a percentage of national wealth increased from 22.1% to 42% and, in 2002, was twice as high as the value of all life insurance and pension funds. The distribution of wealth is much more unequal than the distribution of income, having a Gini coefficient of 0.7 compared to 0.35 for income (Inland Revenue, 2005).

Homeownership involves a number of sacrifices. Most people with mortgages have been obliged to make a downpayment on their homes involving some reduction in living standards while the deposit is saved, in the early years mortgage repayments are high relative to earnings, and the mortgagee is responsible for maintenance. Homeowners are more prone to risk than in the past. Any sustained downturn in house prices or upturn in interest rates can have a marked impact on the finances of homeowners and there is little state protection against income reduction. Nevertheless, the historic gains from homeownership have been considerable and, in part, this yield has been created by the state rather than by the free market. The state planning system has restricted new house building thereby forcing up the price of existing dwellings. In the past tax relief on mortgage interest provided high subsidies to homeowners who have also been exempt from Capital Gains Tax. These tax concessions need to be set against the incidence of Inheritance Tax and Stamp Duty Tax.

It can be argued that the positive equity arising from real increases in house prices is illusionary; the capital gains made from house price increases above general inflation cannot be spent because, when a house is sold, the owner must buy a replacement property at the new, higher price. However, the capital gains from homeownership can be realised in four ways:

- use of the enhanced housing equity to raise income – in 2003, £60.8 billion was taken out of housing equity for consumption;
- sale of the house and then renting for the remainder of a life span;
- moving 'downmarket';
- inheritance, which provides the beneficiary with a home or a capital sum raised from the dwelling sale.

These avenues of gain have been modified in recent years by a reduction in the real threshold at which Inheritance Tax has to be paid and by the increased use of capital tests to determine eligibility for social care (the value of a house is taken into account in assessing residential and nursing home charges and this can result in the rapid erosion of housing wealth).

Long-term tenants cannot benefit from positive equity and hence the Right to Buy, with its discounts based on length of tenancy, had a justification in terms of historical justice. When considering restrictions on the Right to Buy, New Labour explored the possibility of helping tenants gain an equity stake in the value of their homes. This proposal was included in its 2001 Manifesto but an examination of potential schemes concluded that because equity shares in council housing would be expensive – up to £7 billion pounds over 30 years – therefore no scheme would be introduced (ODPM, 2003g). However, New Labour third-term proposals to extend homeownership contain modest equity sharing schemes.

The potential injustice of positive equity is not confined to tenure divisions. The diversity *within* homeownership means that the capital gain it produces depends on a number of variables: when the house was purchased, its location and the quality of the dwelling. Holmans and Frosztega (1994) demonstrated that wealth inheritance from residential property was more equally shared than wealth from other sources such as shares but still reinforced rather than reduced inequality. Saunders (1990) attempted to assess the overall impact of the capital gains derived from homeownership through a survey of homeowners in Burnley, Slough and Derby carried out in 1986. Using a three category division – service, intermediate and working class – he concluded that 'Whether we take the mean, the median, or the range, the service class comes out best, and the working class trails behind on all four measures of total gain....' (Saunders, 1990, p 172). Length of time as a homeowner (the middle class entered the tenure earlier than the working class), regional factors (in 2003, mean equity was £131,000 in Greater London compared to £49,000 in the North West) and the specific location of the home (most inner areas performing far less well than suburbia in terms of absolute gains) help to account for this relationship. Thomas and Dorling (2004, p 12) have calculated that, between 1983 and 2003, house prices increased 20-fold in the most expensive areas whereas in the least expensive areas prices barely doubled.

Land

The 1945 Labour Party Manifesto stated that 'Labour believes in land nationalisation and will work towards it' but, when in power, the Party concentrated on the taxation of development gain arising from planning permission. Labour made attempts to tax 'betterment' value – the difference between the land value with an existing use and its value with planning permission – in each of its periods of office. The last specific attempt was contained in the 1976 Development Land Tax Act, which imposed a tax of 80% on development gain after the first £160,000. Each Labour measure was repealed by a subsequent Conservative government and so the community has received meagre benefit from the substantial increases in the value of land with planning permission.

The pattern of landownership in the UK is opaque: the Land Registry – despite being in existence nearly 80 years – still records the ownership of only half of England's land. Cahill's extensive investigation into landownership has cast some light on the issue (Cahill, 2001). About 6,000 landowners – mainly aristocrats but including some large institutions and the Crown – own about two thirds of the land. As Ferdinand Mount (2004, p 290), former policy advisor to Margaret Thatcher, has commented, land release under the planning system 'is strongly reminiscent of the way De Beers keeps up the price of diamonds, by controlling the supply and releasing gems onto the market in carefully calculated batches so that the price is never in danger of collapse'. In 2002 land costs accounted for about 34% of the value of a new home and, according to Cahill, a high proportion of the land available for residential development is almost wholly owned by aristocrats who make substantial gains from land sales. Between 1983 and 2003 residential land prices in the UK increased by 808% (UK Land Directory, 2003). Recent figures on residential land values are set out in Table 10.1.

Table 10.1: *Residential land prices: 1994-2004*

	Weighted average valuation per hectare (£s) England	Mean density: units/ hectare England and Wales	Weighted average valuation per hectare (£s) London	Mean density: units/ hectare London
1994	731,168	23	1,912,127	41
1995	812,328	25	2,107,732	56
1996	816,828	25	2,104,519	51
1997	921,268	24	2,486,641	42
1998	1,098,965	25	3,059,363	48
1999	1,223,258	26	3,484,825	52
2000	1,514,824	26	4,244,864	55
2001	1,851,505	26	5,410,990	48
2002	2,184,531	27	6,827,319	55
2003	2,590,072	34	7,820,462	72
2004	3,097,773	38	8,138,131	70

Source: Adapted from ODPM (2005a); Department of Environment, Food and Rural Affairs (2005)

Gender

Gender inequality in housing is now part of the political and academic agenda but, in the 1960s, almost all discussions of housing assumed that the 'patriarchal family' was the household form to which policy should be directed. Gender differences in housing outcomes were *not* regarded as a social problem.

The term 'patriarchal family' was devised by a section of the feminism movement to conceptualise the relationships involved in the ideal family form, promoted in the 19th and 20th centuries as the 'natural' form of household structure. The patriarchal family consists of a male breadwinner regarded as the source of authority and a female carer who relies on the male to obtain the resources for her to perform a care and nurturing role in raising children and tending to her husband's physical and emotional needs. Many feminists argue that, rather than accepting this family form as society's basic building block, it is necessary to disaggregate its structure to assess its impact on the status and life chances of women. Such disaggregation is a difficult task. In the past the compilation of data seldom incorporated a gender dimension and, even today, the family is regarded as a private area in which relationships are negotiated on a voluntary basis. Thus, gender divisions in the consumption of housing, such as a study or workroom for many men but for few women, have received scant attention in the housing literature.

One way into the gender inequality and housing issue is to consider the position of women who form separate households. As Morris and Winn (1990, p 180) argue:

> ... it should be recognised that one in four households is headed by a woman and the housing opportunities of such households are also of crucial importance to women living in male headed households. Most women will go through stages in their lives when they either wish to, or are forced to, be part of a household where there is not a man present – such as younger single women, women experiencing relationship breakdown, and older women. The opportunities and constraints for all women are therefore indicated by the housing experiences of the 25% of households which, at any one point in time, are headed by a woman.

Single women

The 1975 Sex Discrimination Act made it illegal to discriminate against a person, directly and indirectly, on grounds of their sex and thereby helped to reduce such practices as refusing to accept a woman's salary as the basis for a mortgage because of her sex – direct discrimination – and mortgage providers insisting that only people who worked full time could be given a mortgage – indirect discrimination because it is more likely to have an adverse effect on women, who are more likely to work part time. In 2001 fewer single women than single men – 40% compared to 54% – were owner-occupiers, mainly because women receive lower pay than men and, as Gilroy and Woods (1994, p 34) have pointed out, 'the British form of home ownership with mortgages which bear down heavily in the early years, favours high or dual earners and therefore generally not women'.

Single women appear to have a lower homelessness risk than single men. A 1993 survey of single homeless people found that 'the great majority of single homeless people interviewed were men ... 23% of people in hostels and Bed and Breakfasts were women as were only 7% in day centres and 13% on soup runs (Anderson et al, 1993, p ix). However, the proportion of 'visible' female homeless single people is increasing (Jones, 1999) and Watson and Austerberry (1986) have argued that female homelessness is not less common than male homelessness, it is simply less conspicuous. Women are more likely to experience homelessness in private – sleeping on a friend's floor for example – than in public. They will strive to avoid becoming street homeless due to the attendant risks of rape, harassment and violence.

Lone parents

Nine out of 10 lone-parent families are headed by a woman. The housing circumstances of lone parents compared to other families are set out in Table 10.2. Half of lone mothers with dependent children live in the social housing sector – the outcome of a number of factors.

A job is one route out of the restricted housing choices that result from low income. In 2002 only 50% of lone parents were in work – a consequence of the spatial segregation of lone parenthood in metropolitan areas where good jobs are relatively scarce, lone parents' relative lack of marketable skills and affordable childcare shortages. Even when in work lone mothers are likely to have a low income, which, in part, explains why only 50% of lone parents have jobs. There is still a gender gap of 19% between the hourly rates of pay of men and women, which means, for example, that some lone mothers, even when they manage to remain in the matrimonial home, cannot afford the mortgage repayments. In 2001, 42% of lone fathers compared to 25% of lone mothers were buying a home with a mortgage.

Losing a home because of domestic violence is a further reason why lone parents are more likely to be found in the social housing sector. There are a number of procedures available to enable the victim of domestic violence to remain in her home and to remove the perpetrator but these can be difficult to enforce. Thus the most viable option for many women needing to escape from domestic violence is to seek temporary accommodation through the homelessness legislation with a view to securing permanent housing in the social housing sector.

Table 10.2: *Lone-parent families: housing profile*

	Lone-parent families (%)	Other families (%)
Tenure		
Owner-occupied	33	79
'Social' housing	51	14
Private rented	15	7
Type of accommodation		
Detached house	8	28
Semi-detached house	30	37
Terraced house	40	28
Flat or maisonette	22	7
Bedroom standard		
One or more below	9	4

Source: National Statistics Online (2005)

Women, housing design and planning

Some feminists have explored the implications of the male dominance of architecture and planning for the everyday lives of women. Roberts (1991) notes the low level of female representation on the committees that determined the design of working-class housing (the Tudor Walters Committee 1918; the Central Housing Advisory Committee, 1944), and the ways that patriarchal family forms have been reflected in housing layouts such as the absence of adequate space in which children can play and the reluctance to include labour-saving amenities in working-class housing. However, attempts to change the basic patterns of domestic living have not been successful. Colonies, established by Robert Owen between 1821 and 1845, based on cooking rotas and communal nurseries, were short-lived, although this may have been due to the rigid gender labour division that was practised in the colonies: domestic labour was collectivised but not divided equally between men and women. Unwin and Parker, two pioneers of the Garden City, included communal kitchens in two areas of Letchworth, but proposals to include such facilities in working-class estates when investigated by the Women's Sub-Committee of the Tudor Walters Committee found limited support from women. The available evidence suggests that the homes built by speculative developers in the period between the wars with their parlours, gardens and provision for the installation of labour-saving devices according to personal preference – were what women wanted. Greed (1994) draws attention to the ways in which the needs of women have been ignored by the planning system. The reluctance to build houses with parlours in the local authority sector has deprived women of the opportunity for private space away from the family. Women's personal safety has been neglected in the decisions made about public space, and the zoning of areas for different purposes (for example residential/industrial) has emphasised the division between work and home and thereby created inconvenience for many women, especially those without access to a car.

Ethnicity

Ethnicity refers to the characteristics that connect a particular group or groups of people to each other. It is self-perceived and people can belong to more than one ethnic group. Thus an ethnic group is a social group whose members have the following characteristics:

• they share a sense of common origins;
• they identify with a common and distinctive history and destiny;
• they feel a sense of unique collective solidarity.

Although 'race' is sometimes used as a surrogate for ethnicity it is usually used to refer to people who are believed to belong to the same genetic stock.

However, since most biologists doubt that there are important genetic differences between 'races' of human beings, in this chapter 'race' will be interpreted as a socially constucted term.

Explanations of ethnic differences in housing outcomes

Box 10.2 examines the relationship between ethnicity and homelessness and Table 10.3 sets out some of the statistical evidence on differences in housing outcomes according to ethnicity. In explaining these outcomes many social commentators have used the concept of 'racist discrimination', defined by the United Nations in 1965 as:

> any distinction, exclusion, restriction or preference based on race, colour, descent, or national or ethnic origin which has the purpose or effect of nullifying or impairing the recognition, enjoyment or exercise, on an equal footing, of human rights and fundamental freedoms in the political, economic, social, cultural or any other field of public life. (Office of the High Commission for Human Rights, 2004, Part 1, Article 1)

Ginsburg (1992), although careful to point out the interactions between the categories, makes a useful distinction between subjective racism, institutional racism and structural racism. Although the importance of these forms of racism in determining housing outcomes may be diminishing, housing circumstances change slowly so past discrimination affects current outcomes.

Box 10.2: Ethnicity and homelessness

The relationship between ethnicity and homelessness – the extreme manifestation of the difficulty in accessing decent housing – illustrates the multiple, interacting factors involved in producing housing outcomes.

People of minority ethnic backgrounds are about three times more likely to become statutory homeless than the white majority (Gervais and Rehman, 2005) and this disparity may be an underestimate because there is evidence to suggest that minority ethnic groups may be less likely to contact their local authority for help. Although part of the recorded difference can be explained by settlement patterns – proportionately more people from minority ethnic groups live in London where homelessness is higher – in all regions minority ethnic groups are more likely to become homeless. This is a reflection of the social exclusion and discrimination experienced by minority ethnic groups, which limits the opportunity to avoid homelessness.

Factors such as pregnancy involving family disputes, relationship breakdown sometimes connected to domestic violence, overcrowding, and having to leave private rented accommodation, that is, the common causes of homelessness across all ethnicities affect the range of ethnic communities in different ways. With regard to South Asian and Black Caribbean communities, Gervais and Rehman (2005, p 6) summarise these differences as:

- Among South Asians, domestic violence, forced marriages and family disputes were the main causes of homelessness among single female-headed households. The most common cause of homelessness amongst South Asian couples with children was being forced by private landlords to leave their accommodation. Overcrowding was a common housing need; many South Asian households lived in large three-generational households before becoming homeless.
- Among Black Caribbeans, many young, single women became homeless when pregnancy led to family disputes, overcrowding and family and friends were no longer able to accommodate them. Homelessness due to multiple and complex problems related to child abuse, time in care, drug abuse, school exclusion, crime and mental health problems was also present. Other less common causes included being forced to leave private rented accommodation, domestic violence, and financial difficulties leading to rent arrears.

Subjective racism

Applied to housing, subjective racism refers to overt racial prejudice and discrimination by individual landlords, estate agents, homeowners and tenants. It can take a variety of forms such as racially motivated attacks, harassment, the steering of minorities to certain geographical areas and the refusal to sell or rent a property to a member of a particular ethnic group. Subjective racism by landlords and estate agents was investigated by Daniel (1968) who arranged for three testers, one English, one West Indian and one Hungarian to apply for rented accommodation or buy a house. Discrimination was found in 60% of the tests, a finding which was influential in the passing of the 1968 Race Relations Act outlawing discrimination in employment and housing. A replication of the tests in 1973 found that discrimination had been reduced to 12% in the sales sector and 27% in the private landlord sector (Riach and Rich, 2002). There was some use of these types of discrimination test in the late 1980s as part of formal investigations by the Commission for Racial Equality (CRE). Evidence of 'steering' – estate agents directing minority ethnic groups to particular areas, a practice common in the 1970s – was identified. In 1990 the CRE examined the practices of accommodation agencies, landlords and landladies, small hotels and guest houses. Testers differing only in their ethnic origin visited agencies asking for details of accommodation, and testers

Table 10.3: *Ethnicity and housing outcomes*

	White	African Caribbean	Indian	Bangladeshi	Pakistani
% owner-occupiers (2001)	74	50	82	39	73
% renting from a private landlord (2001)	9	7	10	10	12
% renting from a local authority (2001)	12	26	5	34	9
% renting from a registered social landlord (2001)	5	16	3	16	6
% of overcrowding (one or more rooms below bedroom standard: 2000-03 combined)	1.7	6.8	8.8	30.5	21.2
% below 'decent' standard (2001)	31.9	35.6	44.5	44.5	44.5
Without central heating – % of children (2001)	5.6	4.6	4.4	8.7	18.5
One or more rooms below occupancy standard – % of children (2001)	8.5	29.9	35.5	56.6	36
Does not have sole use of bath/shower and toilet – % of children (2001)	0.14	0.5	0.4	0.72	0.79
% with flat or maisonette (2001)	12	48	14	38	36
Statutory homeless (% of total, 2001)	68	9	6	6	6
% of total population (England and Wales, 2001)	94.8	1.1	2	0.6	1.4
% slightly dissatisfied or very dissatisfied with the area in which they live (2001)	9	13	8	13	20
% saying services were bad (crime, 2001)	33	41	39	55	52
% dissatisfied with their home (1996)	10.7	19.1	33.2	41.7	41.7
% who wish to move (1996)	4.8	51.8	45.5	52.1	52.1

Note: Where the figure given for Bangladeshi, Indian and Pakistani households is the same this is because separate figures are not available for each community.

Sources: Adapted from ODPM (2004i, 2005e); ONS (2004b, 2004c); Reynolds et al (2004)

with pronounced African Caribbean or Asian accents telephoned to request details of a property and, if told none was available, a white tester telephoned 10 minutes later. They found that 20.5% of accommodation agencies, 5.5% of landlords and 5% of small hotels and guest houses discriminated against minority ethnic groups (CRE, 1990). There have been no such investigations for many years, hopefully a sign that such practices have been eliminated.

Racially motivated crime is an important factor in restricting housing opportunities because fear of crime restricts the choices available in where to live. The British Crime Survey of 2001/02 (Home Office, 2002) revealed that the following were fairly or very worried about racially motivated assaults:

- 60% of Asian respondents;
- 51% of black respondents;
- 12% of white respondents.

Women were particularly concerned. About four in ten Asian women and a third of black women were 'very' worried about racial attacks.

Institutional racism

Institutional racism has been defined by the Stephen Lawrence Inquiry (Macpherson, 1999, para 6.34) as:

> The collective failure of an organization to provide an appropriate and professional service to people because of their colour, culture or ethnic origin. It can be seen or detected in processes, attitudes and behaviour which amount to discrimination through unwitting prejudice, ignorance, thoughtlessness and racist stereotyping which disadvantage Black and Minority Ethnic people.

The 1976 Race Relations Act extended the anti-discrimination legislation of the 1960s. Under the Act it became unlawful to discriminate, both directly and indirectly, on racial grounds. Racial grounds were defined as those of 'race, colour, nationality and ethnic or national origins' but did not include religion. Direct discrimination was defined as treating a person less favourably than another on the grounds of race and included segregation on racial grounds. Indirect racial discrimination was defined as applying a condition such that the proportion of persons of the victim's racial group who could comply with it was considerably smaller than the proportion of persons not of that group who could comply. The condition had to be to the detriment of the victim and the discriminator had to fail to demonstrate that the practice was justifiable irrespective of race, colour, nationality or the ethnic or national origins of the person to whom it applied. Individuals who believed they were victims of discrimination could bring civil proceedings against the alleged discriminator through the courts. In addition, the CRE acquired the power to instigate a formal investigation into an organisation in which it had a reasonable belief that discriminatory procedures was being practised. On completion of the formal investigation the CRE was obliged to prepare a report on its findings and, if it concluded that an act of unlawful discrimination had been committed, it could issue a non-discrimination notice. This notice could require the organisation to change its practices and gave the CRE the power to monitor these changes over a period of time. If an organisation did not comply with the terms of a confirmed notice then the Commission could start proceedings to obtain an injunction prohibiting the respondent from continuing to breach the terms of the notice.

The idea of indirect discrimination, incorporated into the 1976 Race Relations Act, prompted a number of academic studies and CRE investigations into the practices of social landlords. The main findings of these investigations were that the formal and, more significantly, the informal processes involved in the allocation of council houses and the activities of estate agents discriminated against minority ethnic groups. These findings formed the basis of two codes of practice covering rented and owner-occupied housing published by the CRE in the early 1990s, giving examples of direct and indirect discrimination (CRE, 1991, 1992). The codes were updated in 2005. The 2000 Race Relations (Amendment) Act placed a duty on public authorities to promote equal opportunities and good race relations and gave the CRE the power to issue compliance notices.

Structural racism

This refers to the overall context of housing policy set by the government that results in racial inequality. Although academics and the CRE have concentrated their attention on local authorities, 'national legislation has been influential in determining the location and quality of black peoples' housing opportunities....' (Smith, 1989, p 49). There are a number of examples of what might be called 'structural racism':

- The Right to Buy has resulted in many of the most desirable council homes being sold on those estates 'populated mostly by white working-class households who benefited from the racialised allocation policies of previous decades' (Ginsburg, 1992, p 121).
- Central government cutbacks in the allocation of borrowing approvals to local authorities in the 1980s and 1990s prevented them from meeting the housing needs of minority ethnic groups. A stark example of this relates to the system of means-tested mandatory improvement grants set up in 1989. People from minority ethnic groups tend to have low incomes and to live in dwellings requiring major repairs to bring them up to the fitness standard (see Table 10.3 and Table 10.4). Financial allocations to local government to

meet the demand for grants were below the amount necessary, declining from £317 million in 1990 to £232 million in 1997 (Wilcox, 2004, p 109) and, because need as a resource distribution principle from central to local government was partially replaced by performance criteria, the resources were not distributed to the areas with the highest unfitness rates.

Choice and housing outcomes

The specific patterns of settlement of minority ethnic groups in the UK are the product of factors such as employment opportunities, income, various forms of racism and the choices made by members of minority ethnic communities. Initial migration was influenced by the community networks in the country of origin with kinship and local affiliations affecting the places where people settled in the UK. Thus, for example, the 1962 'voucher system', whereby employers in the UK could apply for vouchers to admit workers for specific jobs, gave the opportunity for those who were already in Britain to arrange jobs and vouchers for their relatives and friends. Over time the pull of identity and the push of constraints created areas where many members of minority ethnic groups felt secure, at ease, at home and hence reluctant to leave. Research by MORI on behalf of the CRE (2002) found that 57% of people belonging to minority ethnic groups, compared to 45% of the 'general public', identified with their local area and a study of the Asian communities in Rochdale concluded that the most important features of a neighbourhood were easy access to the town, security of living in the area, the presence of family in the area and the proximity of the mosque (Habeebullah and Slater, 1990). Bowes et al (2002) in an examination of differentiation in the housing careers of Pakistanis in the UK noted a similar tendency to prefer the familiar but there was a minority of households who actively preferred not to live in a 'Pakistani area'. This differentiation of preferences *within* minority ethnic categories also had gender, class and locality dimensions.

In recent years Britain seems to have become a more ethnically spatially integrated society but only modestly so. Based on an analysis of Census statistics for 1991 and 2001 Simpson concluded that the number of 'mixed' electoral wards (more than one tenth White population and more than one tenth Black and Asian population) had increased from 964 to 1070 and that 'what the census counts as Non-white residents are on balance leaving inner cities rather than moving to them' (Simpson, 2005, p 1). As Phillips (2005, p 30) has remarked, 'increasing numbers of young middle class people from all ethnic minority groups, but particularly those of Indian origin, are pursuing suburban ideals of good housing, spacious and low crime neighbourhoods, and access to good schools'.

Explaining diversity in housing outcomes

Examination of the statistics on ethnicity and housing given in Table 10.3 demonstrates considerable diversity in housing outcomes between different minority groups. This diversity has led some authors to conclude that:

> ... the operation of racism, elaborated in its subjective, institutional and structural forms, provides an 'easy' explanation for the development and persistence of racial inequality. The development of a more complex and holistic account of racial inequalities in the housing market must also address a range of other factors.... (Law et al, 1999, p 142)

Given that 80% of the UK housing stock is distributed by market forces, that is, according to the ability to pay, then explaining this diversity involves examining the market position of minority ethnic groups. Table 10.4 sets out some of the economic and related educational variables that may influence the housing circumstances of minority ethnic groups.

The initial settlement patterns of minority ethnic groups were determined by the availability of jobs and accommodation and their homes became concentrated in the inner areas of towns and cities in London, the Midlands, the North West and parts of Yorkshire. The economic decline of these inner areas had started before the newcomers arrived (which partially accounts for the pattern of initial settlement) but structural change in the economy accelerated the decline during the 1970s, 1980s and 1990s. Since 1977 these inner areas have been subject to a large variety of social and economic initiatives but such policies have had only a marginal impact on the economic and the associated housing problems of inner areas. Thus, although there are variations in the unemployment and wages rates of different minority ethnic groups according to locality (Bowes et al, 2002), a disproportionate number of people from minority ethnic groups remain in areas with limited employment opportunities and where pay rates are low. Moreover, a significant percentage of the people who have managed to become homeowners have only modest levels of equity in their property, which places constraints on their ability to move within the owner-occupied sector (Smith, 1989).

Disability

In the 1970s a paradigm of social justice, linked to the idea of social construction (see Chapter One), began to emerge that stressed 'identity' politics. It argued that social justice was not just a matter of command over resources but was also related to 'disrespect' towards a person's authenticity. It emphasised the importance of including marginalised groups in the process of decision making in order to strengthen 'recognition' of their identity (Young, 1990). Although

Table 10.4: *Ethnicity: social and economic circumstances*

	White	Afro-Caribbean	Indian	Bangladeshi	Pakistani
% of households on a low income after housing costs (2000/01)	21	31	30	68	68
Index of segregation[a] (1991)	4	62	57	61	61
Index of segregation (2001)	5	62	55	61	61
% living in most deprived wards	29[b]	44	22	54	51
Economic activity rate (men)	83	78	79	69	72
Economic activity rate (women)	74	72	62	22	29
Unemployment rate (men)	5	14	7	20	16
Unemployment rate (women)	4	9	7	24	16
Average hourly pay – men (1999-2002) (£s)	10.63	9.88	11.16	7.61	7.61
Average hourly pay – women (1999-2002) (£s)	8.21	8.72	8.09	5.90	5.90
Proportion of boys achieving 5 or more GCSEs/GNVQs A* to C (2002)	47	23	58	40	33
Proportion of girls achieving 5 or more GCSEs/GNVQs A* to C (2002)	57	48	70	50	47

Notes:

[a] The percentage of people who would need to move their residence for the spatial distribution to be evenly spread.

[b] All households.

Sources: Adapted from: Cabinet Office (2003); Mason (2003); Department of Trade and Industry Women and Equality Unit (2004); Dorling and Thomas (2004); ONS (2004b, 2004c)

'identity politics' is pertinent to the issues of ethnicity and gender in this chapter it will be elaborated with reference to disability.

What is disability?

Historically disability has been equated with impairment, that is, the condition of being unable to perform specified tasks as a consequence of physical or mental unfitness. This definition is related to the medical model of disability characterised by:

- a focus on the individual, specifically on the body;
- reliance on a strong notion of normality as being able-bodied;
- an emphasis on rehabilitation to ensure the disabled person is as 'normal' as possible;
- the medical profession as the 'expert' on impairment and hence on disability.

On the medical definition of disability there are 6.7 million people of working age who have a physical, sensory or mental impairment that seriously affects their day-to-day activities.

In the 1970s a different definition of disability emerged that made a distinction between 'impairment' and 'disability', with disability meaning 'the disadvantage or restriction caused by contemporary social organisation which takes no or little account of people who have physical impairments and thus excludes them from the mainstream of social activities' (Union of the Physically Impaired Against Segregation, quoted in Oliver and Barnes, 1998, p 17). This notion of disability as the consequence of a disabling process was embodied in a 'social' model that regarded disability as a set of challenges faced by people whose requirements have not been accommodated by the dominant culture. The social model generated two approaches to the disability and housing issue. 'Independent living' tended to stress the availability of cash benefits to enable disabled people to make choices about where they lived and the nature of their personal assistance whereas 'integrated living' emphasised the collective involvement of disabled people in making choices about the overall pattern of accommodation.

The pattern of housing provision for disabled people

For most of the 20th century the pattern of housing provision for disabled people was influenced by the medical model and the idea that disability was a personal tragedy to be mitigated by raising money to reduce the 'suffering' of 'the disabled'. Disabled people were hidden at home or lodged in state or voluntary sector institutions. The advent of a community care policy in the 1960s started to shift this residence pattern but, under the tutelage of the medical model, the accommodation was often supplied in 'clustered' or 'group' units. This spatial exclusion of disabled people was compounded by the tendency to provide adapted property on council estates. From the 1970s the accommodation necessary for 'community care' evolved under a number of different capital and revenue funding streams involving social services departments, health authorities, housing departments and housing associations. These income sources were often supplemented by Housing Benefit used to meet the revenue costs of providing housing-related support. In 2003 an attempt was made to bring some order into the funding of accommodation for disabled people. The current system is outlined in Box 10.3.

Despite the progress made in providing more integrated housing for disabled people, with more support 'floating' to the person rather than the person being moved to the available support, a number of problems remain.

Box 10.3: Housing and disabled people

Lifetime homes

In the early 1990s the Joseph Rowntree Foundation developed the concept of lifetime homes, with 16 design features chosen to ensure that a new house will meet the requirements of a lifetime and, in so doing, meet the requirements of people with temporary or permanent disabilities. If all new homes were built to this standard then, over time, disabled people would not have to move to secure suitable accommodation and they would find it easier to visit friends and relatives. In 1999 new building regulations were introduced covering the accessibility requirements of lifetime homes, and the Housing Corporation's development standards incorporate other lifetime homes criteria.

Disabled Facilities Grant

This is a mandatory grant, that is, it must be awarded if the relevant criteria of being 'necessary', 'appropriate', 'reasonable' and 'practicable' are met. It is paid for essential adaptations to allow disabled people better freedom of movement into and around their homes and to access the essential facilities within it. When necessary it can also provide the essential facilities themselves. Until December 2005 it was means tested but, in response to criticism that the means test excluded 'some people in great need' and that the £25,000 maximum payment was 'not sufficient in most areas to provide an extension' (Heywood et al, 2005, p 6), the means test – but not the grant limit – was abolished.

Supporting People

Over the years social housing providers identified a requirement to provide support for some of their tenants in addition to the normal landlord role of repairs and rent collection: help from wardens in sheltered accommodation is an example. However, funding for housing-related support evolved piecemeal in the 1980s and, by 1998, the nine different funding streams available had produced a pattern of service provision that was 'seen to be uncoordinated, unrelated to local priorities and frequently provider and funding driven' (Foord and Simic, 2005, p 7). In 1998 the government announced that the existing funding schemes for housing-related support would be amalgamated into a single stream, to be known as Supporting People, and would be allocated to local authorities for distribution to a range of suppliers of housing-related support. Supporting People would cover a range of circumstances including physical disability, homelessness, alcohol and drug dependency, mental illness, learning disability and old age.

Supporting People went live in April 2003 at a cost of £1.8 billion compared to the original estimate of £700 million. An immediate independent review of the scheme was ordered by the government (Sullivan, 2004). This found that 'floating support', that is, taking help to a person's home rather than supplying the assistance in a special residential facility – a form of provision in accordance with independent and integrated living – had developed but not to the extent anticipated. Moreover there was evidence of 'cost-shunting' from social services and health budgets into the new scheme: it had always been difficult to make distinctions between 'treatment' (provided by the National Health Service), 'care' (provided by social services departments) and 'support' (supplied by social landlords). In response to the review, the government announced that, in future, resources for Supporting People would be distributed according to a needs-based formula and that the total funding available would be reduced.

- Households with a disabled child experience far greater difficulties with their housing than households with non-disabled children. 90% of families with a disabled child have at least one housing problem and many have multiple difficulties (Beresford and Oldham, 2002).
- There are no routine procedures in place for measuring the requirements of disabled people or the suitability of existing provision that could be used to plan future supply (Housing Corporation, 2002). Thus, for example, there is no reliable information on the requirements for housing for wheelchair users (Harris et al, 1997). The review of Supporting People (Sullivan, 2004) revealed large unexplainable variations in the level of support in different areas with 80% of provision led by the supplier rather than the commissioner.
- More than 8,000 young adults are living in care homes designed primarily for a different client group, usually elderly people (John Grooms Housing Association, 2004).
- Services take-up is poor among black and minority ethnic disabled people (Housing Corporation, 2002).
- Suitable accommodation for disabled people is concentrated in the social sector with only 2% of owner-occupied houses having an even threshold, level access, a bathroom/WC at entrance level and a 750 millimetre doorway

opening compared to 7% of local authority dwellings and 12% of housing association properties (ODPM, 2005c, para 3.7).

- 'There is a grave shortage of housing stock suitable for re-housing.... For families a wait of three years or more would be likely in 70% of all authorities' (Heywood et al, 2005, p 6).
- Only a third of working-age wheelchair users, compared to 70% of the equivalent household heads, are homeowners.

Overview

- Social justice is about the whether or not the distribution of the goods and services within a particular political entity is equitable. The idea has also been linked to the respect given to different members of the community.
- Class as a dimension of inequality has been mediated by tenure divisions, landownership and the way the planning system has operated.
- Gender differences in housing outcomes have been influenced by the dominance of the patriarchal family form.
- Discrimination in the housing system, choice, location factors and economic variables have influenced ethnic variations in housing outcomes.
- The housing choices of disabled people have been affected by the dominance of the medical model of disability.

Questions for discussion

(1) What is the difference between social justice and social exclusion?

(2) How has social class influenced access to good-quality housing?

(3) Distinguish between subjective, institutional and structural racism and give examples of the operation of each form of racism in access to housing.

(4) What have been the major objections of the disabled persons' movement to the dominant form and location of the housing provision made for disabled people?

(5) What evidence is there to support the contention that gender inequality is reflected in access to good-quality accommodation?

Further reading

The relationship between class and housing outcomes is explained in *Housing and Social Inequality* by **Morris and Winn (1990)**. A good exposition of the operations of various forms of racism in the housing system can be found in **Smith's (1989)** *The Politics of 'Race' and Residence*. *Housing Women*, edited by **Gilroy and Woods (1994)**, supplies a sound account of gender inequalities in access to housing.

Harrison et al (2005) *Housing, 'Race' and Community Cohesion*, provides an overview of the relationship between housing and ethnicity.

Website resources

A comprehensive bibliography on women and housing can be found at www.nottingham.ac.uk/sbe/planbiblios/bibs/local/LP05.html

The Commission for Racial Equality has a section on 'Housing and Local Government' at its website (www.cre.gov.uk).

A number of research findings about disabled people and housing can be found at the website of the Joseph Rowntree Foundation (www.jrf.org.uk).

eleven

Conclusion: the future of housing policy

Housing supply is capital intensive and countries build up their housing stock incrementally. Given the need to replace the built environment in new locations during the industrial revolution, the continued population growth and household formation throughout the 20th century, the loss of 10 years' house production during two total wars and the destruction of homes in the Second World War, it is understandable why housing was *the* political issue in 1945. Politicians responded in terms of numbers, their objective being to put people into new or refurbished houses as quickly as possible by subsidising production and consumption. During the 1945 election campaign Labour promised 'Five million houses in quick time' and Harold Macmillan, Housing Minister in the early 1950s, remembered that the monthly housing figures provided 'a scorecard on which the eyes of all the critics, friendly and hostile' were focused (Timmins, 2001, pp 141, 182). Dame Evelyn Sharp, the senior civil servant responsible for housing in the 1960s, noted that 'for successive Ministers the number of houses built each year has been the critical test' (Sharp, 1969, p 69).

During the late 1970s housing policy started to become more selective and targeted – less concerned with increasing supply and directed more to specific housing problems and highly selective consumer subsidies to protect the poorest from the housing market's most extreme outcomes. A number of factors produced this policy shift: the gradual abatement of the national housing shortage; the New Right emphasis on market forces; the recognition that choice was becoming more important to the electorate; and the Labour Party's gradual abandonment of steeply progressive taxation plus general state support for life's essentials as Labour's route to a more just society.

Although New Labour's 'big idea' is difficult to identify, the closest synopsis of its core ideas is contained in the expression 'The Third Way'. Third Way politics accepts – even welcomes – global market forces based on individual choice as the primary resource distributor but, as Bill Clinton, a Third Way advocate, has stated, it wants to use state power to foster 'opportunity, community and responsibility' (Clinton, 1996, p 3).

Consumerism

Phillip Gould, one of Tony Blair's spin doctors in the 1997 General Election, noted that 'The old working class was becoming a new middle class: aspiring, consuming, choosing what was best for themselves and their families. They had outgrown crude collectivism and left it behind in the supermarket car-park' (Gould, 1998, p 4). Consumerism has played an increasingly important role in New Labour's housing policies. Choice-based lettings and paying Housing Benefit directly to tenants have explicit consumerist rationales whereas stock transfer to housing associations can be interpreted as an attempt to promote consumerism by allowing more opportunity to 'exit' between competing rented accommodation suppliers. Homeownership has a central place in this consumerist approach. When used as a noun, 'housing' is commensurate with 'home' and therefore it can be argued that homeownership is the most direct way to foster the secure enjoyment of a lifestyle choice. Moreover there is some evidence, mainly from the US (Maxwell, 2005) and not necessarily applicable to the UK, that owner-occupation also encourages people to become more involved in their local community, promotes educational attainment and leads to more personal investment in a dwelling.

In preparing its 2005 Manifesto there were indications that New Labour intended to pursue a more proactive homeownership policy by granting housing association tenants the Right to Buy on the same terms as council tenants (Weaver, 2004). Resistance to this proposal from Cabinet members more associated with 'Old' Labour led to its dilution to become a revamped Homebuy scheme (see Chapter Five). Rather than grant housing association tenants a Right to Buy, the Chancellor and the Deputy Prime Minister, noting that 90% of people wish to be homeowners, have put their faith in steering the housing market towards higher production as the principal means to create a million new homeowners by 2010 (HM Treasury and ODPM, 2005). The Chancellor of the Exchequer's Pre-budget Report set a target of 200,000 new houses per year – 25% more than the 2004/05 total (HM Treasury, 2005b). This target was based on the implications for affordability of the current anticipated house construction level compared to the new target. The projections showed an improvement in the proportion of typical house-buying couples aged 30-34 able to afford homeownership if housing supply increased to an average of 200,000 per year by 2016 (ODPM, 2005k) However, despite the fall in the annual output of new social housing in England from 30,983 in 1995/96 to 16,737 in 2004/05, no projections were made on the requirements for social housing up to 2016. Such an exercise was postponed until the Chancellor's 2007 Comprehensive Spending Review.

Steering the market

Between 1979 and 1997 the Conservative Party applied market forces to housing supply and distribution but retained a planning system that restricted land supply and hence new house building. In its first term of office, New Labour merely tweaked Conservative policies but mounting evidence that the housing situation was deteriorating led to a more proactive attempt to steer the housing market. Although steering the housing market seems at odds with Third Way politics, direct state intervention in the housing market can be justified if one accepts that, in the past, the physical planning system has placed limitations on the market's capacity to respond to demand. As Ed Balls, former Chief Economic Advisor to the Treasury, has noted, housing, unlike any other privately supplied good, is controlled and regulated by the local democratic process (Balls et al, 2004) and hence there is no automatic relationship between demand and supply.

Influencing the housing market's course requires an understanding of its operations. The Barker Review (2004) was a valuable contribution to understanding how the national housing market works, demonstrating how the planning system and other factors have placed constraints on the market's response to changes in demand. However, spatial variations in demand/supply balance mean that, if possible, a more sophisticated understanding of regional and local markets is required. The proposal to merge Regional Housing Boards with Regional Planning Bodies, the setting up of a national advice unit to provide demographic and economic information and the creation of the housing market renewal pathfinders whose spheres of influence cut across local authority boundaries indicate that the machinery required to secure a firmer grasp of market drivers is being established. Nevertheless, even if it is possible to understand the ways that complex markets operate, steering the market will require more than understanding. In the absence of negative controls on job location – still regarded by New Labour as going against the grain of global market forces – sufficient infrastructure resources to create sustainable communities will be required alongside the robust national and regional affordability targets recommended by Barker. In addition, further planning system reform will be necessary to load its operations towards new housing construction in accordance with demand rather than favouring the interests of established well-housed and well-organised residents. *Planning for housing provision* (ODPM, 2005l) indicated that, in future, local authorities will have to ensure that a rolling five-year supply of developable land, planned over a 15-year time period, is available to meet demand predictions. Given the 'implementation gap' in the existing policies to allocate land for future development – land allocated for building may not be developed due to local objections, site problems and so on – then an allocated land oversupply will be necessary.

Social inclusion

In England New Labour adopted the term social exclusion to direct attention to the processes involved in preventing people from participating in the normal activities of the society in which they live. In Scotland social inclusion was used to emphasise the positive policies designed to diminish social exclusion and, in England, social inclusion is now becoming the accepted term.

Housing policy has been adapted in a number of ways to promote social inclusion. The benchmarks used to assess housing problems have been raised to bring them closer to normal citizen activity. The decent home standard, for example, is a more relative benchmark than unfitness yardsticks and marks a shift away from the sanitary tradition that has influenced housing policy since the time of Edwin Chadwick. However, the decent homes standard is aspirational rather than mandatory; citizens lack enforceable rights to obtain the standard and are reliant on managerial targets rather than mandatory entitlements.

As noted in Chapter Nine, New Labour altered the emphasis of regeneration projects from 'bricks and mortar' to investment in human and social capital; New Deal for Communities and The National Strategy for Neighbourhood Renewal replaced the Estate Action Initiative and Housing Action Trusts. Information on the outcomes of these 'people change' projects is sparse but the available evidence indicates that the initiatives have had, at best, only a modest impact. The switch back to 'bricks and mortar', reflected in the Housing Market Renewal Fund, indicates that New Labour now accepts that a combination of investment in physical, human and social capital at the local level is required. Future regeneration projects may attempt such a combination from the outset and resist the demands from each state department to have its own specific area initiative. The attempt to create more balanced communities in new developments and thereby nurture social inclusion on a spatial basis has also produced limited gains mainly because too few affordable homes have been secured through section 106 planning agreements. Given the rapid increase in land prices between 1996 and 2004 this looks like an opportunity lost and the Barker proposal for a Planning-gain Supplement Tax on which the Chancellor issued a consultation paper in December 2005 (HM Treasury, 2005c) may not produce significant income for investment in affordable housing if the housing market slows down.

Constructing housing problems

Housing policy formation begins with the identification of a condition as a social problem, causation is then attributed and solutions are adopted in accordance with the dominant causal notion. Because Third Way thinking stresses 'community' – symbolised by the appointment of a Cabinet Minister for Communities and Local Government – the externalities of individual behaviour are important to New Labour's recognition of social problems. This is manifest in the emphasis on getting rough sleepers off the streets and in the way antisocial behaviour has been constructed as a specific social problem. Similarly, the lack of externalities flowing from a condition may result in its downgrading as a social problem. Overcrowding, for example, lacks visibility and its sexual morality dimension – important in its designation as a social problem in the past – has lost its impact. The research commissioned by the ODPM on overcrowding (ODPM, 2004g) attempted to establish its externalities but, from a social justice perspective, overcrowding would be regarded as a social problem regardless of its connections to health and education. Using the findings of a survey of overcrowded families in social housing and, on the assumption that the survey findings were applicable to homeowners and private tenants, Shelter estimates that 98,000 children in England are forced to sleep in rooms other than bedrooms, 268,000 children are sharing a bedroom with their parents and 72,000 teenagers of different sexes are forced to share the same bedroom (Shelter, 2005). The decline in the number of new social housing dwellings – from 189,232 between 1992/93 and 1996/97 to 109,315 between 1999/2000 and 2003/04 – and the sharp fall in the proportion of new social houses with three or more bedrooms (ODPM, 2005a) reveals the neglect of overcrowding as a social problem.

The notion of responsibility involved in Third Way politics reintroduces a causative idea into the ways housing problems are constructed and hence to their proposed solutions. Thus the identification of rough sleepers as a specific grouping, separate from the broader category of the single homelessness, and government studies of rough sleepers' personal biographies has produced a more coercive response to tackling the 'street homelessness' problem (Fitzpatrick and Jones, 2005). Statutory homelessness is being subject to a similar process – greater attention is now being given to repeat homelessness and the personal circumstances that surround the loss of the family home with the implication that people deemed 'statutory homeless' bear some responsibility for their predicament.

The emphasis on 'community' as the locale of social problems can direct attention away from resource constraints and a shortage of good employment opportunities towards the local inhabitants as the cause of neighbourhood problems – their dearth of community spirit, their volitional detachment from mainstream society and their lack of enterprise. In expecting the people who remain in 'deprived neighbourhoods' to recapture 'the communities we have lost' (Young and Lemos, 1997), New Labour may have set an impossible task. The 'lost' communities were a product of a former order in which 'place communities' developed around long-term employment in a particular 'firm' – a prospect no longer open to a large section of the working population. Moreover, in attaching people who live in a deprived area to an imagined 'community', New Labour may be denying them the opportunity to break away into the 'modern' world of labour mobility and detachment from 'community' ties (Sprigings and Allen, 2005). Third Way politics, in downplaying the structural context of housing problems, also sets limits to the identification of social issues from a social justice perspective. Land is a salient example. Towards the end of the 19th century the unjustifiable gains accruing from landownership was construed as a major *housing* issue and, until the late 1970s, the restoration to the community of the 'social surplus' created by the enhanced land values was regarded by the Labour Party as an important element in its social justice agenda. Under New Labour the capture of development gain has become merely a replacement for the existing limited planning obligations imposed on developers rather than an instrument for the pursuit of social justice.

Looking back at the evolution of housing policy over 150 years it is possible to identify five broad stages. In the first stage, unhygienic housing was regarded as a social problem because of its impact on the moral and physical health of the nation. The state responded by setting standards for the construction of the built environment and by trying to purge the slum as a source of social pathology. The second stage was marked by the identification of a 'housing famine' and the attempt to boost housing construction by central state sponsorship of local authority housing as an adjunct to the private sector and as a way to contain the working class in urban areas. In the third stage the magnitude of the housing shortage prompted the expansion of both local authority housing and homeownership by state production and consumption subsidies. During the fourth stage, a belief in market forces prompted a retreat from direct state involvement but, because planning controls remained, supply failed to match demand. Housing policy is now entering a fifth phase characterised by:

- a recognition that an ample housing supply is vital to the security necessary for the 'quiet enjoyment' of a chosen lifestyle and hence a state requirement to ensure that supply is more responsive to demand;
- consensus on the virtues of homeownership;
- the identification of the planning system as a restriction on the exercise of consumer choice;
- the selective use of state resources to supply the infrastructure for sustainable housing both in low-demand and high-demand areas;
- promoting social inclusion by investment in human and social capital in selected areas and by an emphasis on enforcing obligations.

Further reading

Housing Policy: An Overview (2005) published jointly by **HM Treasury and ODPM (2005)** sets out New Labour's housing policy.

The second edition of *The Inclusive Society: Social Exclusion and New Labour* by **Levitas (2005)** contains an analysis of New Labour's social inclusion agenda, and a critique of Third Way politics can be found in *The 'Third Way' and Beyond: Criticisms, Futures and Alternatives* edited by **Hale et al (2004)**.

References

Aassve, A., Billari, F.C., Mazzuco, S. and Ongaro, F. (2002) 'Leaving home: a comparative analysis of ECHP data', *Journal of European Social Policy*, vol 12, no 4, pp 259-75.

Adamczuk, H. (1992) *Sleeping Rough in Birmingham*, Birmingham: Birmingham City Council.

Allen, C., Camina, M., Casey, R., Coward, S. and Wood, M. (2005) *Mixed Tenure, Twenty Years On: Nothing Out Of the Ordinary*, York: Joseph Rowntree Foundation/Chartered Institute of Housing.

Allen, J., Barlow, J., Leal, J., Maloutas, T. and Padovani, L. (2004) *Housing and Welfare in Southern Europe*, London: Blackwell.

Alwash, R. and McCarthy, M. (1988) 'Accidents in the home among children under 5: ethnic differences or social disadvantage?', *British Medical Journal*, no 296, pp 1450-3.

Anderson, E. (1992) *Streetwise: Race, Class and Change in an Urban Community*, Chicago, IL: University of Chicago Press.

Anderson, I., Kemp, P. and Quilgars, D. (1993) *Single Homeless People*, London: HMSO.

Atkinson, R. and Kintrea, K. (2000) 'Owner-occupation, social mix and neighbourhood impacts', *Policy & Politics*, vol 28, no 1, pp 93-108.

Atkinson, R. and Kintrea, K. (2001) 'Disentangling area effects: evidence from deprived and non-deprived neighbourhoods', *Urban Studies*, vol 38, no 12, pp 2277-98.

Audit Commission (2003) *Homelessness: Responding to the New Agenda*, London: Audit Commission.

Audit Commission (2004) *Housing: Improving Services through Resident Involvement*, London: Audit Commission.

Audit Commission (2005a) *Financing Council Housing*, London: Audit Commission.

Audit Commission (2005b) *Housing Market Renewal*, London: Audit Commission.

Ball, M. (2005) *RICS European Housing Review 2005* (www.rics.org/).

Balls, E., Healey, J. and Pilch, T. (2004) 'Housing and the progressive economy – building a progressive consensus', in P. Bill (ed) *Affordable Housing*, London: Smith Institute, pp 30-41.

Barker, K. (2003) *Delivering Stability: Securing Our Future Housing Needs; Interim Report* (www.hm-treasury.gov.uk/consultations_and_legislation/barker/consult_barker_background.cfm).

Barker, K. (2004) *Delivering Stability: Securing Our Future Housing Needs; Final Report, Recommendations* (www.hm-treasury.gov.uk/consultations_and_legislation/barker/consult_barker_index.cfm).

Barlow, J. and Duncan, S. (1994) *Success and Failure in Housing Provision: European States Compared*, London: Pergamon.

Barnard, H. and Pettigrew, N. (2004) *Applicants' Perspectives on Choice-Based Lettings*, London: Office of the Deputy Prime Minister.

Barr, N.A., Glennerster, H. and Hills, J. (eds) (1998) *The State of Welfare: The Economics of Social Spending*, Oxford: Oxford University Press.

BBC News Online (2001) 'Workers Back Homeless Survey Concerns', BBC News Online (http://news.bbc.co.uk/1/low/england/1705416.stm).

Belsky, E. and Retsinas, N. (2004) *History of Housing Finance and Policy in Spain* (www.housingfinance.org/pdfstorage/Europe_Spain%202004.pdf).

Bentham, G. (1986) 'Socio-tenurial polarisation in the United Kingdom, 1953-1983: the income evidence', *Urban Studies*, vol 23, no 2, pp 157-62.

Beresford, B. and Oldham, C. (2002) *Housing Matters: National Evidence Relating to Disabled Children and their Housing*, Bristol: The Policy Press.

Berube, A. (2005) *Mixed Communities in England: A US Perspective on Evidence and Policy Prospects*, York: Joseph Rowntree Foundation.

Beveridge, W. (1942) *Social Insurance and Allied Services*, London: HMSO.

Blair, T. (1997) Speech by Prime Minister, Aylesbury Estate, 2 June.

Blair, T. (1998) *Leading the Way: A New Vision for Local Government*, London: Institute for Public Policy Research.

Boddy, M. (1980) *The Building Societies*, London: Macmillan.

Boddy, M. and Gray, F. (1979) 'Filtering theory: housing policy and the legitimation of inequality', *Policy & Politics*, vol 7, no 1, pp 39-54.

Bolster, A., Burgess, S., Johnstone, R., Jones, K., Propper, C. and Sarker, R. (2004) *Neighbourhoods, Households and Income Dynamics: A Semi-parametric Investigation of Neighbourhood Effects*, Bristol: University of Bristol.

Booth, C. (1902) *The Life and Labour of the People of London*, London: Macmillan.

Bovenkerk, K. (1984) 'The rehabilitation of the rabble: how and why Marx and Engels wrongly depicted the lumpen-proletariat as a reactionary force', *The Netherlands Journal of Sociology*, vol 20, no 1, pp 13-42.

Bowes, A.M., Dar, N.S. and Sim, D.F. (2002) 'Differentiation in housing careers: the case of Pakistanis in the UK', *Housing Studies*, vol 17, no 3, pp 381-99.

Bowley, M. (1945) *Housing and the State 1919-1944*, London: George Allen and Unwin.

Bowmaker, E. (1900) *The Facts as to Urban Overcrowding*, Fabian Tract 101, London: Fabian Society.

Boyne, G., Farrell, C., Law, J., Powell, M. and Walker, R. (2003) *Evaluating Public Management Reforms: Principles and Practice*, Buckingham: Open University Press.

Bradshaw, J. and Finch, N. (2004) 'Housing Benefit in 22 countries', *Benefits*, vol 12, no 2, pp 87-94.

Bramley, G. (2004) *Increasing Housing Supply: Achieving Increases and Estimating Their Impact on Price, Affordability and Need* (www.hm-treasury.gov.uk/media/83A4A/Bramley_of_0304.pdf.pdf).

Bramley, G. and Karley, N.K. (2005) 'How much extra affordable housing is needed in England', *Housing Studies*, vol 20, no 5, pp 685-715.

Bramley, G. and Pawson, H. (2002) 'Low demand for housing: incidence, causes and UK national policy implications', *Urban Studies*, vol 39, no 3, pp 393-422.

Bramley, G. and Pawson, H., with Parker, J. (2000) *Responding to Low Demand Housing and Unpopular Neighbourhoods: A Guide to Good Practice*, London: DETR.

Bramley, G., Munro, M. and Pawson, H. (2004) *Key Issues in Housing: Policies and Markets in 21st-Century Britain*, London: Palgrave.

Branson, N. and Heinemann, M. (1973) *Britain in the Nineteen Thirties*, St Albans: Panther.

Brennan, A.J.E. (1976) *Vagrancy and Street Offences*, London, HMSO.

Bruce, M. (1973) *The Rise of the Welfare State: English Social Policy 1601-1971*, London: Weidenfeld and Nicolson.

Burchardt, T. (2005) 'Selective inclusion: asylum seekers and other marginalised groups', in J. Hills and K. Stewart (eds) *A More Equal Society?: New Labour, Poverty, Inequality and Exclusion*, Bristol: The Policy Press, pp 209-30.

Burnett, J. (1986) *A Social History of Housing*, London: Routledge.

Burney, E. (2005) *Making People Behave: Anti-social behaviour, politics and policy*, Devon: Willan Publishing.

Burrows, R (1997) 'The social distribution of the homelessness experience', in R. Burrows, N. Pleace and D. Quilgars (eds) *Homelessness and Social Policy*, London: Routledge, pp 50-68.

Burrows, R. (2000) *Poverty and Home Ownership in Contemporary Britain*, York: Joseph Rowntree Foundation.

Cabinet Office (2003) *Ethnic Minorities and the Labour Market: Final Report*, (www.strategy.gov.uk/work_areas/ethnic_minorities/index.asp).

Cahill, K. (2001) *Who Owns Britain: The Hidden Facts behind Landownership in the UK and Ireland*, Edinburgh: Canongate Books.

Cairncross, L., Morrell, C., Darke, J. and Brownhill, S. (2002) *Tenant Managing: An Evaluation of Tenant Management Organisations in England*, London: ODPM.

Cameron, Lord (1969) *Disturbances in Northern Ireland: Report of the Commission under the Chairmanship of Lord Cameron*, Belfast: HMSO.

Campbell, S. (2002) *A Review of Anti-social Behaviour Orders*, London: Home Office Research.

Carmona, M., Carmona, S. and Gallent, N. (2003) *Delivering Homes: Processes, Planners and Providers*, London: Routledge.

Carter, M. (1997) *The Last Resort: Living in Bed and Breakfast in the 1990s*, London: Shelter.

Central Housing Advisory Committee (1944) *The Design of Dwellings*, London: HMSO.

Century Foundation Task Force on the Common School (2002) *Divided We Fall: Coming Together Through Public School Choice*, New York, NY: Century Foundation.

Chadwick, E. (1842) *Report on the Sanitary Condition of the Labouring Population of Great Britain*, London: HMSO.

Chartered Institute of Housing (2002) *Empowering Communities: The Community Gateway Model*, London: Chartered Institute of Housing.

Cheltenham and Gloucester (2005) 'Housing Affordability Index', (www.cheltglos.co.uk/pdfs/affordIndex230904.pdf).

Churchill, W. (1909) Speech delivered at King's Theatre, Edinburgh, 17 July 1909, (www.cooperativeindividualism.org/churchill_monopolyspeech.html).

Clinton, B. (1996) 'Between Hope and History', (http://usinfo.state.gov/journals/itsv/0197/ijse/clintn.htm).

Cole, I., Green, S., Hickman, P. and McCoulough, E. (2003) *A Review of NDC Strategies for Tackling Low Demand and Unpopular Housing*, Sheffield: Sheffield Centre for Regional Economic and Social Research.

Coleman, A. (1985) *Utopia on Trial*, London: Hilary Shipman.

Commission on Social Justice (1994) *Social Justice: Strategies for National Renewal*, London: Vintage.

Congdon, P., Campos, R.M., Curtis, S.E., Southall, H.R., Gregory, I.N. and Jones, I.R. (2001) 'Quantifying and explaining changes in geographical inequality of infant mortality in England and Wales since the 1890s', *International Journal of Population Geography*, vol 7, no 1, pp 35-51.

Conservative Party (1951) *Conservative Party Manifesto 1951*, London: Conservative Party.

Controller of HMSO (2002) *Regulatory Reform (Housing Assistance) (England and Wales) Order*, SI No 2002/1860, London: The Stationery Office.

CRE (Commission for Racial Equality) (1990) *Sorry, It's Gone: Testing for Racial Discrimination in the Private Sector*, London: CRE.

CRE (1991) *Code of Practice in Rented Housing for the Elimination of Racial Discrimination and the Promotion of Equal Opportunities*, London: CRE.

CRE (1992) *Code of Practice in Non-Rented (Owner-occupied) Housing for the Elimination of Racial Discrimination and the Promotion of Equal Opportunities*, London: CRE.

CRE (2002) *The Voice of Britain: A Research Study Conducted for the Commission for Racial Equality by MORI*, London: CRE.

Crisis (2002) 'Hidden Homelessness: Britain's Invisible City', (www.crisis.org.uk/).

Crisis (2003) *Homelessness Factfile*, London: Crisis.

Crook, A.D.H. (2002) 'Private renting in the 21st century', in S. Lowe and D. Hughes (eds) *The Private Rented Sector in a New Century*, Bristol: The Policy Press, pp 90-130.

CSR Partnership (2004) *Terraced Housing in Rochdale: Main Drivers and Implications*, (www.nwrhb.org.uk/articleimages/04%20rochdale%20terraced%20housing%20report.pdf).

Cullingworth, J.B. (1969) *Council Housing: Purposes, Procedures and Priorities*, London: Ministry of Housing and Local Government/Welsh Office.

Daunton, M.J. (1983) *House and Home in the Victorian City: Working Class Housing 1850-1914*, London: Edward Arnold.

Dennis, R. (1984) *English Industrial Cities of the Nineteenth Century: A Social Geography*, Cambridge: Cambridge University Press.

Department of Environment, Food and Rural Affairs (2005) *Sustainable Development: The Government's Approach – Delivering UK Sustainable Development Together*, (www.sustainable-development.gov.uk/performance/26.htm).

Department of Trade and Industry (2001) *Opportunity for All in a World of Change*, (www.dti.gov.uk/opportunityforall).

Department of Trade and Industry Women and Equality Unit (2004) *Individual Incomes of Men and Women by Ethnicity*, (www.womenandequalityunit.gov.uk/publications/II_ethnicity_factsheets.pdf).

Depastino, T. (2003) *Citizen Hobo: How a Century of Homelessness Shaped America*, Chicago, IL: University of Chicago Press.

Deputy Prime Minister (2004) *Government Response to the ODPM: Housing, Planning, Local Government and the Regions Committee's Report on Decent Homes*, Cm 6266, London: The Stationery Office.

DETR (Department of the Environment, Transport and the Regions) (1998) *Circular 6/98*, April, London: DETR.

DETR (1999a) *National Framework for Tenant Participation Compacts*, London: DETR.

DETR (1999b) *Rough Sleeping: The Government's Strategy: Coming In Out of the Cold*, London: DETR

DETR (1999c) *Report by the Unpopular Housing Action Team*, London: DETR.

DETR (2000a) *Quality and Choice: A Decent Home For All: The Way Forward for Housing*, London: DETR.

DETR (2000b) *Quality and Choice: A Decent Home For All: The Housing Green Paper*, London: DETR.

DETR (2000c) *Stepping Stones: An Evaluation of Foyers and Other Schemes*, (www.odpm.gov.uk/index.asp?id=1155807).

DETR (2001) *Private Sector Renewal: A Consultation Paper*, London: DETR.

Dickens, C. (1888) *Dickens's Directory of London*, London: Macmillan.

Dickens, P., Duncan, S., Goodwin, M. and Gray, F. (1985) *Housing, States and Localities*, London: Methuen.

DoE (Department of the Environment) (1971) *Fair Deal for Housing*, Cmnd 4728, London: HMSO.

DoE (1973) *Better Homes: The Next Priorities*, Cmnd 5339, London: HMSO.

DoE (1974) *Circular 18/74*, London: DoE.

DoE (1977) *Housing Policy: A Consultative Document*, Cmnd 6851, London: HMSO.

DoE (1981) *An Investigation into Hard to Let Housing*, London: HMSO.

DoE (1985) *Home Improvement: A New Approach*, Cmnd 9513, London: HMSO.

DoE (1987) *Housing: The Government's Proposals*, London: HMSO.

DoE (1994) *Access to Local Authority and Housing Association Tenancies*, London: DoE.

DoE (1995) *The Rough Sleepers Initiative: Future Plans*, London: HMSO

DoE (1996) *An Evaluation of Six Early Estate Action Schemes*, Urban Research Summary No 5, London: DoE.

DoE (1997) *An Evaluation of DICE (Design Improved Controlled Experiment) Schemes*, Regeneration Research Summary No 11, London: DoE.

Doling, J. (1997) *Comparative Housing Policy: Government and Housing in Advanced Industrialized Countries*, Basingstoke: Macmillan.

Doling, J. and Ford, J. (2003) (eds) *Globalisation and Home Ownership: Experiences in Eight Member States of the European Union*, Delft: Delft University Press.

Donner, C. (2002) *Housing Policies in the European Union*, Vienna: Christian Donner.

Donnison, D. (1967) *The Government of Housing*, Harmondsworth: Penguin.

Dorling, D. and Rees, P. (2003) 'A nation still dividing: the British Census and social polarisation 1971-2001', *Environment and Planning A: International Journal of Urban and Regional Research*, vol 35, no 7, pp 1287-313.

Dorling, D. and Thomas, B. (2004) *People and Places: A 2001 Census Atlas of the UK*, Bristol: The Policy Press.

Dunleavy, P. (1981) *The Politics of Mass Housing in Britain: A Study of Corporate Power and Professional Influence in the Welfare State*, Oxford: Clarendon Press.

Durlauf, S. (2004) 'Neighborhood effects', in V. Henderson and J.F. Thisse (eds) *Handbook of Regional and Urban Economics 4*, North Holland: Elsevier, pp 2178-227.

DWP (Department for Work and Pensions) (2002) *Building Choice and Responsibility: A Radical Agenda for Housing Benefit*, www.dwp.gov.uk/housingbenefit/publications/2002/building_choice/prospectus.pdf

DWP (2005) *Housing Benefit and Council Tax Benefit: Quarterly Summary Statistics*, www.dwp.gov.uk/asd/asd1/hb_ctb/ht_ctb_quarterly_feb05.asp

Economist, The (2005) 'The global housing boom', 16 June.

Edgar, B., Doherty, J. and Meert, H. (2002) *Access to Housing*, Bristol: The Policy Press.

Engels, F. (1872) *The Housing Question Part Two: How the Bourgeoisie Solves the Housing Question*, www.marxists.org/archive/marx/works/1872/housing-question/

Esping-Andersen, G. (1990) *The Three Worlds of Welfare Capitalism*, Cambridge: Polity Press.

Esping-Andersen, G. (1999) *Social Foundations of Postindustrial Economics*, Oxford: Oxford University.

Evans, A. (1988) *No Room! No Room!: The Costs of the British Town and Country Planning System*, London: Institute of Economic Affairs.

Evans, G.W., Saltzman, H. and Cooperman, J. (2001) 'Housing quality and children's socio-emotional health', *Environment and Behaviour*, vol 33, no 3, pp 389-99.

Faggio, G. and Nickell, S. (2003) 'The rise in inactivity among adult men', in R. Dickens, P. Gregg and J. Wadsworth (eds) *The Labour Market under New Labour: The State of Working Britain*, London: Centre for Economic Performance, London School of Economics and Political Science, pp 40-52.

Farrelly, C. (2004) *An Introduction to Contemporary Political Theory*, London: Sage Publications.

FEANTSA (European Federation of National Organisations Working with the Homeless) (2004) *Third Review of Statistics on Homelessness in Europe: Developing an Operational Definition of Homelessness*, (www.feantsa.org/files/transnational_reports/EN_StatisticsReview_2004.pdf).

Ferrera, M. (1996) 'The 'southern model' of welfare in Social Europe', *Journal of European Social Policy*, vol 6, no 1, pp 17-37.

Field, F. (2003) *Neighbours from Hell: The Politics of Behaviour*, London: Politico's Publishing.

Fitzpatrick, S. (2004) *Poverty of Place*, York: Joseph Rowntree Foundation.

Fitzpatrick, S. and Jones, A. (2005) 'Pursuing social justice or social cohesion? Coercion in street homelessness policies in England', *Journal of Social Policy*, vol 34, no 3, pp 389-406.

Foord, M. and Simic, P. (eds) (2005) *Housing, Community Care and Supported Housing: Resolving Contradictions*, London: Chartered Institute of Housing.

Foot, M. (1975) *Aneurin Bevan: 1945-60, vol 2*, London: Paladin.

Foucault, M. (1991) 'Governmentality', in G. Burchell, C. Gordon and P. Miller (eds) *The Foucault Effect: Studies in Governmentality*, Hemel Hempstead: Harvester Wheatsheaf, pp 87-104.

Garnett, D. and Perry, J. (2005) *Housing Finance*, London: Chartered Institute of Housing.

Gaubatz, K.T (2001) 'Family homelessness in Britain: more than just a housing issue', *Journal of Children and Poverty*, vol 7, no 1, pp 3-22.

Gauldie, E. (1974) *Cruel Habitations: A History of Working-class Housing 1780-1918*, London: Allen and Unwin.

George, H. (1979 [1879]) *Progress and Poverty*, London: Hogarth Press.

Gervais, M. and Rehman, H. (2005) *Causes of Homelessness Amongst Ethnic Minority Populations: Research*, London: Office of the Deputy Prime Minister.

Gilmour, I. (1992) *Dancing With Dogma: Britain Under Thatcher*, London: Simon and Schuster.

Gilroy, R. and Woods R. (eds) (1994) *Housing Women*, London: Routledge.

Ginsburg, N. (1992) 'Racism and housing: concepts and reality', in P. Braham, A. Rattans and R. Skellington (eds) *Racism and Antiracism*, London: Sage Publications, pp 109-33.

Glendinning, C., Powell, M. and Rummery, K. (2002) *Partnerships, New Labour and the Governance of Welfare*, Bristol: The Policy Press.

Glennerster, H. (2003) *Understanding the Finance of Welfare*, Bristol: The Policy Press.

Glennerster, H. and Turner, T. (1993) *Estate Based Housing Management: An Evaluation*, London: Department of the Environment.

Glynn, S. and Oxborrow, J. (1976) *Interwar Britain: A Social and Economic History*, London: George Allen and Unwin.

Goodwin, J. and Grant, C. (1997) *Built to Last*, London: Shelter.

Gould, P. (1998) *The Unfinished Revolution: How the Modernisers Saved the Labour Party*, London: Little Brown.

Goux, D. and Maurin, E. (2003) *The effect of overcrowded housing on children's performance at school*, Paris: INSEE, (www.cepr.org/pubs/new-dps/dplist.asp?dpno=3818).

Greed, C.H. (1994) *Women and Planning*, London: Routledge.

Groves, R. and Sankey, S. (2005) *Implementing New Powers for Private Sector Housing Renewal*, York: Joseph Rowntree Foundation.

Habeebullah, M. and Slater, D. (1990) *Equal Access: Asian Access to Council Housing in Rochdale*, London: Community Development Foundation.

Haines, J. (1977) *The Politics of Power*, London: Jonathan Cape.

Hale, S., Leggett, W. and Martell, L. (eds) (2004) *The 'Third Way' and Beyond: Criticisms, Futures and Alternatives*, Manchester: Manchester University Press.

Hamlin, C. (1998) *Public Health and Social Justice in the Age of Chadwick: Britain, 1800-54*, Cambridge: Cambridge University Press.

Harloe, M. (1995) *The People's Home: Social Rented Housing in Europe and America*, Oxford: Blackwell.

Harris, J., Sapey, B. and Stewart, J. (1997) *Wheelchair Housing and the Estimation of Need*, Preston: University of Central Lancashire/National Wheelchair Housing Association Group.

Harrison, J.L., Barlow, S. and Creed, F. (1998) 'Mental health in the north west region of England: association with deprivation', *Social Psychiatry and Psychiatric Epidemiology*, vol 33, pp 124-8.

Harrison, M., Phillips, D., Chahal, K., Hunt, L. and J. Perry (2005) *Housing, 'Race' and Community Cohesion*, London: Chartered Institute of Housing.

Hayek, F.V. (1960) *The Constitution of Liberty*, London: Routledge.

Hayek, F.V. (1973) *Law, Legislation and Liberty: A New Statement of the Liberal Principles of Justice and Political Economy*, London: Routledge and Kegan Paul.

Heywood, F., Gangoli, G., Hamilton, J., Hodges, M., Langan, J., March, A., Moyers, S., Smith, R. and Sutton, E. (2005) *Reviewing the Disabled Facilities Grant Programme*, London: Office of the Deputy Prime Minister.

Hill, A. (2003) 'Council estate decline spawns new underclass', *The Observer*, 30 November.

Hill, O. (1883) *Homes of the London Poor 1: Four Years' Management of a London Court*, London: Cass.

Hillier, B. (1986) 'City of Alice's dreams', *The Architects Journal*, 9 July.

Hills, J. (ed) (1990) *The State of Welfare: The Welfare State in Britain since 1974*, Oxford: Clarendon.

Hills, J. (1998) 'Housing: a decent home within the reach of every family', in N.A. Barr, H. Glennerster and J. Hills (eds) *The State of Welfare: The Economics of Social Spending*, Oxford: Oxford University Press, pp 122-88.

Hills, J. (2004) *Inequality and the State*, Oxford: Oxford University Press.

HM Treasury (1998) *Modern Public Services for Britain: Investing in Reform*, London: HM Treasury.

HM Treasury (2000) *2000 Spending Review: Prudent for a Purpose: Building Opportunity and Security for All*, London: HM Treasury.

HM Treasury (2004) *2004 Spending Review: Stability, Security and Opportunity for All*, London: HM Treasury.

HM Treasury (2005a) *Delivering High Quality Public Services*, London: HM Treasury.

HM Treasury (2005b) *Britain Meeting the Global Challenge: Enterprise, Fairness and Responsibility, Pre-Budget Report, December 2005*, London: HM Treasury.

HM Treasury (2005c) *Planning-gain Supplement: A Consultation*, London: HM Treasury.

HM Treasury and ODPM (Office of the Deputy Prime Minister) (2005) *Housing Policy: An Overview*, London: HM Treasury and ODPM.

HM Treasury, ODPM (Office of the Deputy Prime Minister), DTI (Department of Trade and Industry) and DoT (Department of Transport) (2004) *Devolving Decision Making: A Consultation on Regional Funding Allocations*, London: HM Treasury.

Hodgkinson, R. (1980) *Science and the Rise of Technology since 1800*, Block V, Unit 10, Milton Keynes: Open University.

Hoekstra, J. (2005) 'Is there a connection between welfare state regime and dwelling type?: an exploratory statistical analysis', *Housing Studies*, vol 20, no 3, pp 475-96.

Holman, R., Lafitte, F., Spencer, F. and Wilson, H. (1970) *Socially Deprived Families in Britain*, London: Bedford Square Press.

Holmans, A.E. (1987) *Housing Policy in Britain: A History*, London: Croom Helm.

Holmans, A.E (1995) *Housing Demand and Need 1991-2011*, York: Joseph Rowntree Foundation.

Holmans, A.E. (2000) 'Housing', in A.H. Halsey and J. Webb (eds) *Twentieth Century British Social Trends*, Basingstoke, Macmillan, pp 465-510.

Holmans, A.E. and Frosztega, M. (1994) *House Property and Inheritance in the UK*, London: Department of the Environment.

Holmans, A.E., Monk, S. and Whitehead, C. (2004) *Building for the Future*, London: Shelter.

Home Office (2002) *Crime in England and Wales 2001/02*, London: Home Office.

Home Office (2003) *Together Tackling Anti-Social Behaviour: Action Plan*, London: Home Office.

Homelessness Directorate (2003) *Achieving Positive Outcomes on Homelessness: A Homelessness Directorate Advice Note to Local Authorities*, London: Office of the Deputy Prime Minister.

House of Commons (2005) *Hansard Written Answers for 13th June 2005*, col 113W, London: House of Commons.

House of Commons Northern Ireland Affairs Committee (2004) *Social Housing Provision in Northern Ireland: Sixth Report of Session 2003-04*, vol 1, London: The Stationery Office.

Housing Corporation, The (2002) *The Big Picture: Housing and Disability*, (www.housingcorplibrary.org.uk/HousingCorp.nsf/AllDocuments/ 0DA7CCB06BA5D1AA80256C4B003761A6).

Housing Corporation, The (2003) *A Home of My Own: The Report of the Government's Low Cost Home Ownership Task Force*, London: The Housing Corporation.

Housing Corporation, The (2004a) *What are The Housing Corporation's Aims and Objectives?*, (www.housingcorp.gov.uk/aboutus/whoweare.htm#1).

Housing Corporation, The (2004b) *Involvement Policy for the Housing Association Sector*, (www.housingcorplibrary.org.uk/HousingCorp.nsf/AllDocuments/ 1AE04680095F313980256E37004282B7).

Housing Corporation, The (2005a) *Profile of the Housing Association Sector 2003*, (www.rsrsurvey.co.uk/).

Housing Corporation, The (2005b) *Guide to Local Rents*, London: The Housing Corporation.

Housing Quality Network (2005) *Homelessness: What's New*, London: Housing Quality Network.

Housing Today (2004) 'Prescott to rethink ODPM definition of homelessness', 26 November.

Housing Today (2005) 'Homeless kept out of stock transfer homes', 29 April.

Howard, E. (1902) *Garden Cities of Tomorrow*, London: Faber.

Humphreys, R. (1999) *No Fixed Abode: A History of Responses to the Roofless and Rootless in Britain*, Basingstoke: Macmillan.

Ineichen, B (1993) *Homes and Health: How Housing and Health Interact*, London: E and FN Spon.

Inland Revenue (2005) Statistics, www.ir.gov.uk/stats/index.htm

Inside Housing (2004) 'Lack of move-on places jams up emergency hostels', 9 December.

Jacobs, K., Kemeny, J. and Manzi, T. (2003) 'Power, discursive space and institutional practices in the construction of housing problems', *Housing Studies*, vol 18, no 4, pp 429-46.

Jacobs, K., Kemeny, J. and Manzi, T. (2004) *Social Constructionism in Housing Research*, Aldershot: Ashgate.

John Grooms Housing Association (2004) *Report of the John Grooms Enquiry into the Future of Young Disabled People*, www.johngrooms.org.uk/html/futures/summary.html

Johnson, P.B. (1968) *Land Fit for Heroes*, Chicago, IL: University of Chicago Press.

Joint Centre for Housing Studies of Harvard University (2004) *The State of the Nation's Housing, 2004*, www.jchs.harvard.edu/publications/markets/son2004.pdf

Jones, A. (1999) *Out of Sight, Out of Mind? The Experiences of Homeless Women*, London: Crisis.

Jones, C. and Murie, A. (1998) *Reviewing the Right to Buy*, York: Joseph Rowntree Foundation.

Jones, G.S. (1976) *Outcast London: Study in the Relationship between Classes in Victorian Society*, Harmondsworth: Penguin.

Jones, M. (1988) 'Utopia and reality: the utopia of public housing and its reality at Broadwater Farm', in M. Teymur, T. Marcus, and T. Woolley (eds) *Rehumanizing Housing*, London: Butterworths, pp 89-101.

Jupp, B. (1999) *Living Together: Community Life on Mixed Estates*, London: Demos.

Katz, B. (2004) *Neighbourhoods of Choice and Connection: The Evolution of American Neighbourhood Policy and What it Means for the United Kingdom*, York: Joseph Rowntree Foundation.

Kemeny, J. (1994) *From Public Housing to the Social Market*, London: Taylor and Francis.

Kemeny, J. (2005) "The really big trade-off" between home ownership and welfare: Castles' evaluation of the 1980 thesis, and a reformulation 25 years on', *Housing, Theory and Society*, vol 22, no 2, pp 59-75.

Kemeny, J. and Lowe, S. (1998) 'Schools of comparative housing research: from convergence to divergence', *Housing Studies*, vol 13, no 2, pp 161-76.

Kemp, P. (1992) *Housing Benefit: An Appraisal*, London: Social Security Advisory Committee.

Kemp, P. (2004) *Private Renting in Transition*, London: Chartered Institute of Housing.

Kemp, P. (2006) 'Up to the job?', *Roof*, January/February, pp 27-29.

Kempson, E (1999) *Overcrowding in Bangladeshi Households: A Case Study of Tower Hamlets*, London: Policy Studies Institute.

Kleinhans, R. (2004) 'Social implications of housing diversification in urban renewal: a review of recent literature', *Journal of Housing and the Built Environment*, vol 19, no 4, pp 367-90.

Kleinman, M.A. (1996) *Housing, Welfare and the State in Europe: A Comparative Analysis of Britain, France and Germany*, Cheltenham: Edward Elgar.

Kling, J.R., Jens, L. and Katz, L.F. (2005) 'Neighborhood effects on crime for female and male youth: evidence from a randomized housing voucher experiment', *The Quarterly Journal of Economics*, vol 120, no 1, pp 87-130.

Knutt, E. (2003) 'It was never meant to be like this', *Housing Today*, 13 June.

Labour Party (1951) *Labour Party Manifesto*, London: Labour Party.

Labour Party (1997) *New Labour because Britain deserves better*, London: Labour Party.

Law, I., Davies, J., Lyle, S. and Deacon, A. (1999) 'Race, ethnicity and youth homelessness', in F.E. Spiers (ed) *Housing and Social Exclusion*, London: Jessica Kingsley Publications, pp 141-62.

Le Corbusier (1927) *Towards a New Architecture*, London: Architectural Press.

Le Grand, J. (2001) *The Quasi-Market Experiments in Public Service Delivery: Did They Work?*, Paper for presentation at the Pontigano Conference 2001, London: Department of Social Policy, London School of Economics and Political Science.

Le Grand, J. (2003) *Motivation, Agency and Public Policy: Of Knights and Knaves, Pawns and Queens*, Oxford: Oxford University Press.

Levitas, R. (2005) *The Inclusive Society: Social Exclusion and New Labour*, Basingstoke: Palgrave Macmillan.

Lund, B. (1999) '"The poor in a loomp is bad": New Labour and neighbourhood renewal', *Political Quarterly*, vol 70, no 3, pp 280-4.

Lund, B. (2002) *Understanding State Welfare*, London: Sage Publications.

Lupton, R. (2003) *Poverty Street*, Bristol: The Policy Press.

Lupton, R. and Power, A. (2002) 'Social exclusion and neighbourhoods', in J. Hills, J. Le Grand and D. Piachaud (eds) *Understanding Social Exclusion*, Oxford: Oxford University Press, pp 118-40.

Lux, M. (2003a) 'Efficiency and effectiveness of housing policies in the Central and Eastern European countries', *European Journal of Housing Policy*, vol 3, no 3, pp 243-63.

Lux, M. (2003b) *Housing Policy: An End or New Beginning*, Prague: Central European Press.

Lux, M., Sunega, P., Kostelecký, T. and Èermák, D. (2003) *Housing Standards 2002/03: Financial Affordability and Attitudes to Housing*, Prague: Institute of Sociology, Academy of Sciences of the Czech Republic.

Macdonald, S. (2004) 'Now you have it, now you don't: the saga of the decency deadline', *Housing Today*, 11 June.

Macpherson, W. (2004) *The Stephen Lawrence Inquiry*, Cm 4262, London: The Stationery Office.

Maile, S. and Hoggett, P. (2001) 'Best value and the politics of pragmatism', *Policy & Politics*, vol 29, no 4, pp 509-16.

Malpass, P. (2000) *Housing Associations and Housing Policy: A Historical Perspective*, Basingstoke: Macmillan.

Malthus, T.R. (1803) *An Essay on the Principle of Population*, Cambridge: Cambridge University Press.

Mann, S.L., Wadsworth, M.E.J. and Colley, J.R.T. (1992) 'Accumulation of factors influencing respiratory illness in members of a national birth cohort and their offspring', *Journal of Epidemiology and Community Health*, no 46, pp 286-92.

Manzi, T. and Smith Bowers, B. (2004) 'So many managers, so little vision: registered social landlords and consortium schemes in the UK', *European Journal of Housing Policy*, vol 4, no 1, pp 57-75.

Marquand, D. (1996) 'Moralists and hedonists', in D. Marquand and A. Seldon (eds) *The Ideas that Shaped Post-War Britain*, London: Fontana, pp 5-28.

Marx, K. and Engels, F. (1969) *Basic Writings on Politics and Philosophy*, London: Collins.

Mason, D. (2003) *Explaining Ethnic Differences*, Bristol: The Policy Press.

May, J., Cloke, P. and Johnsen, S. (2004) *Re-phasing Neo-liberalism: From Governance to 'Governmentality': New Labour and Britain's Crisis of Street Homelessness*, www.geog.qmul.ac.uk/homeless/homelessplaces/re-phasingneo-liberalism.pdf

Mayne, A. (1993) *The Imagined Slum: Newspaper Representation in Three Cities, 1870-1914*, Leicester: Leicester University Press.

Maxwell, D. (2005) *Shifting Foundations: Home Ownership and Government Objectives*, London: Institute for Public Policy Research.

McKenna, M. (1991) 'The suburbanisation of the working-class population of Liverpool between the wars', *Social History*, vol 16, no 2, pp 173-89.

Meen, G., Gibb, K., Goody, J., McGrath, T. and Mackinnon, J. (2005) *Economic Segregation in England: Causes, Consequences and Policy*, Bristol: The Policy Press.

Mellor, J.R. (1977) *Urban Sociology in an Urbanised Society*, London: Routledge and Kegan Paul.

Mellor, J.R. (1989) 'Transitions in urbanization: twentieth-century Britain', *International Journal of Urban and Regional Research*, vol 13, no 4, pp 573-96.

Ministry of Housing and Local Government (1953) *Housing: The Next Step*, Cmd 8996, London: HMSO.

Ministry of Housing and Local Government (1963) *Housing: Government Proposals for Expanding the Provision of Homes*, Cmnd 2050, London: HMSO.

Ministry of Housing and Local Government (1965) *The Housing Programme 1965 to 1970*, Cmnd 2838, London: HMSO.

Ministry of Housing and Local Government (1968) *Old Houses into New Homes*, Cmnd 3602, London: HMSO.

Ministry of Housing and Local Government (1969) *Circular 65/69*, London: HMSO.

Ministry of Housing and Local Government (1973) *Better Homes: The Next Priorities*, Cmnd 5339, London: HMSO.

Minton, A. (2002) 'Utopia street', *The Guardian*, 27 March.

Mitchell, F., Neuburger, J. and Radebe, D. (2004) *Living in Limbo: Survey of Homeless Households Living in Temporary Accommodation*, London: Shelter .

Monck, E. and Lomas, G. (1980) *Housing Action Areas: Success and Failure*, London: Centre for Environmental Studies.

Monk, S., Crook, T., Lister, D., Rowley, S., Short, C. and Whitehead, C. (2005) *Land and Finance for Affordable Housing*, York: Joseph Rowntree Foundation.

Morgan, K. (2005) 'The problem of the epoch? Labour and housing, 1918-1951', *Twentieth Century British History*, vol 16, no 5, pp 227-56.

Morgan, N. (1993) *Deadly Dwellings: The Shocking Story of Housing and Health in a Lancashire Cotton Town*, Preston: Mullion Books.

Morris, J. and Winn, M. (1990) *Housing and Social Inequality*, London: Hilary Shipman.

Morrison, N. (2000) 'Examining the difficulties in letting social housing within England', *Geojournal*, vol 51, pp 339-49.

Morton, J. (1991) *'Cheaper than Peabody': Local authority housing from 1890 to 1914*, York: Joseph Rowntree Foundation.

Mount, F. (2004) *Mind the Gap: The New Class Divide in Britain*, London: Short Books.

Muñoz, M. and Vázquez, C (1999) 'Homelessness in Spain: psychological aspects', *Psychology in Spain*, vol 3, no 1, pp 104-16.

Murie, A. and Nevin, B. (2001) 'New Labour transfers', in D. Cowan and A. Marsh (eds) *Two Steps Forward: Housing Policy in the New Millennium*, Bristol: The Policy Press, pp 29-46.

Murie, A. and Ferrari, E. (2003) *Reforming the Right to Buy in England*, London: Chartered Institute of Housing.

Murray, C. (1984) *Losing Ground*, New York, NY: Basic Books.

Murray, C. (1992) *The Emerging British Underclass*, London: Institute of Economic Affairs.

National Audit Office (2005) *More than a Roof: Progress in Tackling Homelessness*, London: National Audit Office.

National Audit Office/Audit Commission (2006) *Building More Affordable Homes: Improving the Delivery of Affordable Housing in Areas of High Demand*, London: National Audit Office/Audit Commission.

National Federation of Housing Associations (1995) *Core Lettings Bulletin*, London: National Federation of Housing Associations.

National Housing Federation (2002) *Core Lettings Bulletin*, (www.core.ac.uk/bulletins/Lettings_No_47_all_pages.pdf).

National Housing Federation (2005) *England's Housing Crisis: The Facts*, London: National Housing Federation.

National Statistics Online (2005) (www.nationalstatistics.gov.uk/CCI/nscl.asp?ID=6606).

Neighbourhood Renewal Unit (2005) *New Deal for Communities*, (www.neighbourhood.gov.uk/page.asp?id=617).

Newman, O. (1973) *Defensible Space*, London: Architectural Press.

Newton, J. (1994) *All In One Place: The British Housing Story 1973-1993*, London: Catholic Housing Aid Society.

Niskanen, W.A. (1973) *Bureaucracy: Servant or Master?* London: Institute of Economic Affairs.

Northern Ireland Housing Executive (2003) *Annual Report 2002/3*, (www.nihe.gov.uk/publications/reports/AR2003.pdf).

Nozick, R. (1974) *Anarchy, State and Utopia*, Oxford: Blackwell.

O'Brien, M. and Penna, S. (1998) *Theorising Welfare: Enlightenment and Modern Society*, London: Sage Publications.

ODPM (Office of the Deputy Prime Minister) (2003a) *Sustainable Communities: Building for the Future*, (www.odpm.gov.uk/stellent/groups/odpm_housing/documents/sectionhomepage/odpm_housing_page.hcsp).

ODPM (2003b) *Exploitation of the Right to Buy Scheme by Companies*, London: ODPM.

ODPM (2003c) *English House Condition Survey 2001: Building the Picture*, London: The Stationery Office.

ODPM (2003d) *The Draft Housing Bill – Government Response Paper*, Cm 2000, (www.odpm.gov.uk/index.asp?id=1150664).

ODPM (2003e) *Housing Bill Part 2: Licensing of Houses in Multiple Occupation*, (www.odpm.gov.uk/stellent/groups/odpm_housing/documents/page/odpm_house_026058-01.hcsp).

ODPM (2003f) *New Deal for Communities: Annual Review, 2001/2*, London: ODPM.

ODPM (2003g) *Equity Shares for Social Housing*, (www.odpm.gov.uk).

ODPM (2004a) *Office of the Deputy Prime Annual Report 2004*, Cm 6206, London: The Stationery Office.

ODPM (2004b) *Housing Strategies Guidance*, (www.odpm.gov.uk/index.asp?id–1153792).

ODPM (2004c) *Homelessness Strategies: A Good Practice Handbook*, (www.odpm.gov.uk/stellent/groups/odpm_homelessness/documents/page/odpm_home_601517-02.hcsp#P97_4033).

ODPM (2004d) *English House Conditions Survey 2001: The Private Landlords Survey*, (www.odpm.gov.uk/index.asp?id=1155503).

ODPM (2004e) *Piloting Choice Based Lettings: An Evaluation*, London: ODPM.

ODPM (2004f) *Resource Accounting and the Major Repairs Allowance*, (www.odpm.gov.uk/stellent/groups/odpm_housing/documents/page/odpm_house_602081.hcsp).

ODPM (2004g) *Overcrowding in England: The National and Regional Picture – statistics*, (www.odpm.gov.uk/index.asp?id=1152908).

ODPM (2004h) *The Impact of Overcrowding on Health and Education: A Review of Evidence and Literature*, (www.odpm.gov.uk/embedded_object.asp?id=1152907).

ODPM (2004i) *Research Findings No 180: Housing and Black and Minority Ethnic Communities: Review of evidence base*, (www.odpm.gov.uk/stellent/groups/odpm_housing/documents/page/odpm_house_608529.hcsp).

ODPM (2004j) *Neighbourhood Management Pathfinder Programme National Evaluation: Annual Review 2003/4 Key Findings*, London: ODPM.

ODPM (2005a) *Housing Statistics*, (www.odpm.gov.uk/index.asp?id=1155982).

ODPM (2005b) Evaluation *of English Housing Policy 1975-2000 Theme 2: Finance and Affordability*, London: ODPM.

ODPM (2005c) *Sustainable Communities: Homes for All*, (www.odpm.gov.uk/stellent/groups/odpm_about/documents/divisionhomepage/033927.hcsp).

ODPM (2005d) *The Evaluation of English Housing Policy 1975-2000: Theme 5 Management Effectiveness*, London: ODPM.

ODPM (2005e) Survey of English Housing, (www.odpm.gov.uk/stellent/groups/odpm_housing/documents/divisionhomepage/038398.hcsp).

ODPM (2005f) *Sustainable Communities: Settled Homes; Changing Lives: A Strategy for Tackling Homelessness*, London: ODPM.

ODPM (2005g) A *Decent Home: The Definition and Guidance for Implementation*, (www.odpm.gov.uk/stellent/groups/odpm_housing/documents/page/odpm_house_027427.hcsp).

ODPM (2005h) *English House Conditions Survey Key Findings for 2003: Decent Homes and Decent Places*, London: ODPM.

ODPM (2005i) *New Deal for Communities National Evaluation: An Overview of the 2002 and 2004 Household Surveys*, London: ODPM.

ODPM (2005j) *Making it Happen in Neighbourhoods: The National Strategy for Neighbourhood Renewal – Four Years On*, London: ODPM.

ODPM (2005k) *Affordability Targets: Implications for Housing Supply*, London: ODPM.

ODPM (2005l) *Planning for Housing Provision*, London: ODPM.

ODPM Select Committee (2003) *Reducing Regional Disparities in Prosperity, Ninth Report of Session 2002-3, Volume 1: Report*, London: House of Commons.

ODPM Select Committee (2004a) *Written Evidence*, (www.publications.parliament.uk/pa/cm200203/cmselect/cmodpm/46/46we02.htm).

ODPM Select Committee (2004b) *Decent Homes*, London: House of Commons.

ODPM Select Committee (2005a) *Homelessness*, (www.publications.parliament.uk/pa/cm200405/cmselect/cmodpm/61/61i.pdf).

ODPM Select Committee (2005b) *Empty Homes and Low-demand Pathfinders*, (www.publications.parliament.uk/pa/cm200405/cmselect/cmodpm/295/295.pdf).

Offer, A. (2003) *Why has the Public Sector Grown Large in Market Societies?*, Oxford: Oxford University Press.

Office of the High Commission for Human Rights (2004) *International Convention on the Elimination of All Forms of Racial Discrimination*, (www.unhchr.ch/html/menu3/b/d_icerd.htm).

Olecnowicz, A. (1997) *Working-Class Housing in England between the Wars: The Becontree Estate*, Oxford: Clarendon Press.

Oliver, M. and Barnes, C. (1998) *Disabled People and Social Policy*, Harlow: Longman.

Oliver, P., Davis, I. and Bentley, I. (1981) *Dunroamin: Suburban Semi and its Enemies*, London: Barrie and Jenkins.

ONS (Office for National Statistics) (2004a) *Population Trends*, no 118, Winter.

ONS (2004b) *Focus on Ethnicity and Identity*, (www.statistics.gov.uk/focuson/ethnicity/).

ONS (2004c) *Census Focus*, (www.statistics.gov.uk/cci/nugget.asp?id=269).

ONS (2005a) *Regional Trends 38 – 2004 Edition*, (www.statistics.gov.uk/statbase/Product.asp?vlnk=836).

ONS (2005b) *Social Trends 35*, London: ONS.

Orbach, L. (1977) *Homes for Heroes*, London: Seely Service.

Ormandy, D. (1991) 'Overcrowding', *Roof*, March/April, pp 9-11.

Ormerod, R. and Alexander, E. (2005) *Prevention Works: London Councils' Homelessness Prevention Initiatives*, London: Association of London Councils.

Orwell, G. (1937) *The Road to Wigan Pier*, London: Left Book Club.

Packer, I. (2001) *Lloyd George, Liberalism and the Land: The Land Issue and Party Politics in England, 1906-1914*, Suffolk: Boydell Press.

Page, D. (1993) *Building for Communities: A Study of New Housing Association Estates*, York: Joseph Rowntree Foundation.

Paris, C. (ed) (2001) *Housing in Northern Ireland – and Comparisons with the Republic of Ireland*, London: Chartered Institute of Housing.

Pawson, H. (2004) 'Reviewing stock transfer', in S. Wilcox (ed) *UK Housing Review 2004/05*, London: Chartered Institute of Housing, pp 11-20.

Perry, J. (2005) 'The end of council housing – a premature obituary' in S. Wilcox (2005) *UK Housing Review 2005/6*, London: Chartered Institute of Housing/Council of Mortgage Lenders.

Phillips, D. (2005) 'Housing achievements, diversity and constraints' in M. Harrison, D. Phillips, K. Chahal, L. Hunt and J. Perry, *Housing, 'Race' and Community Cohesion*, London: Chartered Institute of Housing.

Poor Law Commissioners (1834) *Poor Law Commissioners' Report of 1834*, London: HMSO.

Powell, M. (ed) (1999) *New Labour, New Welfare State*, Bristol: The Policy Press.

Powell, M. (ed) (2002) *Evaluating New Labour's Welfare Reforms*, Bristol: The Policy Press.

Power, A. (1993) *Hovels to High Rise: State Housing in Europe since 1850*, London: Routledge.

Power, A. (2004) 'Housing as a problem', in P. Bill (ed) *Affordable Housing*, London: Smith Institute, pp 20-9.

Power, A. and Tunstall, R. (1995) *Swimming Against the Tide: Polarisation or Progress on 20 Unpopular Council Estates, 1980-1995*, York: Joseph Rowntree Foundation.

Power, A. and Willmot, H. (2005) 'Bringing up families in poor neighbourhoods under New Labour', in J. Hills and K. Stewart (eds) *A More Equal Society?: New Labour, Poverty, Inequality and Exclusion'*, Bristol: The Policy Press, pp 277-96.

Power, S., White, G. and Youdall, D. (1995) *No Place to Learn: Homelessness and Education*, London: Shelter.

Price Waterhouse (1995) *Tenants in Control: An Evaluation of Tenant-led Housing Management Organisations*, London: Department of the Environment .

Prime Minister's Strategy Unit (2005) *Improving the Prospects of People Living in Areas of Multiple Deprivation in England*, London: Cabinet Office.

Putman, R. (2001) *Bowling Alone: The Collapse and Revival of American Community*, New York, NY: Simon and Schuster.

Quilgars, D. and Anderson, I. (1995) *Foyers for Young People*, Housing Research 142, York: Joseph Rowntree Foundation.

Ranelagh, J. (1991) *Thatcher's People*, London: Fontana.

Rashleigh, B. (2004) 'Keeping the numbers down', *Roof*, January/February, pp 18-21.

Ravetz, A. (2001) *Council Housing and Culture: The History of a Social Experiment*, London: Routledge.

Ravetz, A. and Turkington, R. (1995) *The Place of Home*, London: Spon and Co.

Rawls, J. (1971) *A Theory of Justice*, Oxford: Oxford University Press.

Reeves, P. (2005) *An Introduction to Social Housing*, Oxford: Elsevier.

Reynolds, L., Robinson, N. and Diaz, R. (2004) *Crowded House: Cramped Living in England's Housing*, London: Shelter.

Riach, P.A and Rich, J. (2002) 'Field experiments of discrimination in the marketplace', *The Economic Journal*, vol 112, no 483, pp 480-518.

Ridley, N. (1991) *'My Style of Government': The Thatcher Years*, London: Hutchinson.

Roberts, M. (1991) *Living in a Man-made World*, London: Routledge.

Roof (2006) 'Pathfinder Pain', January/February, p 7.

Rowntree, S. (1941) *Poverty and Progress: A Second Social Survey of York*, London: Longman.

Royal College of Physicians of London (1994) *Homelessness and Ill Health*, London: Royal College of Physicians of London.

Royal Commission on the Housing of the Working Classes (1885) *Reports, with Minutes of Evidence*, London: HMSO.

Royal Commission on the Poor Laws and Relief of Poverty (1909) *Minority Report of the Royal Commission on the Poor Laws and Relief of Distress*, Cd 4499, HMSO: London.

Rubinowitz, L. and Rosenbaum, J. (2001) *Crossing the Class and Color Lines: From Public Housing to White Suburbia*, Chicago, IL: University of Chicago Press.

Ruming, K.J., Mee, K.J. and McGuirk, P.M. (2004) 'Questioning the rhetoric of social mix: courteous community or hidden hostility', *Australian Geographical Studies*, vol 42, no 2, pp 234-48.

Saraga, E. (1998) *Embodying the Social: Constructions of Difference*, London: Routledge.

Saunders, P. (1990) *A Nation of Home Owners*, London: Routledge.

Scanlon, K. (2004) *Housing Tenure in 19 Industrialised Countries*, (www.enhr2004.org/files/plenary_sessions/ K%20Scanlon%20plenary%20presentation.pdf)

Scanlon, K. and Whitehead, C. (2004) 'Housing tenure and mortgage systems: how the UK compares', *Housing Finance*, no 60, pp 41-51.

Schmidt, S. (1989) 'Convergence theory, labour movements and corporatism: the case of housing', *Scandinavian Housing and Planning Research*, vol 6, pp 83-101.

Scottish Executive (2002) *Structural Trends and Homelessness: A Qualitative Analysis*, (www.scotland.gov.uk/cru/kd01/red/sthqa-02.asp).

Scottish Executive (2005) *Homes for Scotland's People: A Scottish Housing Policy Statement*, Edinburgh: Scottish Executive.

SEU (Social Exclusion Unit) (1998a) *Rough Sleeping*, Cm 4008, London: The Stationery Office.

SEU (1998b) *Bringing Britain Together: A National Strategy for Neighbourhood Renewal*, London: Cabinet Office.

SEU (2000) *National Strategy for Neighbourhood Renewal: A Framework for Consultation*, London: SEU.

SEU (2001) *A New Commitment to Neighbourhood Renewal: National Strategy Action Plan*, London: Cabinet Office.

SEU (2002a) *Reducing Re-offending by Ex-prisoners*, London: The Stationery Office.

SEU (2002b) *National Strategy for Neighbourhood Renewal: Report of Action Team 8: Anti-social Behaviour*, London: SEU.

Sharp, E. (1969) *The Ministry of Housing and Local Government*, London: George Allen and Unwin.

Shelter (1969) *Face the Facts*, London: Shelter.

Shelter (2004) *On the Up: The Housing Crisis in the North*, London: Shelter.

Shelter (2005) *Full House*, London: Shelter.

Shephard, A. (2003) *Inequality and Poverty*, (www.ifs.org.uk/conferences/andrews_notes.pdf).

Sim, D. (ed) (2004) *Housing and Public Policy in Post-devolution Scotland*, London: Chartered Institute of Housing.

Simon, E.D. (1933) *The Anti-slum Campaign*, London: Longman.

Simpson, L. (2005) *Segregation*, University of Manchester, (www.manchester.ac.uk/aboutus/news/pressreleases/segregation/).

Smith, A. (1970 [1776]) *Inquiry into the Nature and Causes of the Wealth of Nations*, Harmondsworth: Penguin.

Smith, R., Stirling, T. and Williams, P. (2000) *Housing in Wales in an Era of Devolution*, London: Chartered Institute of Housing.

Smith, S. (1989) *The Politics of 'Race' and Residence*, London: Polity Press.

Speight, G. (2000) *Who Bought the Inter-war Semi? The Socio-economic Characteristics of New House Buyers in the 1930s*, Discussion Papers in Economic and Social History, no 38, Oxford: University of Oxford.

Sprigings, N. and Allen, C. (2005) 'The communities we are regaining but need to lose', *Community, Work and Family*, vol 8, no 4, pp 389-411.

Stephens, M. (2005a) 'Lessons from the past, challenges for the future', Paper to the Housing Studies Association Conference, York, 2005.

Stephens, M. (2005b) 'An assessment of the British Housing Benefit system', *European Journal of Housing Policy*, vol 5, no 2, pp 111-29.

Sullivan, E. (2004) *Review of the Supporting People Programme: Independent Report*, London: ODPM.

Thatcher, M. (1993) *The Downing Street Years*, London: HarperCollins.

Thatcher, M. (1995) *The Path to Power*, London: HarperCollins.

Thomas, B. and Dorling, D. (2004) *Know your Place: Housing Wealth and Inequality in Great Britain 1980-2003 and Beyond*, (www.shelter.org.uk).

Thompson, W. (1903) *The Housing Handbook*, London: National Housing Reform Council.

Thorpe, K. and Wood, M. (2004) 'Antisocial behaviour', in S. Nicholas and A. Walker (eds) *Crime in England and Wales 2002/2003 Supplementary Volume 2: Crime, Disorder and the Criminal Justice System – Public Attitudes and Perceptions*, London: Home Office, pp 65-77.

Timmins, N. (2001) *The Five Giants: A Biography of the Welfare State*, London: HarperCollins.

Torgersen, U (1987) 'Housing: the wobbly pillar under the welfare state', in B. Turner, J. Kemeny and L. Lundqvist (eds) *Between State and Market: Housing in the Post-industrial Era*, Stockholm: Almqvist and Wiksell, pp 116-26.

Tudor Walters, J. (1918) *Building Construction in Connection with the Provision of Dwellings for the Working Classes*, Cmd 9191, London: HMSO.

Tunstall, R. (2003) ''Mixed tenure' policy in the UK: privatisation, pluralism or euphemism', *Housing, Theory and Society*, vol 20, no 3, pp 152-9.

Turok, I. and Edge, N. (1999) 'The jobs gap in Britain's cities', *Findings 569*, York: Joseph Rowntree Foundation.

UK Land Directory (2003) 'UK Land Prices Studied by Halifax', (www.uklanddirectory.org.uk/land-prices-england-uk.htm).

United Nations Economic Commission for Europe (2005) *Trends in Europe and North America*, (www.unece.org/stats/trends2005/Welcome.html).

Vass, J. (2004) 'Affordability: testing times ahead', *Housing Finance No 63*, Autumn, pp 34-44.

Vass, J. and Pannell, B. (2004) 'Positive about housing equity', *Housing Finance No 61*, Spring, pp 11-19.

Waldron, J. (1993) 'Homelessness and the issue of freedom', in J. Waldron (ed) *Liberal Rights: Collected Papers 1981-91*, Cambridge: Cambridge University Press, pp 309-38.

Warnes, A., Crane, M., Whitehead, N. and Fu, R. (2003) *Homelessness Factfile*, London: Crisis.

Watkinson, J. (2004) *Rebalancing Communities: Introducing Mixed Incomes into Existing Housing Estates*, Chartered Institute of Housing, (www.cih.org/branches/york/JudyWatkinson.pdf).

Watson, S. with Austerberry, H. (1986) *Housing and Homelessness: A Feminist Perspective*, London: Routledge.

Watts, D. (1992) *Joseph Chamberlain and the Challenge of Radicalism*, London: Hodder and Stoughton.

Weaver, M. (2004) 'Milburn Proposes To Extend The Right to Buy', *The Guardian*, 9 September.

Weber, M. (1924) 'Class, status and party', in H. Gerth and C.W. Mills (eds) (1948) *Essays from Max Weber*, London: Routledge and Kegan Paul, pp 180-95.

Weiler, P. (2003) 'The Conservatives' search for a middle way in housing, 1951-64', *Twentieth Century British History*, vol 14, no 4, pp 260-390.

Weiss, L. (1998) *The Myth of the Powerless State: Governing the Economy in a Global Era*, Cambridge: Polity Press.

Wilcox, S. (1998) *Housing Finance Review 1998/9*, York: Joseph Rowntree Foundation.

Wilcox, S. (2003) *UK Housing Review 2003/4*, London: Chartered Institute of Housing.

Wilcox, S. (2004) *UK Housing Review 2004/5*, London: Chartered Institute of Housing.

Wilcox, S. (2005a) *UK Housing Review 2005/6*, London: Chartered Institute of Housing/Council of Mortgage Lenders

Wilcox, S. (2005b) *Affordability and the Intermediate Housing Market*, York: Joseph Rowntree Foundation.

Wilcox, S. (2005c) 'Trends in housing affordability', in D. Dorling, J. Ford, A. Holmans, C. Sharp, B. Thomas and S. Wilcox (eds) *The Great Divide: An Analysis of Housing Inequality*, London: Shelter, pp 117-44.

Williams, F. and Popay, J. (1999) 'Balancing polarities: developing a new framework for welfare research', in F. Williams, J. Popay and A. Oakley (eds) *Welfare Research: A Critical Review*, London: UCL Press.

Wilmott, P. and Young, M. (1960) *Family and Class in a London Suburb*, London: New English Library.

Wilson, W. (2001) *The Homelessness Bill*, House of Commons Research Paper 01/58, London: House of Commons.

Wilson, S. and Burbidge, M. (1978) 'An Investigation of Difficult to Let Housing', *Housing Review*, July/August, pp 7-10.

Wohl, A.S. (1977) *The Eternal Slum: Housing and Social Policy in Victorian London*, London: Edward Arnold.

Wohl, A.S. (1983) *Endangered Lives: Public Health in Victorian Britain*, London: Methuen.

Wordnet (2004) http://wordnet.princeton.edu/

World Bank (2000) *World Development Report 2000-2001*, Washington, DC: World Bank.

Wynn, M. (1984) 'Spain', in M. Wynn (ed) *Housing in Europe*, Beckenham: Croom Helm, pp 121-49.

Yelling, J.A. (1982) *Slums and Slum Clearance in Victorian London*, London: Allen and Unwin.

Yelling, J.A. (1992) *Slums and Redevelopment: Policy and Practice in England, 1918-45, with particular reference to London*, London: UCL Press.

Young, I. (1990) *Justice and the Politics of Difference*, Princeton, NJ: Princeton University Press.

Young, M. and Lemos, G. (1997) *The Communities We Have Lost and Can Regain*, London: Lemos and Crane.

Index